be

D1187023

# Secularization

# Secularization

## In Defence of an Unfashionable Theory

Steve Bruce

OXFORD
UNIVERSITY PRESS

*This book has been printed digitally and produced in a standard specification
in order to ensure its continuing availability*

# OXFORD
UNIVERSITY PRESS

Great Clarendon Street, Oxford OX2 6DP
United Kingdom

Oxford University Press is a department of the University of Oxford.
It furthers the University's objective of excellence in research, scholarship,
and education by publishing worldwide. Oxford is a registered trade mark of
Oxford University Press in the UK and in certain other countries

© Steve Bruce 2011

The moral rights of the author have been asserted

First published 2011
Reprinted 2012

British Library Cataloguing in Publication Data
Data available

Library of Congress Cataloging in Publication Data
Library of Congress Control Number: 2010935041

ISBN 978-0-19-958440-6

# Contents

# Preface

Readers may find an explanation of why a book was written helpful in understanding and judging it. It hardly reflects well on my character, but this was written out of frustration and annoyance. I am often asked to speak on secularization and equally often confronted with the same ill-informed arguments from young scholars who have read no further back than the work of their supervisors, who caricature the secularization paradigm as predicting the rapid eradication of all religious sentiment, who present a small case study as rebuttal of a story about large-scale social change, or who assume that I am too naive to have considered and rejected for good reason some trifling objection that has just occurred to them.

So grumpy old man is the bad reason for writing this. There are three good reasons. Since the 1990s there has been a welcome growth in large-scale empirical studies of religion in the modern world: we are now better able to judge the secularization story. Secondly, critics have advanced new reasons for rejecting the paradigm, and these need to be addressed. The final reason is that, after decades of pottering around in the subject, I think I finally understand what I wanted to say all along and can now say it fairly clearly.

That I have written a great deal about secularization inevitably means that parts of this book may seem familiar to that tiny band of scholars who know my work. When one has spent twenty years honing an explanation, it is hard to find new ways of saying the same things that are as clear as the old ones. I hope that clarity trumps novelty.

A final note of introduction: this book is a work of social science. For those who care about such distinctions, I come from a phenomenological and symbolic interactionist background: as a student my heroes were Alfred Schutz, Herbert Blumer, and Peter Berger. I have since become ever more of an old-fashioned positivist as I have become frustrated with the subversion of sociology by imports from literature, media studies, and psychoanalysis, by the confusion of analysis and partisanship, and by capitulation to various forms of relativism. The job of the sociologist is the accurate description, interpretation, and explanation of real social phenomena. Although complete objectivity is impossible, it remains our goal. And anyone who uses the terms 'more' and 'less' can have no objection to quantification, to measurement, and to statistical analysis. Here endeth the lesson.

# Acknowledgements

Although there is little direct reference to it, my thinking about the large issues discussed here has been much helped by the detailed research on 'Religion in Britain since 1945' that I conducted between 2007 and 2009 as a Leverhulme Trust Senior Research Fellow. I am extremely grateful to the Leverhulme Trust, to the Carnegie Trust for the Universities of Scotland, and to the University of Aberdeen for supporting my work. I am also grateful to the many librarians, archivists, local historians, clergy, and lay people who have assisted me in that research.

More technical versions of elements of this book have been published elsewhere and I am grateful to the referees, editors, and publishers of the *British Journal of Sociology*, the *Journal of Contemporary Religion*, and the *Journal of Ecclesiastical History* for their assistance in improving my ideas and allowing me to draw on those studies for this work.

Some of the key ideas in the book have been presented at public lectures and seminars over the last few years and I would like to thank the following institutions for inviting me to speak and to those audiences for their helpful comments: the University of Wales, Bangor, the University of Lancaster, Birkbeck College, London, the University of Stirling, the University of Oxford, the University of Amsterdam, and the Carl Ossietsky University of Oldenberg.

Particular thanks are due to David Voas of the University of Manchester and my Aberdeen colleague Tony Glendinning, with whom I have co-written a number of essays that inform this presentation. Much of the credit (but none of the blame) for what follows is due to them.

I am also grateful to Walter Nonneman and Chris Timmerman of the University Centre Saint-Ignatius, Antwerp, for inviting me to teach at their 2009 summer school and to Sara Mels and Barbara Segaert for their efficient organization of the event. The students and the other faculty—Robert Hefner of Boston University, John Hutchinson of the London School of Economics, and David Voas—repeatedly challenged my views of secularization and put me in the right frame of mind to write this book.

Finally I would like to make a special mention of Paul Heelas of the University of Lancaster. Heelas has been one of the pioneers in the study of alternative spirituality. He deserves particular credit for devising the Kendal Project as the first attempt to measure the penetration of a community by holistic spirituality ideas and practices. As is clear from Chapter 5, I disagree with many of his conclusions, but he has been a kind friend to me for over twenty years and an inspiration to all of us working in this field. In an impressively open spirit of scholarly collaboration, he regularly invited me to explain to his students why I disagreed with him. I am not sure that it helped them, but our arguments certainly helped me.

# 1

# Describing Secularization

## Introduction

The secularization paradigm aims to explain one of the greatest changes in social structure and culture: the displacement of religion from the centre of human life.[1] Social scientists spend far too much time quibbling over words, but it is useful to begin with some idea of the key concepts. We could define religion in terms of the purposes it serves or the needs it meets, but such functional definitions rather assume what ought to be demonstrated. Hence I will define religion substantively, as beliefs, actions, and institutions based on the existence of supernatural entities with powers of agency (that is, Gods) or impersonal processes possessed of moral purpose (the Hindu and Buddhist notion of karma, for example) that set the conditions of, or intervene in, human affairs.[2] Although rather long-winded, that covers most of what we mean when we talk about religion and so offers a reasonable starting place.

---

[1] This chapter owes much to the work of my colleague Tony Glendinning, who has patiently assisted me with statistical analysis for over a decade. It owes even more to David Voas of the University of Manchester, with whom I drafted a long essay on religion in Europe that was never published, and who has kindly shared with me his growing body of analyses of large-scale survey data.

[2] For a technical discussion of this definition and alternatives, see S. Bruce, 'Defining Religion', *Revue internationale de sociologie* (2010).

Defining secularization in advance of explaining it is less easy because scholars often conflate definitions and explanations, but we can start with Bryan Wilson's succinct definition of secularization as the decline in the social significance of religion. He also offered a more detailed definition, which I paraphrase as follows.[3]

Secularization includes:

- the decay of religious institutions;
- the displacement, in matters of behaviour, of religious rules and principles by demands that accord with strictly technical criteria;
- the sequestration by political powers of the property and facilities of religious agencies;
- the replacement of a specifically religious consciousness (which might range from dependence on charms, rites, spells, or prayers, to a broadly spiritually inspired ethical concern) by an empirical, rational, instrumental orientation;
- the shift from religious to secular control of a variety of social activities and functions;
- the decline in the proportion of their time, energy, and resources that people devote to supernatural concerns.

Wilson was usually careful to distinguish between the social significance of religion and religion as such. We should not foreclose on the possibility that religion may cease to be of any great social importance while remaining a matter of some import for those who have some. However, as I will argue, there is a very clear implication that three things—the social power of religion, the number of people who take it seriously, and how seriously anyone takes it—are causally related. It is possible that a country that is formally and publicly secular may contain among its populace a large number of people who are deeply religious. But, in a number of these chapters, I will show that the declining power of religion causes a decline in the number of religious people and the extent to which people are religious. As religious faith loses social power, it becomes harder for each generation to socialize its children in the faith. It also becomes progressively harder for those who remain religious to preserve the cohesion

---

[3] B. R. Wilson, *Religion in Sociological Perspective* (Oxford: Oxford University Press, 1982), 149.

and integrity of their particular belief system. As religion becomes increasingly a matter of free choice, it becomes harder to maintain boundaries. Alternative reworkings of once-dominant ideologies proliferate, and increasing variation encourages first relativism—all roads lead to God—and then indifference as it becomes harder to persuade people that there is special merit in any particular road.

As a preliminary observation, we may note that the secularization paradigm is concerned largely with the demand for religion. It supposes that, if fewer people worship and churches lose influence, the underlying explanation is probably a loss of faith or a loss of interest. When pressed, people often give alternative proximate explanations. They no longer attend church because they are too busy or they do not like the priest or they moved and never quite got round to finding a new church.[4] But, as the stated reasons for defection usually cite some obstacle that could have been overcome with the merest effort, we can suppose that they no longer believe there is a creator God who will punish them for failing to worship him in the way he demands. As we shall see in the following chapters, much criticism of the paradigm is less a challenge to specific propositions and more a blanket rejection of that underlying assumption of loss of faith. For example, Rodney Stark and his associates argue that the main determinants of religious vitality lie not in causes of varying demand (which they take to be fairly stable) but in features of the religious market place that affect the 'supply' of religious goods.[5] The supply-side alternative to the secularization paradigm will be considered in detail after the more common 'demand-side' model has been explained.

A final preliminary point: the secularization paradigm is not like Boyle's law in physics (which asserts that, if the temperature of a gas is held constant, pressure and volume are inversely related; that is, if pressure increases, volume decreases, and vice versa). We do not think we have discovered some unvarying law of social development that must apply to all societies. The secularization paradigm is an attempt to explain common features of the recent past of modern

[4] P. Richter and L. J. Francis, *Gone but not Forgotten: Church Leaving and Returning* (London: Darton, Longman and Todd, 2005).

[5] R. Stark and R. Finke, *Acts of Faith: Explaining the Human Side of Religion* (Berkeley and Los Angeles: University of California Press, 2000).

industrial liberal democracies. In the first place, it is an exercise in historical explanation and has no application to the future. Of course, if the explanation is reasonable, it follows that, to the extent that other societies experience the changes that we think caused the decline of religion in the West, they too will experience secularization. However, for the reasons I will elaborate in Chapter 9, history can never repeat itself. Even if every other circumstance were the same (and that is very unlikely), there would always be one key difference: other societies have already done it. As there are now societies where relatively few people are religious, where religion has little impact on social life, and where religious affiliation and degree of commitment are matters of personal choice, any currently religious society has a model of its possible future that can attract either admiration or loathing, and that model is not passive. It can intervene. For example, Western powers may insist that states in the developing world receive some benefit (economic aid, for example, or admission to the European Union) only if they adopt some of our values (by, for example, permitting religious liberty). The net result is that it is difficult to distinguish 'naturally occurring' from externally inspired or imposed change. This problem will be explored later. It is enough to note here that, while the nineteenth-century founding fathers of sociology (Auguste Comte, in particular) may have thought that secularization was inevitable, no modern sociologist has taken this view, and it forms no part of my approach.

## Religion in Western Europe

The secularization paradigm is an attempt to provide an overarching sociological explanation of the history of religion since the Middle Ages. Later chapters consider the USA and the developing world. I will start with Europe and then consider settler offshoots. Because religion in Europe and its settler offshoot societies is still overwhelmingly Christian, this chapter will concentrate on the decline of Christianity. The effects of and on other religions will be discussed in subsequent chapters.

It is sometimes claimed that the empirical prerequisite for the secularization paradigm—proving that religiosity has declined—is impossible, because we cannot know how religious people were before the advent of social surveys and social statistics. That can be a constraint only if we put unusual weight on the word 'know'. Thanks to work of historians, we actually know a great deal about the past. And, because religious institutions were often pioneers of statistical reporting and record-keeping and because religion was of great importance or interest to those who wrote diaries and travelogues, we probably know more about religion than about any other sphere of human life.

It is easy to see the power of religious institutions in the Middle Ages: just look at the cathedrals. It is less easy to be sure how far institutionally promoted beliefs penetrated the consciousness of ordinary people, but we can be fairly confident that the peoples of pre-industrial Europe were deeply religious. The extent to which they were orthodox Christians varied, but most understood the world through basically Christian lenses. They knew the Lord's Prayer and the Hail Mary and could make the sign of the Cross. They knew the Ten Commandments, the Four Cardinal Virtues, the Seven Deadly Sins, and the Seven Works of Mercy. They sometimes grumbled, but they paid their taxes to the church. They were baptized, christened, married, and buried by the church. They believed sufficiently in hell and in the status of Holy Writ for swearing oaths on the Bible to be an effective means of control. They avoided blaspheming. Even the most humble left something in their wills for the church, and the wealthy willed large sums for priests to say masses post-mortem on their behalf. Most knew they had to make reparation to God for their sins, in this life or in the next. When the clergy of the Middle Ages complained of irreligion (and they did so frequently), their target was not secularity but the persistence of pre-Christian superstitions and the use of the church's rituals in an instrumental magical manner.[6]

In one sense secularization is not new. Since the initial conversion of Europe, the Christian churches have gained and lost influence, and popular religiosity has ebbed and flowed. David Martin suggests that there were four major waves of Christianization in Europe, each of which brought with it a new tendency to secularization, which in turn encouraged or allowed a new wave of revival. The first wave

[6] K. Thomas, *Religion and the Decline of Magic* (Harmondsworth: Penguin, 1978).

resulted from the conversion of princes and kings. Clovis, for example, who united the Frankish tribes under one king, converted in 486 AD and imposed his new religion on his people. The downside of this wave was that the faith became firmly associated with power, hierarchy, war, compulsion, and violence. The second wave resulted from the work of the friars in the cities and towns of medieval Europe, and its cost was the division of the people into the seriously religious and the rest. The third wave was the Protestant Reformation of the sixteenth century: an attempt to overcome that division and encourage in the common people the degree of piety formerly expected only of religious officials and monks and nuns. When the religious enthusiasm of that era become institutionalized and waned, Europe experienced the evangelical and pietist revivals.[7]

Martin is right that the history of European Christianity is not a linear decline from an all-pervasive world view in the Middle Ages to a marginal minority interest in the twenty-first century. However, it does not follow that, because the tide of religion ebbs and flows, that the peak wave of every tide will reach equally high up the beach. Martin is right that some secularizing forces themselves contain the possibility of a further wave of Christianization. The Reformation's fragmentation of a single church into competing organizations, for example, allowed new social classes the opportunity to rework Christianity into styles that well fitted their circumstances and thus encouraged greater commitment. The post-Reformation arguments (which often developed into wars) encouraged people to take sides and thus become more knowledgeable about their faith.

However, it is also reasonable to argue that some secularizing forces prevent the successive waves having anything like the power of their predecessors. An example is the increase in personal freedom. When Clovis converted to Christianity, the social structure he dominated permitted his people to be coerced into a nominal attachment to the new religion and then gradually socialized into a real and enduring faith. By the time of the Reformation the social forces of coercion and socialization were far weaker and by the time of the evangelical and pietist revivals of the late eighteenth and nineteenth centuries they were almost entirely absent. Clovis could convert his

---

[7] D. Martin, *On Secularization: Toward a Revised General Theory* (Aldershot: Ashgate, 2005), 3–7.

Franks. John Wesley, the founder of Methodism, could only persuade his hearers and he persuaded only some of them.

The 1648 Treaty of Westphalia, which ended the Thirty Years War, is conventionally taken as the start of the modern accommodation of the nation state to the problem of religious competition. It marks what, to borrow Winston Churchill's fine distinction of stages in the Second World War, we might call the 'beginning of the end' of attempts to enforce religious homogeneity across Europe.[8] Thereafter, each principality or kingdom would follow the religion of its sovereign. That gradually became democratized, with the people displacing the monarch as the determinant of the national faith. With the rise of modern nationalism it became common for countries to promote a dominant religion as an essential part of the national identity. Hence at the start of the nineteenth century almost all European states were dominated by a single Christian church.[9] The precise legal status of those churches varied with accidents of political history and with features of the confession in question. The Lutheran churches of northern Europe were officially recognized and privileged as state churches, and the early constitutions written to limit the power of monarchies still required government officials to be active members of the state church. The Catholic Church in countries such as Italy, France, Spain, and Portugal enjoyed greater popular influence than their Lutheran counterparts (whose penetration of the general culture was weakened by competing reformist movements and by a more humble attitude to their status), but they had a formally weaker constitutional position. Being international in organization and mission, the Catholic Church did not normally seek the status of state church but instead tried to have its privileges protected by treaties negotiated by the Vatican.

The type of Christianity is important, because different confessions offered different opportunities for dissent and hence for accommodating radical social and political upheaval. Seeing itself as having a mission to encompass an entire people rather than as a body of those who choose to be its members, the Catholic Church, like the

---

[8] W. S. Churchill, Speech to the Lord Mayor's Luncheon, Mansion House, 10 Nov. 1942.

[9] J. T. S. Madeley and Z. Enyedi (eds), *Church and State in Contemporary Europe: The Chimera of Neutrality* (London: Cass, 2003).

Orthodox Churches of the east, has usually been conservative and firmly allied to the ruling elites of any society. The core claim that its papal hierarchy offers unique access to the will of God makes dissent difficult. The result was that the political conflicts that came with the rise of democracy tended to split Catholic countries: progressives rejected the church as they rejected the state. Although the great divide occurs at different times, France, Italy, Spain, and Portugal all show this pattern of a radical division between a conservative Catholic bloc and a secular progressive bloc. While the French Revolution produced the prototype in the 1790s, we still see the residue of the great divide in the 1970s, when those countries had large and powerful communist movements. In contrast, because Protestantism offers little theological support for the notion of a hierarchy of discernment, it permits the formation of equally valid competing expressions of Christianity. As happened in the English Civil War, rejection of rulers could be channelled into support for radical Protestant sects: it did not need to become a rejection of religion as such. Hence, in the Britain Isles, democratization produced challenges to the privileges enjoyed by the state Church of England, Ireland and Wales and the separate state Church of Scotland, but religion as such did not become a point of contention. Instead of following the French model of an organic communal communist movement, the British left produced an individualist liberal social democratic tradition that was heavily influenced by the values and practices of the dissenting Protestant sects. The British labour movement always owed far more to the Methodists and Baptists than it did to Karl Marx.

Two major variables in the recent religious history of the West are economic development and democratization. In the older and more prosperous democracies the post-1945 period was relatively free of religious controversies. In part because its educational demands were met and in part because the horror of fascism had discredited its preferred conservative model of social organization, the Catholic Church had finally abandoned its long opposition to representative democracy and endorsed Christian Democratic politics. Popular involvement in religious organizations started to show significant decline in the 1960s.

In Spain, Portugal, and Greece the legacies of civil wars and dictatorial regimes kept the dominant church (Catholic in the first two cases; Orthodox in the third) in a powerful position. Francisco Franco and Antonio Salazar had misgivings about the reliability of the Catholic Church in Spain and Portugal respectively, but they were happy to support it as a conservative influence. The rapid democratization and economic modernization of those countries from the 1970s brought a profound change in levels of religious observance and in socio-moral climate (so much so that in 2005 Spain displaced the Scandinavian countries from their traditional lead role in sexual liberalization when it legalized same-sex marriages).

The Catholic states of Western Europe still show a nostalgic fondness for restricting religious liberties. Periodically government bodies produce lists of dangerous cults, often defined in such a haphazard manner as to include centuries-old Protestant denominations and sects. But the religious economies of the West gradually liberalized, and by the 1990s we can find representatives of a very wide variety of alternative Christian and post-Christian organizations. However (as we will see in Chapter 5), these recruited very few adherents. Although there was a considerable increase in the range of religious options on offer, there was a marked decline in total take-up.

Some figures can illustrate the decline of Christianity in Western Europe. We cannot be sure when churchgoing started to decline in Britain, but we can be certain that it was before 1851, because the census of that year collected remarkably detailed information on the numbers of people who attended all the services of almost all churches and chapels on Sunday, 30 March. The census enumerators collected data for attendances (and many people attended more than once), so we can be sure only of the upper and lower limits, but we know that between 40 and 60 per cent of the population attended public worship that day. In 2001 the comparable figure was around 9 per cent.[10] Furthermore, a large body of survey evidence shows that, contrary to the popular notion that Britons are 'believing without belonging', 'belief has in fact eroded in Britain at the same rate as two key aspects of belonging: religious affiliation and attendance'.[11] In countries such as Ireland, that have conventionally been taken as exceptionally religious, decline in church involvement started later but has been more rapid.

---

[10] P. Brierley, *Pulling out of the Nosedive: A Contemporary Picture of Church-going: What the 2005 English Church Census Reveals* (London: Christian Research, 2006).

[11] D. Voas and A. D. Crockett, 'Religion in Britain: Neither Believing nor Belonging', *Sociology*, 39 (2005), 11–28.

Surveys in the early 1980s produced mass attendance figures of over 80 per cent. Those taken twenty years later show figures in the low 40s. One extremely robust statistic is the number of religious vocations. In 1965 1,375 men in Ireland joined the priesthood; in 1994 it was 201; in 2000, it was 61.[12] In Holland, the percentage of adults describing themselves as having no denomination rose from 14 per cent in 1930 to 39 per cent in 1997 and 42 per cent in 2003.[13] An overwhelming majority of Swedes (some 95 per cent) seldom or never attend public worship, and Hamberg finds no evidence of revival in a situation that she describes as follows: 'the share of the population who adhere to Christian beliefs or who devote themselves to such traditional religious activities as prayer and church attendance declined in Sweden during the twentieth century…data indicate a decline not only in the prevalence of religious beliefs but also in the saliency of these beliefs.'[14] According to the Mannheim Eurobarometer, the percentage of the population attending church once a week or more often changed between 1970 and 1999 as follows: in France from 23 to 5 per cent; in Belgium from 52 to 10 per cent; in Holland from 41 to 14 per cent; in Germany from 29 to 15 per cent; in Italy from 56 to 39 per cent; and in Ireland from 91 to 65 per cent.[15] The actual numbers matter less than the pattern. In no cases has there been a reversal of decline.

## Religion in Eastern Europe

The fate of Christianity in those parts of Europe controlled by communist parties from 1917 (Russia, Ukraine, and Belarus) or from the Second World War (the Baltic states, Poland, East Germany, Hungary,

[12] These data were kindly provided by Dr R. D. Stevens of the Irish Council of Churches.

[13] N. D. De Graaf, A. Need, and W. Ultee, 'Losing my Religion? A New and Comprehensive Examination of Three Empirical Regularities Tested on Data for the Netherlands in 1998', in A. Crockett and R. O'Leary (eds), *Patterns and Processes of Religious Change in Modern Industrial Societies: Europe and the United States* (Lampeter: Edwin Mellen Press, 1998), table 1.

[14] E. Hamberg, 'Christendom in Decline: The Swedish Case', in H. McLeod and W. Ustorf (eds), *The Decline of Christendom in Western Europe 1750–2000* (Cambridge: Cambridge University Press), 47.

[15] P. Norris and R. Inglehart, *Sacred and Secular: Religion and Politics Worldwide* (Cambridge: Cambridge University Press, 2004), 72.

Rumania, Bulgaria and Czechoslovakia, Yugoslavia and Albania) was very different. Rather than gradual weakening, the churches were suppressed. In Marxist theory, religion—memorably described as the opiate of the masses—has no role in a classless society, because there is no class exploitation to disguise and no pain to be dulled by the opiate of religion. Hence it would die out. But, to hasten the process, the state would administer two sorts of poison: persecution and substitution. The communist states severely constrained the churches and they created secular alternatives to religious rites of passage and collective rituals.

The success of the communist strategy varied with the nature of the church and its relationship to the titular nationality. In the Soviet Union the Orthodox Church (which had a history of being co-opted by the state that went back to Peter the Great) was stripped of most of its real and its symbolic estate and its officials were replaced by party hacks. In Poland the much healthier Catholic Church (aided by being the local branch of a powerful international organization) was able to retain the support of the people by acting as an unofficial opposition to the alien and imposed regime. While the Catholic Church in the German Democratic Republic chose to preserve itself in pious isolation, Lutheran Bishop Schönherr announced: 'We do not want to be a church against or alongside, but in socialism.'[16] The state reciprocated. The great Protestant Reformer Martin Luther, who in the 1950s had been denounced as the father of fascism, was rehabilitated as a proto-revolutionary, and Erich Honeker, the communist party boss, gave his approval by serving as the president of the committee organizing the celebrations of the quincentenary of Luther in 1983. In Bulgaria in the 1950s, the communist government sent uncooperative priests for hard labour, encouraged a left-wing League of Orthodox Priests of Bulgaria to assert itself, stripped the church of its lands, put the clergy on state salaries, placed the church under control of an office within the Ministry of Foreign Affairs, and reduced it to being a timid spokesman for Bulgarian foreign-policy initiatives. And, with barely disguised contempt, communist party officials praised the church for its patriotism and stout defence of national culture.[17]

[16] Quoted in S. Bruce, *Choice and Religion: A Critique of Rational Choice* (Oxford: Oxford University Press, 1999), 110.

[17] S. P. Ramet, 'Politics and Religion in Eastern Europe and the Soviet Union', in G. Moyser (ed.), *Politics and Religion in the Modern World* (London: Routledge, 1991), 86.

But, for all that the details differed with such considerations as the level of economic development, the type of Christian church, and the confidence of the ruling communist party, in all communist states churches found it difficult to reproduce and to socialize younger generations. As the secularity of Eastern Europe had been artificially imposed, one might have supposed that the collapse of communism would lead to a religious revival. The churches were given back their buildings and the bones of their saints and the historically dominant faith was often given an honourable mention in the constitutions of the new democracies, but the people did not return in any great numbers.

This simplifies, but we can describe what has happened in the east in two parts. In the wealthier countries—East Germany, the Czech Republic, Slovenia, Hungary, and Poland—there has been no significant revival. In the less-developed countries of Russia, Belorussia, Ukraine, Bulgaria, Serbia, and Romania, there has been some growth. In Russia, for example, at least once a month church attendance went from 6 per cent in 1991 to 11 per cent in 2005.[18] But almost everywhere in Eastern Europe we see the same fundamental driver of decline as we see in the West: younger people are markedly less religious than older people.

The end of communism liberalized the religious economy. Communist states had sometimes tolerated the hegemonic church and, as Stalin did in 1939, sometimes cynically used the national church to mobilize patriotism. No such toleration was shown to those minority denominations and sects that were doubly despised as bourgeois deviation and as alien intrusion. But, as with the restoration of the formerly dominant churches, the opening of the market to new competitors (even ones well funded by European and US supporters) has made little change to the overall levels of Christian belief and observance, because they are on quite a different scale. If we stretch the definition of Christian to admit the Mormons, we can see the point. There were no Mormons in Russia in 1991; there are now 46 groups. This is impressive, but the likely 500 members vanish in the Russian population of 149 million.[19]

---

[18] I am grateful to Detlef Pollack of the University of Munster for these data. See also H. Knippenberg (ed.), *The Changing Religious Landscape of Europe* (Amsterdam: Het Spinhuis, 2005).

[19] I. Y. Kotin and A. D. Krindatch, 'Russia', in Knippenberg, *Changing Religious Landscape*, 156.

# Changes in Christianity

As well as considering the popularity of religion, we should consider its nature. The secularization of Western Europe has had a corresponding resonance within the ranks of the faithful. In brief, the major churches have responded to the liberalization of the general environment by themselves becoming more liberal in doctrine and more ecumenical in inter-church relations. The Second Vatican Council (1962–5) marked a sea change in the Catholic Church's self-image: Latin was replaced in many rituals by the vernacular languages, the traditional gulf between priest and laity was narrowed, demands on practising Catholics were relaxed, and the Church muted its claims to be the sole authentic representative of God on earth. As well as losing many adherents, the Church lost much of its authority over even those who continued regularly to attend its rituals and receive its offices. Catholics became more selective in their attention to official church teaching. As Scots Cardinal Thomas Winning said to me in 1998: 'We have to accept that we can no longer command. We no longer have a "people" who will obey us. Catholics are becoming more and more like the Protestants: they pick and choose.'

The change in attitude to hierarchy and authority, of course, had occurred for Protestants at the time of Reformation, but Western Europe's Protestant churches have seen similar changes in doctrine. All the major churches have become markedly more liberal. Although the historic creeds enjoy an honoured place as part of the heritage, even among the clergy their specific propositions rarely command assent. The changes have been complex, but they can be summarized as an 'internal secularization'. Few Protestants now believe that the Bible is the revealed Word of God, that Christ really was the Son of God, that God created the world in six days, that the Bible miracles really happened, that there is an actual heaven and hell, and so on. Rather, the basic Christian ideas have been internalized and psychologized. Evil and sin have been turned into alienation and unhappiness. The vengeful God has been replaced by Christ the inspiring Big-brother or Christ the therapist. The purpose of religion is no longer to glorify God: it is to help find peace of mind and personal satisfaction.

Although the charismatic movement that influenced Protestant churches in the 1970s is often seen as a conservative reaction to liberalizing trends, the reality is rather different. Although the new emphasis in charismatic fellowships on such 'gifts of the Holy Spirit' as speaking in tongues, healing, and prophesying might seem like a significant injection of supernaturalism, it eroded the doctrinal orthodoxy of conservative Protestant sects and weakened the behavioural codes that had served to distinguish conservative Protestants from the wider population.[20] The new churches recruited primarily from older denominations and sects rather than from the unchurched, and much of their appeal lay in the way they disguised the extent of change with some old language. Far from being a cure for the liberalization of the faith, they made the change easier by providing easy steps away from the old orthodoxies.

To summarize so far, although the post-1945 histories of Western and Eastern Europe have been very different, the outcome for the Christian churches has been sufficiently similar for it to be summarized in a single rubric. The once-hegemonic churches have lost significant power, prestige, and popularity, and the new entrants to the market have made little headway in filling the gaps. Across almost all strands of Christianity there has been a significant decline in doctrinal orthodoxy, a shift in focus from the next world to this one, and a weakening of the ties of obedience.

The same changes can be found in the modern liberal democracies that were founded by European settlers. The case of the United States will be discussed in Chapter 8, but we can note that Australia, New Zealand, and Canada all experienced major declines in church adherence over the twentieth century and, for the period for which we have good survey data, show a decline in the proportion of people who see themselves as religious or claim specific religious beliefs similar to that of Western Europe. The percentage of Canadians with no religion rose from 2 per cent in 1901 to 28 per cent in 2001. Claimed weekly church attendance rate fell from 67 per cent in 1946 to 19 per cent in 2003, with 43 per cent saying they never attended.[21] Australia

[20] This case is argued at length in S. Bruce, *God is Dead* (Oxford: Blackwell, 2001), ch. 9.

[21] D. Voas, 'The Continuing Secular Transition', in D. Pollack and D. V. A. Olson (eds), *The Role of Religion in Modern Societies* (New York: Routledge,

shows similar figures. For fifty years from 1911 to 1961, censuses showed less than 1 per cent of the population declining to choose a religious identity. But the percentage saying 'none' rose to 7 per cent in 1971 and 19 per cent in 2006. To this later figure we probably need to add most of the 11 per cent who either refused to answer or whose answer was unclear.[22] In 1960 weekly church attendance in Australia was 30 per cent. By 1997 it had fallen to 15 per cent and in 2001 it was just 7.5 per cent—much the same level as in Britain.[23] In New Zealand, the percentage of people claiming 'no religion' was 0.5 in 1956, 5.3 per cent in 1981, and 20 per cent in 1991.[24]

## An Aside on Measuring Religious Interest

One common criticism levelled at the proponents of the secularization paradigm is that we make too much of church attendance as an index of popular interest in, and commitment to, religion. In order to make comparisons over time and space, we need some common unit of currency and, for Christians, church attendance is a good measure. For Catholics, canon law made mass attendance an obligation for all the faithful, and the Catechism describes deliberate failure to attend as a 'grave sin'.[25] It was hardly less of a burden

2007), 27. Changes in Canadian religiosity have been tracked by Reginald Bibby in a series of surveys since 1975. See R. Bibby, *Fragmented Gods* (Toronto: Stoddart, 1987); *Unknown Gods* (Toronto: Stoddart, 1991); and *Restless Gods* (Ottawa: Wood Lake Books, 1995). His most recent work sees some signs of revival in the manner of Grace Davie (discussed in Chapter 4) and is criticized in J. Thiessen and L. L. Dawson, 'Is there a "Renaissance" of Religion in Canada? A Critical Look at Bibby and beyond', *Studies in Religion*, 37 (2008), 389–415.

   [22] The Australian census figures are summarized in http://en.wikipedia.org/wiki/Religion_in_Australia#cite_note-ABS_2008_Yr_Bk-3. Accessed 3 March 2010.

   [23] The first two figures come from P. L. Marler and C. K. Hadaway, 'Church Attendance and Membership in Four Nations', unpublished report, 1997, 13. The 2001 figure is from the National Church Life Survey: www.ncls.org.au (accessed 1 Sept. 2009).

   [24] M. Hill and R. Bowman, 'Religious Adherence and Religious Practice in Contemporary New Zealand', *Archives de science sociales des religions*, 58 (1985), 91–112, and http://en.wikipedia.org/wiki/File:Religious_affiliation_in_New_Zealand_1991-2006_-_bar_chart.svg (accessed 3 Mar. 2010).

   [25] T. Horwood, *The Future of the Catholic Church in Britain* (London: Laicos, 2006), 13.

for Protestants. Every Protestant church, sect, and denomination strenuously encourages its adherents to gather together to worship, and until recently most Protestant organizations have had more attenders than members.

We know from years of survey research that, when asked, people will often give opinions on issues about which they actually care little or nothing. They will even assert strong views on entirely fictitious issues. Talk is cheap. Attendance has the value to the researcher that it requires some effort and thus shows some degree of commitment. In the case of juveniles or compliant spouses, the commitment may only be to not offending someone else who thinks churchgoing is important, but even in those instances attendance is evidence that someone cares.

There is a further reason for treating attendance as a reliable index of underlying belief and commitment. Modern surveys allow us to correlate attendance with self-described religiosity (as in answers to a question such as 'Would you describe yourself as religious, spiritual, or neither?'), the holding of specific religious beliefs, responses to salience questions (such as 'How important is religion to you in living your life?'), and the like. At the level of both the group and the individual, such indices tend to fit together in the obvious ways. It is rare to find a large number of survey respondents who describe themselves as religious, say they are Christian, claim to believe in a personal creator God, or say that religion is important to them, but do not attend church regularly. This cohesion is not confined to Christianity. Surveys of Muslims show that high levels of mosque attendance correlate strongly with high frequency of personal prayer and with stating that religion is very important.[26] When we are looking for a single simple measure to convey a general impression, then, for modern Christian societies, church attendance works remarkably well, which is why I have frequently used it.

I should add that, as we will see with US Gallup polls in Chapter 8, actual attendance is a better measure than claimed attendance and that, when we do ask people about their churchgoing, indirect questions such as 'Which of the following did you do last weekend?' tend

[26] P. Heine and R. Spielhaus, 'What do Muslims Believe?', in M. Rieger (ed.), *What the World Believes: Analyses and Commentary on the Religion Monitor 2008* (Gutersloh: Verag Bertelsmann Stiftung, 2009), 595.

to produce more reliable responses than the direct 'How often do you attend a place of religious worship?'.

## Types of Religiosity

However, when we do have a number of different indices, it is sensible to use them all, which is what David Voas has done in a definitive article on changes in European Christianity.[27] The European Social Survey (ESS) includes questions on religious affiliation, frequency of attendance and frequency of prayer, self-rated religiosity, and the importance of religion in the respondent's life. Voas combines responses to these into a single scale of religiosity and divides respondents into five-year age cohorts by year of birth. By comparing those cohorts, he is able to produce a highly detailed picture of change in twenty-one countries. The demographically minded will appreciate that an important assumption is involved in using a single-time snapshot to represent change over time. Ideally data to study change should be longitudinal: they should survey the same people at regular intervals and periodically add a new first generation to the study. Unfortunately such studies are rare, so we often use data from a single survey to draw conclusions about the past by treating each age cohort as if it is representative of its era.

That is fine so long as people do not generally become more religious as they get older and we do have three sorts of evidence that they do not. First, there is ample evidence from non-survey sources that the churches in Europe have indeed been declining, and this would not be the case if most people became more religious as they aged. Second, we have small longitudinal studies that track people over long periods, and those do not show people becoming more religious over the life course.[28] Third, surveys frequently ask respondents if they attend church more or less often than they used to, and very few respondents claim to have become more religiously observant as they aged. Elderly people tend to be more religious than their children,

[27] D. Voas, 'The Rise and Fall of Fuzzy Fidelity in Europe', *European Sociological Review*, 25 (2009), 155–68.

[28] Voas and Crockett, 'Religion in Britain'.

who in turn tend to be more religious than the grandchildren, not because of age *per se* but because they were raised in more religious times. Or, to view the process from the other end, if someone was not raised in a particular faith, the chances of acquiring one later in life are small: about 5 per cent in a 2001 Scottish survey.[29]

When Voas compares the religiosity of Europeans born in the early 1980s with that of their grandparents' generation (born in the late 1920s), he finds a difference of exactly one scale point across the twenty-one countries: the older generation is twice as likely as the younger to be religious. The same two-generation difference is found in most of the countries taken separately. The exceptions are Hungary, Ireland, and Spain (where the gap between the generations is bigger), and Finland, Norway, Denmark, and Slovenia (where it is smaller). To put it another way, the pattern of decline has been similar across Europe, so that the rank ordering of countries by religiosity was largely preserved through the twentieth century. Within that stability, those countries that were most unusual at the start of the period also changed to become more like the others: what statisticians call regression to the mean. The more religious countries (mainly Catholic) declined most; the more secular countries (especially in Scandinavia) declined least.

There is a further and more significant pattern in the data. Voas uses his compound religiosity scale to divide respondents into three groups: the patently religious, the patently unreligious, and those in between. In every country there is an evident decline in the relative size of the religious part of the population as one moves from older to younger generations, accompanied by growth in the wholly secular part. The intermediate group, though, has become larger over time in the most religious countries (for example, Greece and Italy) and slightly smaller in the least religious (for example, Sweden and the Czech Republic), with stability or modest growth in the middle group (for example, Switzerland and Germany). At first sight the three-line graph for each country seems unique, but, once one controls for the point in time when decline begins, the graphs for the majority of countries fit closely on top of each other. There is actually a common

---

[29] S. Bruce and T. Glendinning, 'Religious Beliefs and Differences', in C. Bromley, J. Curtice, K. Hinds, and A. Park (eds), *Devolution: Scottish Answers to Scottish Questions* (Edinburgh: Edinburgh University Press, 2003), 86–115.

trajectory of religious decline. What varies is when the decline began and (to a lesser extent) how rapidly it is proceeding. There is much more that could be said about Voas's attempts to model change, but at this stage it is enough to note that the decline in the seriously religious part of the population is common across Europe and that the patterns of movement from seriously religious to intermediate to secular are regular across such a large number of states that we can be confident that we are looking at evidence of a substantial and real change that calls for a general social explanation.

Before we get to that explanation it is worth spending some time looking more closely at Voas's intermediate category, which in most countries is as large as the religious and the secular combined. These people should interest us, because it allows us to eliminate one common misconception of the secularization paradigm. It would be a mistake to suppose that the decline of religion is best explained by the superior attraction of secularity. This is not a battle between two sides that is being won by secularity's ability to attract defectors from religion. Rather, it is a slow process of generational change in which people gradually lose interest in things that mattered to their parents and in which the possibilities for belief and practice expand while the salience of any of those beliefs and practices declines. In that sense, the religious and the secular are not mirror images of each other. The best way I can convey the change from the religious to the secular is to use the metaphor of an abandoned garden in the countryside. Without constant pruning, selective breeding, and weeding, the garden loses its distinctive character, as it is overtaken by the greater variety of plant species in the surrounding wilderness.

Let us look at the intermediates—the neglected garden in the early stages of assimilation to the infinite possibilities of the wilderness—and begin with beliefs. As Voas puts it: 'Opinion polls in Europe show high levels of belief, not merely in religious or quasi-religious ideas (such as reincarnation) but also in folk superstition: horoscopes, clairvoyance, ghosts, and so on.'[30] Characteristically Christian beliefs have been in decline, and are now held by a minority.[31] For reasons

---

[30] Voas, 'Rise and Fall', 161.
[31] R. Gill, C. Kirk Hadaway, and P. Long Marler, 'Is Religious Belief Declining in Britain?', *Journal for the Scientific Study of Religion*, 37 (1998), 507–16; see also *The Tablet*, 18 Dec. 1999, 1729.

I will pursue in Chapter 5, many people would like to be thought of as spiritual and will therefore acknowledge a belief in something, but that something is less and less likely to be recognizable as religious doctrine. In Scotland in 2001 those who said they believed in God divided fairly equally between 'a personal creator God', 'a higher power or life-force', and the remarkably vague and permissive 'there is something there'.[32]

The numbers of self-conscious seekers is small. Paul Heelas's pioneering attempt to identify all those people in a small English town who were in any way involved in what he called the 'holistic milieu' claimed less than 2 per cent, and over half of them denied that their involvement in meditation, yoga, aromatherapy, and the like was spiritual.[33] Psychological and physical well-being was more common than spiritual seeking. But a more substantial proportion of the population will privately follow a variety of self-spirituality. Those who are most engaged with the process may reject Christianity, but others will see their spirituality as consistent with Christian identification.

More common in the intermediate class is a mix of beliefs about fate, the afterlife, a higher power, and the like that are quasi-religious but inconsistent with the teachings of the major Christian denominations. Elements of astrology, reincarnation, divination, magic, folk religion, and conventional Christianity coexist in packages that are not particularly coherent, but then they do not have to be because those who hold them tend not to reflect deeply on their world views. A woman wrote to the Aberdeen *Press and Journal* to complain that the little roadside shrine she had made to honour her husband who had died in a car crash had been vandalized. A 4-foot-high white stone ornament of a cat had been taken: 'I just want it to be put back and for his things to be left alone because it is the only place I can go to play his favourite CDs for him.'[34] Quite what state she thought her husband now occupied—able to hear music but only when played where he died—is not at all clear, but her shrine was an idiosyncratic construct that did not require the support of a coherent ideology. She had a particular notion and did not require anyone else to validate it.

As for religious activities, between those who attend church regularly and those who never attend, there is a large population that still

[32] Bruce and Glendinning, 'Religious Beliefs and Differences'.

[33] P. Heelas and L. Woodhead, *The Spiritual Revolution: Why Religion is Giving Way to Spirituality* (Oxford: Blackwell, 2004).

[34] *Press and Journal*, 13 Sept. 2002.

uses religious offices for rites of passage such as baptisms, weddings, and funerals and that will attend at Easter and Christmas. Much of that occasional attendance is explained by nostalgia and tradition and by the relative absence of secular ceremonies that confer the same degree of solemnity and seriousness. However, the evidence shows what logic would dictate: as the proportion of the seriously religious declines, so too does the weight of tradition. My father was baptized because everybody was. Along with about half my generation, I was baptized because my parents knew that their parents expected it. My children were not baptized because my parents no longer expected it.

After belief and activity, Voas discusses identity. Even if they have no discernible religious beliefs and do not participate in church services even occasionally, many Europeans still claim a religious identification. There are all sorts of reasons for such nominalism. Some of the non-churchgoers who ticked the 'Christian' box in the 2001 census in England and Wales may, like the successful businessman who describes himself as 'working class', simply have been recognizing their origins. Others may have been making a claim to respectability. Given that the next option for that question was 'Muslim', some may have been making an essential political point: they may have felt that the implied alternatives required a riposte, a form of social positioning.

The important point of Voas's wide-ranging exploration of the intermediate group concerns the salience of what he called their 'fuzzy fidelity': 'What is striking…is how little religion seems to matter to most fuzzy Christians. Only in the most religious countries do more than a quarter think that religion is personally somewhat important rather than unimportant.'[35] In most countries a very large majority of the intermediates see religion as not very important, and for 25 per cent or more, it is very unimportant.

The dominant attitude towards religion…is not one of rejection or hostility. Many of those in the large middle group who are neither religious nor unreligious are willing to identify with a religion, are open to the existence of God or a higher power, may use the church for rites of passage, and might pray at least occasionally. What seems apparent, though, is that religion plays a very minor role (if any) in their lives.[36]

---

[35] Voas, 'Rise and Fall', 164.     [36] Voas, 'Rise and Fall', 164.

This leaves two final issues: the size of the intermediate group and its stability.

Strictly speaking, the number of Europeans who fall between the extremes of religious and unreligious depends on what survey items one uses to define the group and where one places cut-off lines in the responses to questions that permit a scale of answers. Using what seems to the untutored eye to be sensible distinctions, Voas places between 40 and 60 per cent of the population of most European countries in the intermediate category. Which brings us to the vital issue for the secularization paradigm: how stable is this category?

One could argue that, after a period of unusually high religiosity, our societies have simply lapsed into the dull conformity that characterized the religious culture of the Middle Ages and that such a condition of vague supernaturalism and occasional involvement in organizations that worship God on our behalf is the human default position and hence is indefinitely sustainable. Voas's data offer a rare test of this claim. If they are right, then we would expect to see continued growth, or at least stability at a high level, in the neither-religious-nor-secular population. If the secularization paradigm is right, then, not long after wholly secular people outnumber the religious, the proportion of fuzzy Christians will reach a plateau and then start to fall. Ultimately they will be overtaken by the completely secular subpopulation, which will continue to grow steadily. That is what we see in the countries that have travelled furthest along a secularizing trajectory: France, Norway, Sweden, Hungary, and the Czech Republic. Others, including Britain, will soon reach that point. As Voas concludes: 'Fuzzy fidelity is not a new kind of religion, or a proxy for as yet unfocused spiritual seeking; it is a staging post on the road from religious to secular hegemony.'[37]

## Conclusion

A sceptical political scientist colleague dismissed my presentation of the above evidence with two damning assertions: 'all you've got is a trend' and 'you don't have an explanation'. The next chapter will

---

[37] Voas, 'Rise and Fall', 167.

present what I believe to be a decent explanation. It is complex and its causal claims cannot be supported with the sort of experimental demonstration that Boyle could mount when he showed the pressure of his gases rising when he heated them, but in those respects it is no worse (and probably much better) than most of what passes for explanation in the non-experimental social sciences.

Let us consider the 'all you've got is a trend' rebuttal. First, it is a very long-standing trend. In all the states of Western Europe and in Canada, Australia, and New Zealand, once decline has begun, it has proceeded unchecked. In almost no index of popular religiosity is there any reversal. And, for the states where the decline first became apparent, it has proceeded unchecked for almost a century, if we take a complex of measures of religiosity as a package. On some measures the trend of decline has been evident for at least 150 years. In Britain, for example, church attendance has been declining since at least 1851. Second, the trend has defied the most strenuous efforts of church people (who have been well aware of it for the best part of a century) to reverse it. Of course, tomorrow may be different. God may send showers of revival rain, and the social scientist has to remain agnostic about that possibility. Social scientists have been surprised often enough for us to be cautious of betting the house on any trend continuing unchanged. But, unless we have good cause to think otherwise (as distinct from a general reluctance to commit ourselves), it is reasonable to assume that the trend we have seen for a century will continue.

Much more will be said about the details of the decline of religion in the West, but enough evidence has been presented here to suggest that there is some regular relationship between modernization and secularization. The next chapter will present the outline of an explanation of that relationship.

# 2

# Explaining Secularization

## Introduction

The theory of secularization could be presented through an intellectual biography of sociology. Because the founders of the discipline were interested in what distinguished the modern world from previous social formations and cultures, almost all the major figures in the development of sociology made some contribution to our understanding of the changing nature and social roles of religion. However, to present the explanation of secularization as a history of ideas is to show a lack of confidence in our enterprise. By implying that sociology cannot transcend its history, such an approach encourages those who deny the possibility of social science.[1] We cannot pretend to the confidence of physics, but sociology is more than a series of intellectual fashions.

In what follows I present a synthesis of various attempts to explain the general observation that modernization undermines the power, popularity, and prestige of religious beliefs, behaviour, and institutions. As the authorship of ideas is less important than how well those ideas stand up to critical and empirical scrutiny, the elements of the synthesis will be grouped around the aspect of social reality to which

---

[1] For an excellent account of the evolution of the key ideas involved in the secularization paradigm, see O. Tschannen, 'The Secularization Paradigm: A Systematization', *Journal for the Scientific Study of Religion*, 30 (1991), 395–415.

they relate rather than around schools of social theory or the legacy of particular scholars. This leaves me open to the accusation of trying to give unwarranted authority to my own invention by attributing it to others. To the extent that there is anything original in what follows, it lies in two things: sidestepping the issue of the origins of religion and treating the related question of what purposes religion serves as secondary to the question of why people believe it.[2] Rather than try to explain why societies have religions, I simply note that almost all agrarian societies were pervaded by religious sentiments, that most modern societies are not, and that our task is to understand the change. The first difficulty of explaining the invention or the persistence of religion by the needs it is supposed to serve is that the list of candidate needs is long, and, given the near universality of religion, it is difficult to know how we would establish which items on that list were most effective. A second problem is the role of culture in defining needs. Unless we root the idea of needs in some invariant element of human psychology or in some perpetual problem of social organization—and any such rooting is challenged by the fact of secularization—we have to recognize needs are created by shared cultures. It is what we are raised to believe that shapes our sense of what we (or our societies) require. So we are back to where we started. We still have to explain why societies differ in the extent to which people feel needs that they seek to satisfy through religious beliefs and rituals (rather than in some secular manner). The sociological way out of this tautology is to recognize that belief systems are social products that are socially created, maintained, and transmitted and that their plausibility and persuasiveness depend on social-structural features. To give the simplest example (and one to which we will frequently return), parents who are equally committed to the same religion are more likely than parents who differ to succeed in raising their children to share their beliefs. In sum, the presentation that follows concentrates on identifying those features of social structures and social relationships that make beliefs more or less plausible.

---

[2] For a discussion of a variety of definitions of religion that attempt to explain both origins and persistence, see E. Durkheim, 'Concerning the Definition of Religious Phenomena', in W. S. F. Pickering (ed.), *Durkheim on Religion* (London: Routledge and Kegan Paul, 1975), 74–99.

The details of what is meant by modernization will be presented shortly, but it is worth offering a brief introductory definition and clearing away one source of confusion. Marion Levy identified technology as the key driver when he defined modernization as the growing ratio between inanimate and animate sources of power.[3] My ancestors worked the fields with their own muscles and with horses. The man I hire to plough my field drives a tractor that runs on fossil fuels. Hence my method of cultivation is more modern than that of my great-grandfather. Technology brings economic growth. It also brings new ways of organizing social life, and, in recognition of that fact, it makes sense to add to Levy's definition. For my purposes modernization 'consists of the growth and diffusion of a set of institutions rooted in the transformation of the economy by means of technology'.[4] As modernization refers to a process, a specific series of linked changes, there is strictly speaking no such thing as a modern society; there are only societies that are more or less advanced on the continuum of modernization. And, more importantly, 'modern' does not mean 'existing now'; it means having certain characteristics. Some contemporary societies are thoroughly modern; others are not. This needs to be stated clearly, because it is still common for critics to rebut the secularization paradigm by showing that this or that un-modern society is religious. Modernity does not come just with the passage of time.

## Understanding Secularization

Although it adds an extra syllable, 'paradigm' is preferable to 'theory' because it reminds us of the complexity of what is involved. Figure 2.1 attempts a diagrammatic representation of the key elements of the

---

[3] M. Levy, *Modernization: Latecomers and Survivors* (New York: Basic Books, 1972). My general approach to social evolution is greatly informed by E. Gellner, *Plough, Sword and Book: The Structure of Human History* (London: Collins Harvill, 1988), and M. Mann, *The Sources of Social Power*: i. *A History of Power from the Beginning to AD 1760* (Cambridge: Cambridge University Press, 1986), and ii. *Rise of Classes and Nation States, 1760–1914* (Cambridge: Cambridge University Press, 1993).

[4] P. L. Berger, B. Berger, and H. Kellner, *The Homeless Mind: Modernization and Consciousness* (Harmondsworth: Penguin, 1974), 15.

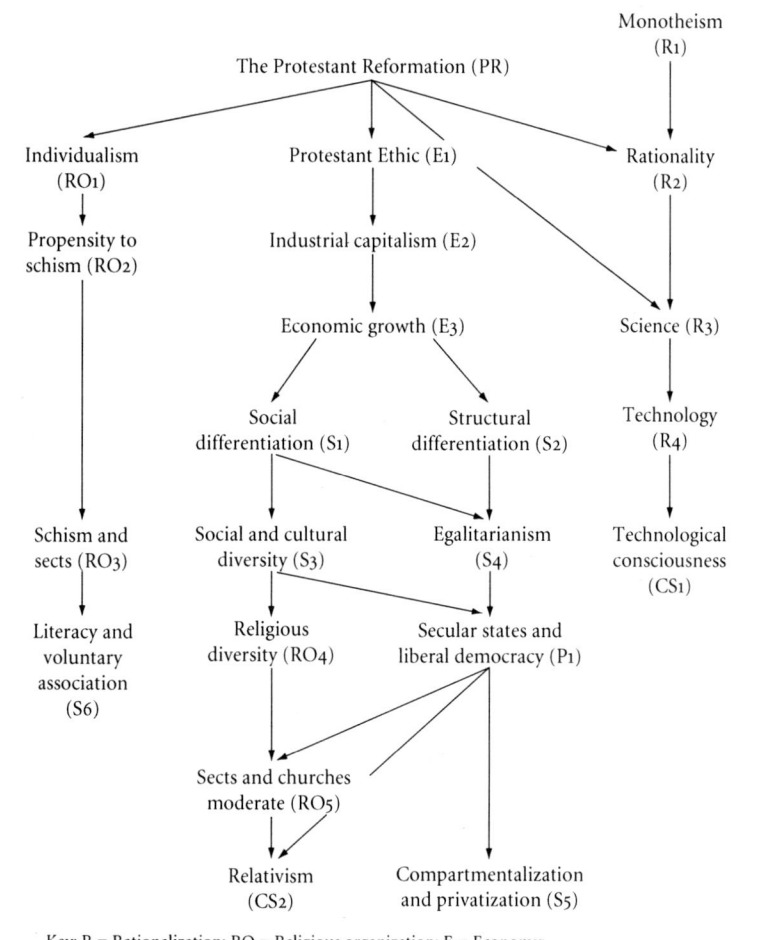

Figure 2.1. The secularization paradigm

secularization paradigm, which I will now present in roughly chronological order.

## Monotheism (R1)

I will begin with the oldest part of what sociologists, following Max Weber, regard as a foundational element of the secularization

✝ story: the rationalization of consciousness and social organization.[5] Monotheism makes a major difference to how people think about the natural and supernatural worlds and their interconnection.[6] The Egyptian, Roman, and Greek worlds were embedded in a cosmic order that made no sharp distinction between the human and the non-human or the natural and supernatural worlds. Gods had sex with people and produced demi-God offspring. In contrast, the single Jewish God was remote. He had created the world, at some point he would end it, and he visited periodically to call us to order, but his remoteness meant that it was easier for the world to be seen as having its own structure and logic. He made consistent ethical demands—for example, with the Ten Commandments—and he was beyond magical manipulation. We could learn his laws and obey them, but we could not bribe, cajole, or trick him. As the Christian Church evolved from its Jewish roots, the cosmos was remythologized with angels and semi-divine saints. The idea that God could be manipulated through ritual, confession, and penance undermined the tendency to regulate behaviour with a standardized ethical code. However, this trend was reversed as the Protestant Reformation of the sixteenth century stripped away the angels and saints, eliminated the ritual and sacramental manipulation of God, and restored the process of ethical rationalization.

Making formal what pleased God made it possible for ethics to become detached from beliefs about the supernatural. Codes could be followed for their own sake and could even attract alternative justifications. In that sense, the rationalizing tendency of Christianity created space for secular alternatives.

## The Protestant Ethic (E1)

Weber believed that the Reformation of the sixteenth century inadvertently created new attitudes to work and capital accumulation.[7]

---

[5] A vast industry has grown around interpreting Weber's often fragmented works. Two of the best commentaries on rationalization are G. Roth, 'Rationalization in Max Weber's Developmental History', in S. Lash and S. Whimster (eds), *Max Weber, Rationality and Modernity* (London: Allen and Unwin, 1987), 75–91, and A. Sica, 'Rationalization and Culture', in B. S. Turner (ed.), *The Cambridge Companion to Weber* (Cambridge: Cambridge University Press, 2000), 42–58.

[6] P. L. Berger, *The Social Reality of Religion* (London: Faber and Faber, 1969).

[7] M. Weber, *The Protestant Ethic and the Spirit of Capitalism* (London: George Allen and Unwin, 1976); G. Marshall, *In Search of the Spirit of Capitalism* (London: Hutchinson, 1982).

The pre-Reformation model of piety was generally one of other-worldly asceticism: the unusually Godly cultivated the purity of their souls by cutting themselves off from the world in monasteries and in hermitages. In his attempt to break the division between the religious virtuosi and the common people, so that everyone would be as pious as the monk and the nun, Martin Luther argued that any legitimate occupation, performed diligently, glorified God. There was no need to withdraw from the world. By arguing against confession, penance, and absolution, the Reformers deprived people of a way of periodically wiping away their sins. They thus increased the strain of trying to live a Christian life and made it all the more important to avoid temptation; hence the additional premium on work, which both glorifies God and distracts us from sin. With other changes, the result was what Weber called 'this-worldly asceticism'—an attitude of disciplined self-control that was well suited to the rise of rational capitalism. The link from E2 to E3 represents the fact that those countries that first adopted industrial capitalism prospered ahead of their rivals, and, as we will see, prosperity itself weakens religious commitments.

## Structural Differentiation (S2)

One of the most far-reaching elements of modernization is the structural and functional differentiation that comes with size and wealth. As societies became larger and more affluent, they become more internally varied and specialized. Durkheim neatly expressed this point in a contrast between mechanical and organic societies.[8] Small simple societies (his examples were the tribes studied by early anthropologists) hang together through the similarity of their parts: everyone is much the same. Large complex societies hang together because their component parts are very different: internal differentiation means that no part can survive without the rest. I always have to think twice about Durkheim's labels, because to me 'organic' suggests 'natural' therefore 'simple' or 'primitive', while 'mechanical' suggests modern and complex. That Durkheim calls the simple tribe mechanical and the modern society organic is a nuisance, but the contrast is clear and it is useful. As societies modernize, social life fragments as specialized roles and institutions are created to handle

[8] E. Durkheim, *The Division of Labor in Society* (Glencoe, Ill.: Free Press, 1964).

specific features or functions previously embodied in one role or institution.[9] To give an obvious example, the family was once a unit of production as well as the institution through which society was reproduced. With industrialization, economic activity became increasingly divorced from the home. It also became increasingly informed by its own values—that is, a link could be drawn from R2 to S2. At work we are supposed to be rational, instrumental, and pragmatic. We are also supposed to be universalistic: to treat customers alike, paying attention only to the matter in hand. The private sphere, by contrast, is taken to be expressive, indulgent, and emotional. It is where we make up for what is increasingly missing from the public world.[10]

Increased specialization directly secularized many social functions that were once dominated by the church: education, health care, welfare, and social control. Either the state directly provided such services or, if churches remained the conduit, the work became increasingly governed by secular standards and values.

## Social Differentiation (S1)

As the social structure fragments, so does the people. Economic growth created an ever-greater range of occupation and life situation, and, because it was accompanied by growing egalitarianism (of which more below), led to class avoidance. In feudal societies, masters and servants often lived cheek by jowl. Such proximity was possible because the gentry had no fear that the lower orders would get ideas 'above their station', and both those terms—order and station—give a good idea of rigidity of social divisions. As the social structure became more fluid and the defence of hereditary inequality more difficult, those who could afford to do so replaced the previously effective social distance with literal space. One can see a nice example of this in the geography and architecture of Edinburgh. In the tenements of the Old Town, different floors of the same house were occupied by people of different classes. The construction of the New Town

---

[9] T. Parsons, *Structure and Process in Modern Societies* (Glencoe, Ill.: Free Press, 1960).

[10] T. Parsons and R. F. Bales, *Family, Socialization and Interaction Process* (Glencoe, Ill.: Free Press, 1955).

in the late eighteenth century was the start of a process of quite refined class allocation by town planning.

The idea of a single moral universe in which all people have a place is more plausible the more stable is the social structure. With new social roles and increasing social mobility, communal conceptions of the moral and supernatural order fragmented. As classes became more distinctive, they created salvational systems better suited to their interests. The medieval church's great pyramid of pope, bishops, priests, and laity reflected the feudal social pyramid of king, nobles, gentry, and peasants. Independent small farmers or the rising business class preferred a more democratic religion; hence their attraction to such Protestant sects as the Presbyterians, Baptists, and Quakers.

† Modernization was not simply a matter of religion responding to social, economic, and political changes. Religion itself had a considerable effect on social and cultural diversity (S3). To explain this I must go back a stage to the link between the Reformation, the rise of individualism, and schism.

## Individualism (RO1)

David Martin noted a major effect of the Reformation when he wrote: 'The logic of Protestantism is clearly in favour of the voluntary principle, to a degree that eventually makes it sociologically unrealistic.'[11] Belief systems differ greatly in their propensity to fragment. To simplify, some religions claim a unique truth while others allow that there are many ways to salvation. The Catholic Church claims that Christ's authority was passed to Peter and then fixed in the office of Pope. It claims control of access to salvation and the right to decide disputes about God's will. If those claims are accepted, the Church is relatively immune to fission. As to depart from Rome goes to the very heart of what you believe as a Catholic, such departures are difficult and are associated with extreme upheavals, such as the French Revolution. Thus, as Catholic countries modernized, they split into the religious and the secular: in the twentieth century, Italy, Spain and France had conservative Catholics traditions and powerful Communist parties.

[11] D. Martin, *The Dilemmas of Contemporary Religion* (Oxford: Blackwell, 1978), 9.

Protestantism was vulnerable to schism, because it rejected institutional mechanisms to settle disputes. Asserting that everyone can equally well discern God's will invited fracture. Division might be retarded by tradition, habit, respect for learning, and admiration for piety, but it could not be prevented. The Reformation produced not one church purified and strengthened but a large number of competing churches and sects.

We might add a secular version of RO1. Individualism gradually developed an autonomous dynamic as the egalitarianism located in the Figure 2.1 as S4. It is placed there to suggest that individualism and the closely associated social reality of diversity (S3) could develop only in propitious circumstances and that such circumstances were provided by structural differentiation (S2) and economic growth (E3). The link between modernization and inequality is paradoxical. Industrialization produced both greater social distance and a basic egalitarianism (S4). The Reformers were not democrats, but they inadvertently caused a major change in the relative importance of community and individual. By removing the special status of the priesthood and the possibility that religious merit could be transferred (by, for example, saying masses for the souls of the dead), they reasserted what was implicit in early Christianity: that we are all severally rather than jointly equal in the eyes of God. That equality initially lay in our sinfulness and our responsibilities—we each had to answer for ourselves to God—but the idea of equality could not indefinitely be confined to duty. Equal obligations opened the way for equal rights.

The potential was able to become actual because of changes in the economy.[12] Economic development brought change and the expectation of further change. And it brought occupational mobility. As it became more common for people to better themselves, it also become more common for them to think better of themselves. However badly paid, the industrial worker did not see himself as a serf. The serf of the Middle Ages occupied just one role in an all-embracing hierarchy, and that role shaped his entire life. A tin-miner in Cornwall in 1800 might be oppressed at work, but in the late evening and on Sunday he could change clothes and persona to become a Baptist

---

[12] E. Gellner, *Nations and Nationalism* (Oxford: Basil Blackwell, 1983); *Plough, Sword and Book*.

preacher: a man of prestige. Such alternation marks a crucial change that brings us back to Durkheim's potent contrast of mechanical and organic societies. Where simple societies have clear statuses (such as age bands), these tend to be all-encompassing. An elder is an elder. When social status becomes more task-specific and structural differentiation produces a number of hierarchies, it becomes possible for people to occupy different positions in different spheres. The same person could be above you in one order and below you in another. That fact allowed and encouraged people to distinguish between social roles and the persons who filled them. Roles were still ranked and accorded very different degrees of power or status, but the people behind the roles could be seen as being, in some foundational sense, equal. Or, to put it another way, the more complex and flexible the ranking systems of a society, the more likely it is that people will distinguish between the status of a social position and the person who occupies that position.

## Societalization

Societalization is the term that Bryan Wilson gave to the way in which 'life is increasingly enmeshed and organized, not locally but societally (that society being most evidently, but not uniquely, the nation state)'.[13] If social differentiation (S1) and individualism (RO1) are blows to small-scale communities from below, societalization is the attack from above. Close-knit, integrated, communities gradually lost power and presence to large-scale industrial and commercial enterprises, to modern states coordinated through massive, impersonal bureaucracies, and to cities. This is the classic community-to-society transition delineated by Ferdinand Tönnies.[14]

Following Durkheim, Wilson argued that religion is at its strongest in the small-scale community. As the society rather than the community becomes the locus of the individual's life, so religion is denuded. The parish church of the Middle Ages christened, married, and buried. Its calendar of services mapped onto the seasons. It celebrated

---

[13] B. R. Wilson, *Religion in Sociological Perspective* (Oxford: Oxford University Press, 1982), 154.
[14] F. Tönnies, *Community and Association* (London: Routledge and Kegan Paul, 1955).

and legitimated local life. In turn it drew strength from being frequently reaffirmed by the local people. In 1898 almost everyone in my village celebrated the harvest by bringing tokens of their produce to the church. In 1998 a very small number of people in my village, only one of them a farmer, celebrated by bringing to the church vegetables and tinned goods (many of foreign provenance) bought in a supermarket that was itself part of a multinational combine. Instead of celebrating the harvest, the service thanked God for all his creation. Broadening the symbolism of the celebration solved the problem of relevance but at the price of losing close contact with the lives of those involved. When the all-embracing community of like-situated people working and playing together gives way to the dormitory town or suburb, there is little left in common to celebrate.[15]

Structural differentiation and societalization reduced the plausibility of any single overarching moral and religious system and thus allowed competing convictions to emerge. While any one faith may have had much to say to the private experiences of its adherents, none could have much connection to the performance of social roles or the operation of social systems because none was society-wide. Religion lost its objective taken-for-grantedness. It was now a preference, not a necessity.

Again it is worth stressing the interaction of social and cultural forces. The Reformation's fragmentation of the religious tradition (RO3) hastened the development of the religiously neutral state (P1). A successful economy required a high degree of integration: effective communication, a shared legal code to enforce contracts, a climate of trust, and so on.[16] This required an integrated national culture. Where there was consensus, a national high culture could be provided through the dominant religious tradition. The clergy could continue to be the school teachers, historians, propagandists, and public administrators. Where there was little consensus, the growth of the state was secular.

### Schism and Sects (RO3)

One of the greatest impacts of the Reformation was that it stimulated literacy (S5). With everyone required to answer to God individually,

---

[15] It is too complex a case to argue here, but I am rejecting Bellah's argument that large complex societies can have an effective civil religion. See R. Bellah, *Tokugawa Religion: The Values of Pre-Industrial Japan* (Glencoe, Ill.: Free Press, 1957).

[16] Gellner, *Plough, Sword and Book*.

lay people needed the resources to meet that new responsibility. Hence the translation of the Bible into vernacular languages, the rapid advance in printing, the spread of literacy, and the start of mass education. Competition between sects was a further spur. And, as Gellner and others argue, the spread of education was both essential to, and a consequence of, economic growth. The sectarian competitive spirit of the RO line interacted with the requirements of the E and S line to produce a literate and educated laity, which in turn encouraged the general emphasis on the importance and rights of the individual and the growth of egalitarianism (S4) and liberal democracy (P1).

Protestant sects also had a direct influence on P1 by providing a new model for social organization. Reformed religion was individualistic but it was not lonely. It encouraged individuals to band together for encouragement, edification, evangelism, and social control.[17] As an alternative to the organic community in which position was inherited and ascribed, the sectarians established the voluntary association of like-minded individuals coming together to pursue common goals.

## Social and Cultural Diversity (S3)

That modern states gradually become less and less religious was driven, in part, by diversity. Modernization brought with it increased cultural diversity in three ways. Peoples moved and brought their language, religion, and social mores into a new setting. Secondly, expanding nation states encompassed new peoples. Third, especially common in Protestant settings, economic modernization created classes that created competing sects. Hence the paradox: at the same time as the nation state was trying to create a unified national culture out of thousands of small communities, it was having to come to terms with increasing religious diversity, and it did so by gradually reducing the importance of religion in its operations. The idea of having one legally established state church to which all subjects or citizens should belong was abandoned altogether (the United States) or neutered (the British case). While freedom from entanglements with secular power allowed churches to concentrate on their core task and thus become what Talcott Parsons called 'a more specialized

---

[17] The importance of this is recognized in Weber's *Protestant Ethic* essays, which treat not only the new ideas but also the group structures that supported them.

agency', their removal from the centre of public life reduced their contact with, and relevance for, the general population.[18]

Because it is still common for people to confuse secularism (in the sense of a conscious project to promote the secular) and secularization (the social process of becoming more secular), it is important to stress the inadvertent and often ironic nature of much social change. In trying to compress a great deal of history into a few pages, I may inadvertently suggest the operation of some benign wise causal agent. Quite the opposite is the case. We have already seen one potent example of unintended consequences in Weber's Protestant ethic thesis. He does not suggest that the great Reformers such as Martin Luther and John Calvin deliberately encouraged people to become rational pursuers of material gain. On the contrary, their view of wealth was the standard pious Christian perspective: acquisitiveness is bad because it distracts from the service of the Lord and wealth is a rich source of temptation to sin. Weber's case is that reforms promoted for purely religious reasons, in the long run, had major unanticipated and unsought-for consequences. The same point can be made about the link between religious diversity and toleration. Some religious minorities have always promoted the desirability of religious liberty, but many of the Protestant sects that broke away from their national churches were originally as committed to coercion in the cause of righteousness as the state churches they rejected. The Scottish Covenanters who opposed the national church after 1638 were firmly committed to the idea of a deal or 'Covenant' between religious and political power. The church was obliged to support the state and the state was obliged to ensure (with force if necessary) that the people worshipped the right God in the right manner. The Covenanters left the national church not because they were liberals opposed to imposition but because this particular church was not sufficiently pure to deserve the state's support. The same is true of many of the Puritan groups that fled persecution in England for the New World. Once they were the masters, they tried to impose their faith on the New England colonies with as much enthusiasm as the oppressors from whom they had fled.

---

[18] T. Parsons, *Structure and Process in Modern Societies* (Glencoe, Ill.: Free Press, 1960), 304.

It is a sad reflection on human nature that it took their own failure to be effectively intolerant eventually to persuade most sects that toleration was a good idea. Only after they had tried and failed to become the dominant force did they start to find some virtue in necessity and gradually abandon their vision of a theocracy in favour of the idea of religious liberty.

Separation of church and state was one consequence of diversity. Another was the break between community and religious world view. In sixteenth-century England, every significant event in the life cycle of the individual and the community was celebrated in church and given a religious gloss. The church's techniques were used to bless the sick, sweeten the soil, and increase animal productivity. Testimonies, contracts, and promises were reinforced by oaths sworn on the Bible and before God. But, beyond the special events that saw the vast majority of parishioners troop into the church, a huge amount of credibility was given to the religious world view simply through everyday interaction and conversation. People commented on the weather by saying 'God be praised' and on parting wished each other 'God Speed' or 'Goodbye' (an abbreviation for 'God be with you').

Diversity also had consequences for consciousness. It called into question the certainty that believers could accord their religion.[19] Ideas are most convincing when they are universally shared. If everyone shares the same beliefs, they are not beliefs; they are just how the world is. Any world view is most powerful, not when it is supported by aggressive propaganda but when it is so much taken for granted that it does not require such promotion. The elaboration of alternatives provides a profound challenge. Believers need not fall on their swords when they find that others disagree with them. Where clashes of ideologies occur in the context of social conflict or when alternatives are promoted by people who need not be seriously entertained, the cognitive challenge can be dismissed.[20] It can be managed by creating elaborate explanations of why other cultures have got it wrong. In a Scottish Presbyterian Sunday school I was taught that the races differed in their cognitive competence and that a wise God had

---

[19] P. L. Berger, *The Heretical Imperative: Contemporary Possibilities of Religious Affirmations* (London: Collins, 1980).

[20] P. L. Berger and T. Luckmann, 'Secularization and Pluralism', *International Yearbook for the Sociology of Religion*, 2 (1966), 73–84.

revealed himself to them in ways that they would understand. So the really backward peoples got animism, the fairly backward ones got a multiplicity of Gods, the next strata got Islam, the ones above that got Catholicism, and the northern Europeans, God's finest creation, received the full revelation of God as a Presbyterian. But even such flattering coping strategies cannot disguise the fact that the proliferation of alternative faiths removes the sense of inevitability. When the oracle speaks with a single clear voice, it is easy to believe it is the voice of God. When it speaks with twenty different voices, it is tempting to look behind the screen.

## Compartmentalization and Privatization (S5)

Once society has moved beyond the possibility of restoring religious homogeneity by exterminating the deviants, believers often respond to the fact of variety by supposing that all religions are, in some sense, the same (RO5). Another possibility (and they are not incompatible) is to confine one's faith to a particular compartment of social life (S5). With compartmentalization comes privatization: the sense that the reach of religion is shortened to just those who accept the teachings of this or that faith. As Thomas Luckmann puts it:

This development reflects the dissolution of *one* hierarchy of significance in the world view. Based on the complex institutional structure and social stratification of industrial societies different 'versions' of the world view emerge....With the pervasiveness of the consumer orientation and the sense of autonomy, the individual is more likely to confront the culture and the sacred cosmos as a 'buyer'. Once religion is defined as a 'private affair', the individual may choose from the assortment of 'ultimate' meanings as he sees fit.[21]

In what is often regarded as a challenge to the secularization paradigm, Jose Casanova has argued that social and structural differentiation need not cause privatization.[22] Although many elements of modernization prevent an authoritarian dogmatic church from exercising the power it enjoyed in the Middle Ages, it is not inevitable

---

[21] T. Luckmann, *The Invisible Religion: The Problem of Religion in Modern Society* (New York: Macmillan, 1967), 98–9.

[22] J. Casanova, *Public Religions in the Modern World* (Chicago: University of Chicago Press, 1994).

that religion be enduringly excluded from the public sphere. In the early phases of democratization in the Catholic states of Europe and of Central and South America, the Church had to be stripped of its power, but since 1945 the Catholic Church has accepted the principles of liberal democracy and has again been able to play an important role as one actor among others in civil society. Casanova is right, but his point seems more like an illustration of secularization than refutation. Churches, because they can claim to represent important social values and because they can mobilize large parts of their membership, can still be political actors, but such action requires that they accept secular rules of engagement. No church in a modern society can plausibly claim that its values should predominate because God is on its side. As we will see in Chapter 8's discussion of the Christian Right in the United States, religious interest groups are now forced to present their case in essentially secular terms.

### Secular States and Liberal Democracy (P1)

Social innovations, once established, can have an appeal that goes far beyond the initial motive to innovate. My case that the Reformation played a major part in laying the foundations for liberal democracy rests on the mechanism of unintended consequences. What were initially religious arguments inadvertently encouraged individualism, egalitarianism, and diversity, which in turn combined with growing social and structural differentiation to shift governments in the direction of secular liberal democracy. But, once the accidents had allowed something of the new ethos to become established, it could be promoted as virtuous in its own right, and in the late nineteenth century societies that had no great need for them introduced the same principles as part of wider political reforms. For example, despite dissent being largely contained within the Lutheran tradition, the introduction of representative democracy in the Nordic countries was accompanied by the gradual acceptance of the idea of religious liberty.

### The Moderation of Sects and Churches (RO5)

A crucial turn in the evolution of religion in the West was the scaling-down of the demands that believers made for their faith. In the history of any major religious tradition, we can see phases of moderation alternating with radicalism. Enthusiasts become frustrated with the current lack of piety and whip up a period of radical fervour, which gradually burns out as the mundane necessities of life—the harvest, the fishing season, the family—reassert themselves, and dull conformity again becomes the norm until the next wave of enthusiasm and so on. But, in the modernization of Western Europe, those cycles operated within a general pattern of decline, so that each wave of radicalism was smaller than its predecessor.

A large part of the dynamic for such cycles comes from a certain intrinsic tendency for radical movements to subvert themselves. Almost every Protestant sect since the Reformation has begun with a radical critique of its society (and especially the dominant religious climate), made strict demands of its members, and tried to create 'a new heaven on earth' in the lives of its adherents. And almost every one has gradually moderated its critique, its demand on its members, and the claims it makes for the uniqueness of its access to God. The Quakers, because of their radical egalitarianism, were initially regarded as a threat to the state, but they gradually evolved into a comfortable denomination, on easy terms with the world they had once despised as ungodly. Richard Niebuhr's explanation of that change involves two key observations.[23]

First, the commitment of those born into the sect is generally weaker than that of the founding generation, because they have not chosen to make sacrifices for their faith. Parents may work hard to socialize their children in their principles, but what people inherit will generally be less important to them than what they create themselves. Secondly, through a combination of accident and an unintended consequence of their own characteristics, later generations of sectarians faced a proportionately greater sacrifice. The accident was simply increasing prosperity. There have been temporary and local reversals, but overall the societies of the West have become ever more prosperous, and so over generations the relative cost of puritanical lifestyles increases. The unintended consequence is the potential prosperity that came with puritanism. Partly for the 'Protestant Ethic' reasons elaborated by Weber (E1) and partly because their

---

[23] R. H. Niebuhr, *The Social Sources of Denominationalism* (New York: Meridian, 1962).

asceticism made them widely trusted, many Quakers gradually became extremely wealthy. It is no accident that most of the British banking system developed from family firms run by Quakers: the Barclays, Backhouses, Trittons, and Gurneys. Increasing wealth (and the possibilities of social status and public acceptance that came with it) increased the costs of asceticism. Not surprisingly, most Quakers gradually moderated. By the late nineteenth century, the banking Quakers (and their cousins in the tea and chocolate trade) had shifted to the evangelical wing of the Church of England, and by the 1920s most were mainstream or liberal Anglicans. And those who remained Quakers eventually went the same way, as did most other Protestant sects.

An additional dynamic for moderation is found by the Italian political scientist Robert Michels in his study of oligarchy in left-wing trade unions and political parties, which explains the common pattern of drift to the right by the unintended consequences of professional leadership.[24] Translated to religious sects, the story goes like this. Most sects begin as primitive democracies, with little formal organization, but as they grow they acquire an internal division of labour and a distinct leadership cadre. Especially after the founder has died, there is a need to educate and train the preachers and teachers who will sustain the movement. There is an organization to be coordinated and managed. There are buildings to be managed and insured, laws to be complied with, books to be published and distributed. With organization comes paid officials who have a vested interest in reducing tension between the sect and the wider society. The movement's officers start to compare themselves to the clergy of the established church and (initially for the status of their faith rather than their own reward) desire the same levels of training, remuneration, and social status. The once-radical sect is compromised by its own officials.

Not all sects moderate. If the sect can isolate itself from the wider society so that its culture forms the taken-for-granted backcloth to life, then it can sustain itself relatively unchanged. The Amish, Hutterites, and Doukobhors, who created isolated agricultural communes and consciously adopted distancing strategies such as

---

[24] R. Michels, *Political Parties: A Sociological Study of Oligarchic Tendencies* (New York: Free Press, 1962).

continuing to speak an archaic foreign language, are cases in point. But in most cases the sect is only slightly insulated and cannot avoid the social-psychological effects of diversity described above. Having failed to win over the bulk of the people to its radical message and having to come to terms with being only a 'saved remnant', the sect gradually finds good reasons to moderate its claims and comes to see itself, not as the sole embodiment of God's will, but simply as one expression among others of what is pleasing to God.

The moderation of sects is mirrored in the moderation of the dominant churches. Again we must note that virtue only follows the failure of the vices. The first response of any hegemonic church to dissent is persecution. National churches generally gave up trying to reimpose conformity only when the dissenters successfully resisted and when the egalitarian principle became sufficiently well established that enough members of the ruling classes could no longer stomach the disruption caused by using troopers or oppressive laws to coerce righteousness. Faced with widespread defection and the loss of authority, most churches reduced their claims and came to view themselves as just one religious expression among others. The change was rarely made quickly or willingly, but by the start of the twentieth century most state churches were cooperating with other Christian organizations. By the end of it, most were presenting themselves as the senior spokesman for all religions against a largely secular climate.

## Economic Growth (E3)

The effect of prosperity on Protestants sects noted above can be generalized.[25] Increasing affluence often reduces religious fervour and traditionalism.[26] The poor and dispossessed find solace in a belief system that promises that 'the meek shall inherit the earth', that those who have little in this life will have everything in the next. As they prosper, the no-longer-so-poor rewrite their faith so that its loses much of its distinctiveness. US Pentecostalists such as Oral

---

[25] D. Chirot, 'The Rise of the West', *American Sociological Review*, 50 (1985), 181–95.

[26] See the discussion of the work of Ronald Inglehart in Ch. 9.

Roberts and Tammy Faye Bakker grew up in impoverished conditions that made it easy and satisfying to denounce flashy clothes, make-up, Hollywood movies, social dancing, and television.[27] When they could afford the work of the Devil, they relaxed their disapproval. Divorce, though still regretted, is widely accepted. Of itself, this does not mean that US Pentecostalists are less religious than their grandparents. I am not making asceticism a defining characteristic of religion. But the erosion of distinctive ways of life makes the maintenance of distinctive beliefs harder, because it increases positive interaction with people of more liberal religious views (or none) and hence brings into play the relativizing force of diversity.

## Science (R3) and Technology (R4)

Some critics of the secularization paradigm misrepresent it by elevating science to a central position. Rodney Stark and Roger Finke, for example, say 'it is science that has the most deadly implications for religion'.[28] A zero-sum notion of knowledge, with rational thought and science conquering territory from superstition, was carried into early sociology by Auguste Comte and Karl Marx among others, but it is not part of the modern secularization paradigm. We recognize that modern people are quite capable of believing nonsense and hence that the decreasing plausibility of any one body of ideas cannot be explained simply by the presence of some (to us) more plausible ones.[29] The crucial connections are more subtle and complex than those implied in a science-versus-religion battle and rest on nebulous consequences of assumptions about the orderliness of the world and our mastery over it.

[27] D. E. Harrell, *Oral Roberts: An American Life* (Bloomington, Ind.: Indiana University Press, 1985); T. F. Messner, *Tammy: Telling it my Way* (New York: Villard, 1996).

[28] R. Stark and R. Finke, *Acts of Faith: Explaining the Human Side of Religion* (Berkeley and Los Angeles: University of California Press, 2000), 61.

[29] Originally the sociology of knowledge was the sociology of error: only ideology (that is, the acceptance of bad ideas) needed sociological explanation. Berger and Luckmann's popularizing of phenomenology persuaded most sociologists that all beliefs needed to be explained (P. L. Berger and T. Luckmann, *The Social Construction of Reality* (Harmondsworth: Penguin, 1973)).

More important than science was the development of effective technologies. We should not forget that religion is often practical. Holy water cures ailments and prayers improve crop quality. Wilson argued that technology secularizes by reducing the occasions on which people have recourse to religion. Farmers need not stop praying to save their sheep from maggots because an effective sheep dip becomes available. They can believe that the dip works only if its application is accompanied by prayer. But the experience of their impious neighbours, whose sheep prove equally protected, weakens that holding operation. The more common adaptation is to see the discoveries of agricultural chemists as part of God's bountiful creation. This neatly avoids arguments between the religious and secular spheres and leaves the religious sphere intact, but it also leaves it smaller and increasingly irrelevant. As the accumulation of scientific knowledge gave people insight into, and technological mastery over, areas that had once been mysterious, the need and opportunity for recourse to the religious gradually declined. A perfect example can be seen in the contrasting responses of the Church of England to the Black Death of 1348–50 and the HIV/AIDs 'gay plague' of the 1980s. In the first, the Church called for weeks of fasting and special prayers. In the second, it called for more government investment in medical-scientific research.

More generally, as Martin puts it, with the growth of science and technology 'the general sense of human power is increased, the play of contingency is restricted, and the overwhelming sense of divine limits which afflicted previous generations is much diminished'.[30] To appreciate the implied contrast, we can go back to the famous words of the seventeenth-century philosopher Thomas Hobbes:

Whatsoever therefore is consequent to a time of Warre, where every man is Enemy to every man; the same is consequent to the time, wherein men live without other security, than what their own strength, and their own invention shall furnish them withall. In such condition, there is no place for Industry; because the fruit thereof is uncertain; and consequently no Culture of the Earth; no Navigation, nor use of the commodities that may be imported by Sea; no commodious Building; no Instruments of moving, and

---

[30] D. Martin, *The Religious and the Secular* (London: Routledge and Kegan Paul, 1969), 116.

removing such things as require much force; no Knowledge of the face of the Earth; no account of Time; no Arts; no Letters; no Society; and which is worst of all, continuall feare, and danger of violent death; And the life of man, solitary, poore, nasty, brutish, and short.[31]

Even when people have not been beset by 'continual fear and danger of violent death', most of humanity has had so little control over the circumstances of its existence that the contrast between helpless humanity and an all-powerful God or Gods has seemed entirely plausible. The Sunday school I briefly attended as a child met in a room that was decorated with Victorian etchings of Bible scenes. One showed a gigantic hand of God coming through dark clouds, with its finger pointing accusingly at a tiny cowering and obviously intimidated human figure. I cannot recall the story it was meant to illustrate, but, like the contrast between the mighty medieval cathedral and the hovels that surrounded it, that divine finger neatly conveyed what most religions have traditionally seen as the relative positions of God and humankind. God is great; we are insignificant.

It may well be that our sense of mastery over fate is a dangerous illusion of which we will be disabused when the various chickens of modern technology come home to roost in the form of environmental disaster, but there is no doubt that to date science and technology have played a part in elevating our sense of self-importance.

The precise way in which they combine is complex, but individualism, egalitarianism, liberal democracy, and science and technology all contribute to a general sense of self-importance, of freedom from fate, which makes the traditional authoritarian dogmatic religion, with its vengeful God, generally unpalatable to modern sensibilities. This does not stop modern people being religious, but it does suggest by logical inference what we find by observation: both in the world of the mainstream churches and in the cultic milieu of alternative spirituality people are now generally unwilling to subordinate themselves to external authority.[32]

---

[31] T. Hobbes, *Leviathan*, ch. 13. The text is available at www.fordham.edu/halsall/mod/hobbes-lev13.html (accessed 3 Mar. 2010).

[32] That 'generally' is important. The modern culture of the sovereign individual does not prevent the occasional guru from attracting a small but devoted following.

### Technology and Technological Consciousness (CS1)

Technology has not just increased our mastery over the physical world. It has changed how we think. In a neglected classic, Peter Berger, Brigitte Berger, and Hansfried Kellner combined Weber's emphasis on the rationalization of the modern world with a phenomenological interest in structures of thought to argue that the use of modern technology involves certain novel attitudes that are so pervasive that, even if we are unaware of them, they shape a great deal of how we see the world.[33] One such is 'componentiality'. In contrast to the world of the skilled craftsman, modern work assumes that the most complex entities can be broken down into parts that are infinitely replaceable. When my central heating pump fails, I can replace it by any other pump that has the same size pipe fittings and produces the same pressure. In the same way, technological work assumes that complex activities can be reduced to elements that can be indefinitely repeated. Technological production also assumes that those who participate in it define each other as anonymous functionaries. The man on the assembly line who performs step twelve in the process may be my friend, but he is also infinitely replaceable by anyone else suitably trained.[34] This attitude is carried over from work to workers in the management style known after the legendary car manufacturer Henry Ford as 'Fordism' and into the management of people generally through the prevalence of bureaucracy. Paul Heelas's explanation of the appeal of contemporary spirituality (discussed at length in Chapter 5) rests heavily on the alienated nature of modern work. The prevalence in modern society of such assumptions as componentiality deprives us of authentic human relationships; we have lost our souls and some of us seek to find them again through spiritual therapies and practices. While it is true that modernity creates its own discontents, it also makes certain solutions to that discontentment less likely. While the teachings of most religions do not openly clash with the assumptions of technological consciousness, there are serious incompatibilities of approach. There is little space for the eruption of the divine.

---

[33] P. L. Berger, B. Berger, and H. Kellner, *The Homeless Mind: Modernization and Consciousness* (Harmondsworth: Penguin, 1974).

[34] Berger et al., *Homeless Mind*, 36.

To summarize the R line, the effects of science and technology on the plausibility of religious belief are often misunderstood. The direct clash of religious and scientific knowledge is less significant than the subtle impact of naturalistic ways of thinking. The former was of interest only to the educated elite. The latter is pervasive. Science and technology have not made us atheists, but the underlying rationality and the subtle encouragement to self-aggrandisement make us less likely than our forebears to entertain the notion of a divine force external to our selves.

## Relativism (CS2)

Finally we come to the bottom line. The Christian Church of the Middle Ages was firmly authoritarian and exclusive in its attitude to knowledge. There was a single truth, and it knew what it was. Gradually social and cultural diversity combined with egalitarianism to undermine all claims to authoritative knowledge. Compartmentalization—the idea that my God rules my private life but need not rule the lives of others or govern my engagement in the public sphere—can serve as a holding operation, but it is difficult to live in a world that treats as equally valid a large number of incompatible beliefs, and that shies away from authoritative assertions, without coming to suppose that there is no one truth.

We may continue to prefer our world view, but we find it hard to insist that what is true for us must also be true for everyone else. The tolerance that is necessary for harmony in diverse egalitarian societies weakens religion by forcing us to live as if we could not be sure of God's will. A fine illustration of this is inadvertently given by the Bolton Interfaith Council in a pamphlet designed to encourage people to walk around various worship sites in the town. The pamphlet has pages on 'What Christians believe', 'What Muslims Believe', and 'What Hindus Believe'. All three faiths are presented as if they were equally correct.[35]

The consequence, visible over the twentieth century in liberal democracies, was a decline first in the level of commitment of, and then in the number of, church adherents. Relativism debilitates faith

---

[35] Bolton Interfaith Council pamphlet, 'The Bolton Faith Trail', www.allcommunity.co.uk/sei/s/911/f1.pdf (accessed 3 Mar. 2010).

by removing the best reason to ensure one's children are socialized in the faith. If all faiths (and none) offer a road to God, if there is no hell to which heretics get sent, then there is no need to ensure the transmission of orthodoxy.

## Change versus Decline

The argument will be pursued in subsequent chapters, but it is worth spelling out clearly one place in the above account where analysts can head in very different directions. It would be quite possible to accept most of the above as an explanation of why powerful shared communal religions have been displaced by individualized forms of religion without accepting that such a change also involved numerical decline.[36] In theory, Wilson permits that whenever he defines secularization as religion losing social significance.[37] However, given the mass of evidence that the totality of expressions of religious sentiment has declined with modernization (that is, new forms of religion have failed to compensate for the scale of decline in old ones), this seems like an unnecessary evasion. As this is frequently misrepresented, I stress that I am not saying that individualized forms of religion (such as ultra-liberal Christianity or alternative spirituality) are not 'really' religious. This is not an argument about definition. As Chapter 5 will elaborate, I am making an empirical causal claim: because privatized, compartmentalized, and individualized religion attracts less commitment, is harder to maintain, and is more difficult to pass on intact to the next generation, it fails to make up the ground lost by, and declines faster than, traditional religion. And there is a compounding process at work. Of its very nature, individualized religion does not produce a strongly religious public culture. As there is less consensually shared ambient religion, the work that the new

[36] Niklas Luhmann, for example, agrees that 'the social structure is secularized but not the individual' (N. Luhmann, *Funktion der Religion* (Frankfurt: Suhrkamp, 1977), 172). David Yamane wants to confine the process of secularization to the narrowing scope of religious authority (D. Yamane, 'Secularization on Trial: In Defense of a Neosecularization Paradigm', *Journal for the Social Scientific Study of Religion*, 36 (1997), 109–22).

[37] B. R. Wilson, *Religion in Secular Society* (London: C. A. Watts, 1966), p. xiv.

form of religion would have to do to make up the ground lost by the decline of the previously dominant traditional religion is proportionately greater and it is not up to the task. That is, secularization is change and decline.

## Retarding Tendencies

One of the crassest responses to the secularization paradigm is to suppose that its proponents are so blinkered they see only decline. The secularization paradigm suggests that social and structural differentiation, societalization, rationalization, individualism, egalitarianism, and increasing social and cultural diversity undermine religion. However, because most proponents are fully aware of the many settings in which religion has prospered in modernizing societies, they would add an important qualification: except where religion finds or retains work to do other than relating individuals to the supernatural. The many and varied instances of circumstances that retard secularization can be usefully summarized under the headings of cultural transition and cultural defence.

### Cultural Transition

Where social identity is threatened in the course of major social transitions, religion may help negotiate such changes or help to assert a new claim to a sense of worth. This is particularly evident in migration. Religio-ethnic groups can ease the move between homeland and the new world. The church offers a supportive group that speaks the language and shares the values of the old world but also has contacts with the new social milieu. Hence the common phenomenon of migrants being more religiously observant than they were in the old country, especially once they marry and have children and passing on their culture (with its religious component) becomes an issue.

There is another manifestation of the tendency for religion to retain significance, even temporarily to grow in significance, and that is in the course of modernization itself. Modernization disrupted communities, traditional employment patterns, and status hierarchies.

By extending the range of communication, it made the social peripheries and hinterlands more aware of the manners and mores of the centre and vice versa. Those at the centre of the society were motivated to evangelize the rest, seeking to assimilate them by socializing them to 'respectable' beliefs and practices. Late-eighteenth- and nineteenth-century British evangelicals such as William Wilberforce, Lord Shaftesbury, Hannah More, Dr Thomas Barnardo, and the many members of the sprawling wealthy Quaker families devoted vast amounts of time and money trying to improve the lot and the faith of the poor.[38] Sectors of the social periphery in turn were motivated to embrace the models of respectable performance offered to them, especially when they were already in the process of upward mobility and self-improvement.

## Cultural Defence

Religion often acts as guarantor of group identity. Where culture, identity, and sense of worth are challenged by a source promoting either an alien religion or rampant secularism, and that source is negatively valued, secularization will be inhibited. Religion can provide resources for the defence of a national, local, ethnic, or status-group culture. The role of Catholicism in Polish national resistance to Soviet communism is a good example.[39]

In the process of functional differentiation, the first sphere to become rationalized and freed of cultural encumbrances is the economy, but, in settings where religio-ethnic identity is important, such rationalization is often constrained. Employers will often hire only 'their own'. In 1933, Sir Basil Brooke, who later became Prime Minister of Northern Ireland as Lord Brookeborough, disparagingly noted that 'there was a great number of Protestants and Orangemen who employed Roman Catholics', and, before giving reasons why this was a very bad idea, added that 'he felt he could speak freely on this

[38] D. Smith, *Transforming the World? The Social Impact of British Evangelicalism* (Carlisle: Paternoster Press, 1998); J. Wolffe (ed.), *Evangelical Faith and Public Zeal: Evangelicals and Society in Britain 1780–1980* (London: SPCK Press, 1955); F. K. Brown, *Fathers of the Victorians* (Cambridge: Cambridge University Press, 1961).

[39] B. Szajkowski, *Next to God... Poland: Politics and Religion in Contemporary Poland* (New York: St Martins Press, 1983).

subject as he had not a Roman Catholic about his own place'.[40] Even in consumption, religious affiliation may override rationality. Northern Ireland's small towns often have a Protestant butcher and a Catholic butcher where the market can profitably sustain only one. At times of heightened tension, Protestants and Catholics boycotted each others' businesses and travelled considerable distances to engage in commerce with their own sort.

Cultural defence also inhibits societalization. A beleaguered minority may work hard to prevent community ties being displaced by a wider sense of belonging. Those who order their lives in the societal rather than the community mode may be regarded as traitors and punished accordingly. In ethnic conflicts (Bosnia or Northern Ireland, for example) those who marry across the divide are frequent targets for vigilantes.

Finally, religio-ethnic conflict mutes the relativizing consequences of pluralism because the prevalence of invidious stereotypes allows a much more thorough stigmatizing of alternative cultures. It cannot be too highly stressed that the shift to relativism as a way of accommodating those with whom we differ depends on us taking those people seriously. Where religious differences are strongly embedded in ethnic identities, the cognitive threat of the other is weak. Scottish Protestants in the nineteenth century deployed caricatures of the social vices of the immigrant Irish Catholics as a way of avoiding having to consider them as Christian.

It is worth spelling out why this section is headed 'retarding tendencies' and not 'reasons to abandon the secularization paradigm'. The case is empirical: in most of the examples that I and others have had in mind when we talk of religion remaining popular because of the role it plays in aiding cultural transition or cultural defence, that role has been temporary. Migrants may be initially more religiously observant in the new world than in the old, but they eventually assimilate or find non-religious ways of retaining some thin nostalgic connection to the old life. The nineteenth-century London chapels that provided an ethnic haven for Welsh and Scottish migrants saw their congregations dwindle and then disappear as the migrants married out of their initial religio-ethnic enclaves and

---

[40] A. C. Hepburn, *The Conflict of Nationality in Modern Ireland* (London: Edward Arnold, 1980), 164.

only periodically displayed their roots in the secular activities of annual dinners and support for the London Welsh and London Scottish rugby clubs. The Catholic churches in Liverpool and Glasgow that were filled by Irish settlers gradually emptied as Irish Catholics became indistinguishable, first from English Catholics, and then from the general population. Industrialization and urbanization did give rise to powerful revival and reform movements, but these eventually faded away. If ethnic conflicts are resolved, the rationalizing processes resurface. Although the Northern Ireland conflict is far from a full resolution, government policies have ended labour-market discrimination in the public sector and in large firms. It has sometimes taken the entry of a new player into the market (usually a major international supermarket chain), but after fifteen years of peace much of the parallel pattern of consumption has gone. And every measure of religiosity in Northern Ireland now shows decline.

## An Aside on Functional Explanation

The retarding tendencies have been presented in a functionalist style: religion remains popular where people find it unusually useful. Although it is a convenient shorthand, functional explanation has two paradoxical dangers that I will briefly address. First, it can unduly imply that people have a cynical or utilitarian attitude to their faith. When we note that Methodism was attractive to the upwardly mobile working classes because it allowed them to think themselves superior to their masters, offered opportunities for leadership, and provided the comfort of a close-knit association of like-situated people, we come close to suggesting that these secondary benefits (or latent functions) were the main appeal and that the Methodism was a mere convenience. It is important to appreciate that the people who became Methodists did so because they believed Wesley and his followers to be right. That is, the conversions were genuine. The various beneficial social consequences might have been openly perceived, as when the temperance preacher pointed out the financial advantages of sobriety. They might have been implicitly sensed, as when the potential convert noticed that the born-again Christians were better dressed, had tidier houses, had cleaner children, and seemed more self-confident. But he became a Methodist, not because he wanted those things (though he did), but because he saw those things as evidence that Methodism was right. That is, the beneficial side products were not the primary goal but were taken as circumstantial evidence that the new beliefs should be seriously entertained. The new behavioural patterns were adopted, initially with a degree of 'role distance', and only as the novice felt the new life to be working was the belief system that legitimated it fully accepted. The latent social functions or the good social consequences were not desired separately from the religion but added to the plausibility of the religion.

Similarly when, as in the case of Poland, we explain unusually high church adherence by the political purposes that Catholicism served in retaining an autonomous anti-communist Polish identity, we need to avoid implying that for most churchgoing Poles the main appeal was the latent function of political protest. We need to remember that functional language is a shorthand that saves us the much longer formulation that would go something like this. One good reason Poles had for believing in Catholicism was that its place in their history meant it was validated, legitimated, and reinforced by (that is, made plausible by) almost every aspect of their life-world. That events could be repeatedly interpreted through the lens 'atheist communists are bad; Catholic Poles are good' strengthened that faith. That all of one's friends and neighbours (except the bad communists) were Catholics meant that the occasional desire for personal liberty (for example, to chose not to attend mass or accept the clergy's teaching) was overruled by the knowledge that others whose judgements one respected would disapprove.

The important point to remember is that when we use notions such as needs and functions to explain the popularity of religion we are, for convenience, skipping a vital line in the equation: the plausibility of religion. In the last analysis, personal religiosity rests on belief, on faith. No shorthand explanation that cannot be extended to include a sensible account of why people believe or not should be accepted.

This is important, because many discussions of the rise and fall of religion that refer to functions or needs are based on implausible motivational stories. This brings me back to the paradox

I mentioned at the start of this section. The danger of functionalist explanation I have just discussed is that we assume the people we are trying to understand are cynics. The second danger of functionalist explanation is that it can all too easily assume that people can readily be persuaded of the truth of a belief system that serves some secular purpose. One common version of that argument is the idea that, because societies need shared moral values, people will adopt a shared religion. What is missing from that is any explanation of why recognizing some social need should lead atheists to believe in God.

## The Irreversibility of Secularization

It is always possible that the secularization of the West is merely temporary and that there will be a resurgence of religious interest. Many commentators believe the human condition is such that people will always need religion: that the desire for the supernatural and what it can offer is somehow 'hard-wired' into our constitution. Hence long-term and widespread secularization is impossible. When one religious tradition declines, another will fill the gap. The obvious evidential problem is that, in the British case, Christianity has experienced at least 150 years of decline, and each wave of possible gap fillers (the Pentecostal movements of the 1920s, the charismatic movements of the 1960s, the new religious movements of the 1970s, and the New Age spirituality of the 1990s) has failed to make even a small dent in the growing numbers of people free from any organized religious interest.

Laurence Iannaccone uses retrospective data from thirty-four countries to construct trends in child and adult church attendance over the course of the twentieth century.[41] No country displays steadily increasing attendance, nor does any low-attendance rate country ever shift to a higher long-run level. In no country was religious activity higher at the end of the period than at the beginning, and in most it was significantly lower. As Voas summarizes: 'Nowhere has

[41] L. A. Iannaccone, 'Looking Backward: A Cross-National Study of Religious Trends', working paper, George Mason University, 2003.

demand dropped and later rebounded for any sustained period. Secularization is a one-way street.'[42]

The idea that secularization is temporary and will be reversed when the innate human need for religion finds an appropriate form of expression suffers from a serious logical flaw. It neglects the role of culture in shaping human behaviour. It supposes that individual needs translate into outcomes in an unmediated fashion. It thus misses the point that biological and psychological drives are shaped by and articulated in a particular culture. Even if there are basic questions that most people will ask themselves (such as 'what is the meaning of life?'), we cannot assume that large numbers will frame the question in the same terms, let alone embrace the same answer. On the contrary, the authority of the autonomous individual prevents such consensus. While it is common to ascribe to individualism every manner of social vice and to yearn for a more communal way of life, there is no sign that the people of the West are willing to give up their autonomy. The communalist always want everyone else to 'get back' to his or her basics.

Brevity requires me to state this bluntly: shared belief systems require coercion. The survival of any particular religion requires that individuals be subordinated to the community. In some settings (religio-ethnic conflicts, for example) individual autonomy is constrained by shared identities. In the stable affluent democracies of the West the individual asserts the rights of the sovereign autonomous consumer. We choose our electrical goods; we choose our Gods. Unless we can imagine some social forces that will lead us to give up that freedom, we cannot imagine the creation of detailed ideological consensus. It is not enough to suggest that some calamity may disrupt our complacency: Britain experienced two catastrophic wars and an intervening depression without a religious revival. Without a preexisting common culture, large numbers will not interpret a disaster in the same way and hence will not respond with a collective change of world view. When the common culture of a society consists of operating principles that allow the individual to choose, no amount of vague spiritual yearning will generate a shared belief system.

[42] D. Voas, 'The Continuing Secular Transition', in D. Pollack and D. V. A. Olson (eds), *The Role of Religion in Modern Societies* (New York: Routledge, 2007), 43.

To conclude, the secularization paradigm argues that the decline of religion in the West is not an accident but is an unintended consequence of a variety of complex social changes that for brevity we call modernization. As Figure 2.1 shows, the paradigm is patently not, as critics have claimed, 'a simple-minded theory of inevitable decline'.[43] But, unless we can imagine a reversal of the increasing cultural autonomy of the individual, secularization must be seen as irreversible.

[43] Stark and Finke, *Acts of Faith*, 33.

# 3

# Clarifying Secularization

## Introduction

When what is to be explained—secularization—and what is thought to explain it—modernization—are both complex notions, it is hardly surprising that the secularization paradigm has attracted a deal of critical attention. What is surprising, and disappointing, is that so much of the criticism is directed, not at the ideas advanced in the previous chapter, but at second-hand caricatures. One critic said: 'Theories of secularisation, arguing that religion had all died out and was socially and politically insignificant, have clearly failed,' and added of religion: 'Here was this very, very, live force in western and world societies and people weren't researching it adequately.'[1] Equally dismissive, another summarized the secularization paradigm as arguing that urbanization undermined religion and then proved it false by finding that certain sorts of religious expression grew in the British cities of the nineteenth century; which would hardly be a surprise to Bryan Wilson, who wrote extensively on urban modern Protestant sects.[2] The prolific Rodney Stark routinely reduced the

---

[1] Linda Woodhead, in R. Pigott, 'Lifting the Veil on Religion and Identity', *Edge*, 24, www.esrc.ac.uk/ESRCInfoCentre/about/CI/CP/the_edge/issue24/veil1. aspx (accessed 3 Mar. 2010).

[2] C. G. Brown, 'Did Urbanization Secularize Britain?', *Urban History Yearbook* (1988), 1–14. B. R. Wilson, *Sects and Society* (London: Heinemann, 1978).

paradigm to the proposition that science destroyed religion and frequently imputed to secularizationists the view that secularization was inevitable.[3] And, in the way of these things, Stark's caricature is now taken as a reliable summary by the next generation.[4]

Stark's supply-side alternative to the secularization paradigm will be considered later. The next chapter considers in detail the criticism that the secularization approach overlooks important signs of religious interest outside the churches. In this chapter I will consider a variety of less far-reaching challenges and use those criticisms to clarify what is entailed by the secularization paradigm.

## Inevitability

A very common criticism of the paradigm is that it supposes the decline of religion to be inevitable. Hence it is refuted by showing either that some parts of modern societies are still religious or that many unmodern societies are still thoroughly religious. As this criticism has its strongest foundation and its clearest application in the societies of the Third World, a full response will be left to Chapter 9. Here it is enough to stress the contingent nature of the explanation presented in the previous chapter. The various causes could have been divided up in different ways, but, even in the fairly economic form in which I have presented them, there are still twenty-one elements linking modernization and secularization. Some of them were unlikely; their combination even more so. The great polymath Ernest

---

A likely explanation of Brown's mistake is that he is reacting, not to sociology, but to historical work such as E. R. Wickham, *Church and People in an Industrial City* (London: Lutterworth Press, 1957).

[3] On at least three occasions, Stark offered as compelling proof that sociologists of secularization regarded the demise of religion as inevitable a quotation from a 1966 anthropology textbook written by Anthony Wallace, and the same quotation appears again in C. Smith (ed.), *The Secular Revolution: Power, Interests, and Conflict in the Secularization of American Public Life* (Berkeley and Los Angeles: University of California Press, 2003), 16.

[4] For example, I. Rossi and M. Rossi, 'Religiosity: A Comparison between Latin Europe and Latin America', Department of Economics, Universidad de la Republica Working Paper, 11 July 2008.

Gellner was right when he said that, far from being inevitable, the history of the Western world was fortuitous, because so many critical elements of that history could easily have turned out differently.[5] I sometimes wonder if the mistake here is acoustic: I say 'irreversible' and people hear 'inevitable'. It is easy to imagine that many of the elements of the explanation could easily have been otherwise. For example, had the Counter-Reformation succeeded in suppressing the Reformation and reimposed Catholic orthodoxy on Europe, much of Europe's history would have been different. What is not so easy to imagine is that, once embedded, significant social changes such as the rise of the idea of individual liberty or the replacement of fatalistic resignation by an instrumental attitude to the world will be reversed. I can no more imagine theocracy being imposed on the people of Holland or England than I can imagine the return of slavery or of gender apartheid.

## Partisanship

One common line of criticism is to accuse the proponents of the secularization approach of some purpose that so distorts their work that their conclusions can be dismissed as wishful thinking. In its simplest form this tactic accuses us of secularism. We think we have identified a real change in the social world, but we are really just advocates of a godless society. It is true that Auguste Comte (who invented a rational religion to replace the old illusions), Karl Marx (who also invented a rational religion to replace the old illusions), and Sigmund Freud (who invented a science to explain the old illusions) were engaged in ideological projects, but modern sociologists are not promoters of secularism. David Martin and Peter L. Berger are Christians. Bryan Wilson was an agnostic, but he saw little benefit in the decline of religion. Indeed, his reading of Durkheim led him into an extremely gloomy prognosis. A society without a shared value system internalized in most citizens as conscience would have to rely on external coercion to maintain order. In this somewhat bleak

[5] E. Gellner, *Plough, Sword and Book: The Structure of Human History* (London: Collins Harvill, 1988), 11–15.

dystopia, the all-seeing eye of God would be replaced by the all-seeing eye of the CCTV camera.[6] But, while any scholar's biography may be fascinating, it is no more an acid test for the secularization paradigm than it is for more optimistic alternatives promoted by scholars who happen to be Christians. What matters is not why any of us is persuaded of our explanations but whether those explanations can stand after the appropriate evidence is tested and the internal logic of the explanations is examined for inconsistency.

There is one form of the bias accusation that is not so easily answered and that is the assertion that those who work within the secularization paradigm are unconsciously trapped within the discourse of an 'Enlightenment project': a tradition of thought (stemming from the French Encyclopaedists of the eighteenth century and the Scottish philosophers Adam Smith, Adam Ferguson, and David Hume) that is predicated on the then-novel belief in the rational improvability of humankind and the social condition.[7] At its most general, this critique rests on relativism. Because human perception can never be free of preconceptions and biases, scientific objectivity is impossible; hence all scholars can do is generate equally plausible narratives, discourses, or voices. I was once confronted with an extreme form of this in the question session after a lecture, when an unusually emotional young women insisted that Catholicism in Scotland could not be declining because her church was well attended. When I tried to respond that a national decline in mass attendance was quite compatible with a concentration of mass-goers in a smaller number of popular churches, an elderly female theologian harangued me to the effect that the young lady's 'voice' was as important as my evidence and that I was a patriarchal bully for not accepting her contribution as being every bit as valid as the Catholic Church's own 'male' statistics.

---

[6] B. R. Wilson, 'Morality in the Evolution of the Modern Social System', *British Journal of Sociology*, 36 (1985), 315–32. Weber also struck a dystopian note about the consequences of acquisitiveness freed from its original religiously inspired asceticism (M. Weber, *The Protestant Ethic and the Spirit of Capitalism* (London: George Allen and Unwin, 1976), 181).

[7] For an entertaining discussion and rebuttal of this argument, see E. Gellner, *Relativism and the Social Sciences* (Cambridge: Cambridge University Press, 1985) and *Postmodernism, Reason and Religion* (London: Routledge, 1992).

There are at least three straightforward responses to such relativism. The first, which is the least honourable but the most fun, is to point out that my relativist colleagues are never relativists about their salaries or working conditions. That is, the application of their criticism is inconsistent and therefore we need not take it any more seriously than they do. The second was popularized by the anthropologist Clifford Geertz when he said that, although conditions of complete asepsis are impossible, all sensible people would prefer the theatre of a modern hospital to a sewer if they needed an operation.[8] Though perfect objectivity may be unattainable, work that tries to be objective is generally more useful than that which makes no such effort. A third rebuttal concerns the bluntness of the relativist's claim: it is blanket assumed that interests alter all perceptions. However, if we allow that our interests may distort perceptions of some topics but not others, then we need not abandon the practice of social science. We simply need to do what we should be doing anyway: rigorously testing claims against the best available evidence. In the case of Catholic mass attendance in Scotland, the best available evidence is that collected from all congregations by the church hierarchy, not one person's impression of a single congregation. If we allow that there is a real world that can be studied more or less well, then the issues of bias and preconception become nuisances rather than obstacles: problems to be assessed and overcome by hard work and sound argument.

## Teleology

One particular form of the claim that the secularization paradigm is stuck in the mindset of Adams Smith and Ferguson is the accusation of teleology (from the Greek *telos* meaning a purpose). This is the sin of supposing that human history has an endpoint. Because the early promoters of secularism were inspired by the Enlightenment, the secularization paradigm must be teleological. As it involves a hidden

---

[8] C. Geertz, 'Thick Description: Towards an Interpretative Theory', in his *The Interpretation of Cultures: Selected Essays* (New York: Basic Books, 1973), 30. The original source seems to have been the brilliant economist Robert Solow.

purpose, which is not amenable to empirical testing, it cannot be scientific and hence is in no sense superior to religion. By dismissing the pretensions of sociologists, the reality of the decline of religion can also be disregarded.[9]

Apart from this critique again confusing promoting secularism with describing and explaining secularization, it fails to understand the role of inadvertent and unintended consequences. Whether or not the secularization paradigm is persuasive, it can hardly be teleological when almost every causal connection is inadvertent. The Jewish, Christian, and Islamic promoters of monotheism had no intention of undermining the sacred when they simplified and rationalized the religious culture. The Reformers wished to purify the faith so that they could justify imposing it on everyone. Instead they created diversity, ensured that imposition would be impossible, and opened the way for human rights to become independent of religious rectitude. Even the French case, where the formal secularization of the state was a product of conscious secularism, has elements of the unintended in it. Some of the drive behind French anti-clericalism came from the memory of the conflicts over religion that saw France divided between Huguenots and Catholics creating a subsequent wish to forge a strong national spirit that could not be subverted by religious divisions.

For sociologists of secularization, the changes are rarely directed and there is no specific single endpoint. The apparent symmetry of the terms 'religious' and 'secular' should not disguise the fact that the first is something specific while the second is only the absence of the first. The process of secularization assumed in the sociological paradigm is not an Enlightenment journey from A to B but a broadening-out from a common past.

## Politics versus Sociology

One curious rebuttal of the secularization paradigm involves a contrast between natural and engineered change. American sociologist Christian Smith has edited an excellent collection of studies of early

---

[9] J. Millbank, *Theology and Social Theory: Beyond Secular Reason* (Oxford: Blackwell, 1990).

twentieth-century struggles between religious traditionalists and the promoters of various secularizing agendas in such key fields of US life as education, the law, science and medicine, and the mass media.[10] Although he could have introduced the essays as detailed case studies of how secularization occurred in specific spheres, he instead glossed the collection as refutation of the secularization paradigm. To quote from the publisher's description:

Sociologists, historians, and other social observers have long considered the secularization of American public life over the past hundred and thirty years to be an inevitable and natural outcome of modernization. This groundbreaking work rejects this view and fundamentally rethinks the historical and theoretical causes of the secularization of American public life between 1870 and 1930. Christian Smith and his team of contributors boldly argue that the declining authority of religion was not the by-product of modernization, but rather the intentional achievement of cultural and intellectual elites, including scientists, academics, and literary intellectuals, seeking to gain control of social institutions and increase their own cultural authority.[11]

Smith supposes that the secularization account requires the natural and inevitable decline of religion and so, if people are arguing about the particular rights and privileges of religion, then it is not secularization, even if the end result of such quarrels is precisely the displacement of religious values and beliefs by rational and technical concerns and the end of religious discrimination that the rest of us regard as secularization.

I suspect that Smith mistakes a failure to state the obvious for not knowing the obvious. For brevity, historical sociologists often write in sweeping abstractions, but this does not mean that they think there are mysterious causal processes that can substitute for human conflict as the carrier of change. For example, to say that 'the increasing social and cultural diversity of modern societies, combined with a growing egalitarianism, made impossible the church form of religion' does not mean that we are ignorant of the bitter

---

[10] C. Smith (ed.), *The Secular Revolution: Power, Interests and Conflict in the Secularization of American Public Life* (Berkeley and Los Angeles: University of California Press, 2003).

[11] www.amazon.com/Secular-Revolution-Interests-Conflict-Secularization/dp/0520235614 (accessed 11 Nov. 2009).

struggles for individual liberty, the attempts by state churches to maintain their hegemony, the governments that fell because they failed to reconcile increasing tolerance with maintaining the position of the state church, or the millions of pages of invective that were spent on church–state disputes. Far from being unaware of such conflict, I have explored it at length.[12] Our relative neglect of the details of the conflicts involved in the changes we summarize in the secularization paradigm does not mean that we do not know about them or see them as a threat to our explanations; it simply means that, as the historians have ably documented those details for us, we can take their work as given.

So the response to Smith is simply to note that there is no inherent conflict between the secularization paradigm and the observation that many of the changes to the rights and privileges of religious viewpoints were severely contested. The second response is to challenge one possible interpretation of Smith's position: that the removal of religion from the public sphere was due *only* to the machinations of secular interests. It was not. It was also promoted or acquiesced in by committed Christians who saw the marginalization of religion as a reasonable price to pay for social harmony and for the guarantee of their own liberties. To build an *unum* out of *pluribus*, to take the two key terms of the motto of the United States of America, requires a solution to the problem of sectarian conflict; liberal democracies took some time (and a lot of struggle) to work out that allowing almost everything in private while trying to maintain a religiously neutral public square was an effective solution.

## An Abrupt Alternative to Gradual Decline

In his poem 'Annus Mirabilis' Phillip Larkin wrote: 'Sexual intercourse began in 1963 (which was rather late for me) | Between the end of the Chatterley ban and the Beatles' first LP.'[13] That couplet could stand as a summary of one of the more interesting recent challenges

---

[12] S. Bruce, *A House Divided: Protestantism, Schism and Secularization* (London: Routledge, 1990).

[13] P. Larkin, 'Annus Mirabilis', *High Windows* (London: Faber and Faber, 1979).

to the secularization paradigm. Social historian Callum Brown's *The Death of Christian Britain* argued that Christianity in Britain was in pretty robust health until the 1960s, when it was abruptly undermined by a radically permissive culture. Although the argument may seem parochial, it has implications beyond the religious history of Britain, and a detailed response will allow me to add further detail to the basic secularization explanation outlined in the previous chapter. The dating of church decline is no small matter. The sociological explanation presented in the previous chapter lists as compound causes the rationalization, religious diversification, and increasing egalitarianism and individualism that have accompanied industrialization, democratization, and economic growth. Although we can imagine some sort of threshold effect with these causes, the general assumption is that the plausibility of religion will have declined gradually and that at least some symptoms of it will have been visible in the nineteenth century. If Brown is right that nothing much had changed until the second half of the twentieth century, the secularization paradigm is weakened.

Although he wishes to argue for a very recent date for the *Death of Christian Britain*, Brown begins by recognizing that church attendance was 'historically very high' in 1851, when the Census of Religious Worship suggested that between 40 and 60 per cent of the adult population attended church on 30 March, and that it has declined since.[14] Brown also accepts the conventional account of church membership: it grew through the second half of the nineteenth century 'to reach a peak in England and Wales in 1904 and in Scotland in 1905'.[15] Given the importance I will attach to the recruitment of children, it is worth noting that Sunday school enrolment in England and Wales peaked between 1901 and 1905.[16]

---

[14] C. G. Brown, *The Death of Christian Britain: Understanding Secularization 1800–2000* (London: Routledge 2001), 161. Robin Gill agrees: 'there has been a continuous process of decline of Sunday attendance in the Church of England since...1851' (R. Gill, *The 'Empty Church' Revisited* (Aldershot: Ashgate, 2003), 57).

[15] Brown, *Death of Christian Britain*, 163–4. Brown's radical redating is modified by H. McLeod, *The Religious Crisis of the 1960s* (Oxford: Oxford University Press, 2000).

[16] P. Brierley, *Religious Trends* (London: Christian Research, 1999), ii, table 2.15; Gill, *Empty Church*, 225. Peak dates differ depending on whether we use those under 15 or the entire population as the base for calculating percentages.

Brown's challenge to the conventional view rests on five things: privileging membership over attendance as an index of religious interest; underestimating the change in the meaning of religious activity; concentrating on female piety at the expense of men's involvement; imputing to secularizationists the expectation of rapid decline; and exaggerating the revival post-war. I will consider each in turn.

In Chapter 1 I gave good reasons for treating church attendance as a useful index of interest. It began to decline at least fifty years before membership declined.

Brown's vision of church vitality into the second half of the twentieth century makes much of the continued popularity of religious offices for rites of passage. Baptisms, church weddings, and church funerals did remain more popular than routine churchgoing but this seems perfectly in accord with the secularization approach. We would expect that acts of conformity that require little or no commitment would decline after those that are more obviously symptomatic of a serious faith, especially if the occasional conformity performed important social functions for which secular alternatives were not readily available or suitably sombre. Involvement with the Church of England in the Cumbrian village of Gosforth shows an interesting pattern. Bill Williams reports that, in 1953, only 7.6 per cent of the population regularly attended. However, almost everyone was baptized and almost all the young people of the parish were confirmed in the church. But that ritual completed, the majority only ever attended again for major rites of passage. In July 1950 the Bishop of Penrith confirmed thirty-five candidates but 'six only of the newly-confirmed made their first Communion on the following Sunday'.[17] Williams is clear that the farmers of Gosforth viewed baptism and confirmation as largely social ceremonies. We could, of course, impose the same interpretation on religious rites of passage in the nineteenth century (or any earlier time). Historians such as David Cressy would argue against such a downgrade of the religion of the early modern period, but, so long as we accept that there is a significant difference between regular churchgoers having their children baptized and non-churchgoers going through the same ritual, we

---

[17] W. M. Williams, *The Sociology of an English Village: Gosforth* (London: Routledge and Kegan Paul, 1956), 180–2.

need not pursue that argument here.[18] That rates of religious marriages and funerals fell once secular alternatives had become available suggests that occasional conformity is a residue of core faith rather than a symptom of an enduring and independent popular religious culture.

Brown's explanation of the abrupt decline from the late 1950s involves a complex argument about the feminization of piety making religion largely women's work and then the new opportunities for women causing them to abandon that work for more rewarding secular alternatives. This case actually contains its own refutation. While Brown is right about the changing involvement of women, this does not help establish a late date for decline. The relatively abrupt disaffiliation of women had its dramatic effect because more men had already withdrawn. In 1956—the start of Brown's period of abrupt decline—there were 41 women but only 28 men confirmed in the Church of England for every 1,000 head of population aged 12–20.[19] The difference in confirmation rates for men and women peaked in 1956 and 1958 (at 13 percentage points) but it was already 9 points in 1936.[20] All indices of church involvement show that men dropped out first, which is what we would expect from the argument that the world of industrialized work and the economy were the first sites of secularization.

We come now to the rate of decline. Brown summarizes the popularity of the churches in the first half of the twentieth century thus: 'despite problems in some denominations... the first half of the twentieth century witnessed no great haemorrhage of church membership in Britain.'[21] That assertion of stability loses force when we shift from gross numbers to size relative to the population. As the largest nonconformist body in Britain (and the most punctilious in record-keeping), the Methodist Church offers a good guide to the health of British church life. Methodism had been declining as a proportion of the available population since the middle of the nineteenth century, and the rate of change was fairly regular.[22] Church of Scotland

[18] D. Cressy, *Birth, Death and Marriage: Ritual, Religion, and the Life-Cycle in Tudor and Stuart England* (Oxford: Oxford University Press, 1997).

[19] Brown, *Death of Christian Britain*, 191.

[20] McLeod, *Religious Crisis*, 63.   [21] Brown, *Death of Christian Britain*, 65.

[22] There is a dip in the period 1931–41 that almost certainly reflects the union of the three main bodies of Methodists in 1932. It is impossible to know how

membership, as a proportion of the available population, started declining in the early 1930s.[23] David Voas and Alasdair Crockett's work on the very large British Household Panel and British Social Attitudes datasets shows a gradual decline from the 1930s in affiliation, church attendance, and religious belief.[24]

Much of Brown's claim for the resilience of the churches rests on a contrast between the reality of gradual decline and the expectation of haemorrhage he imputes to sociologists. As there was 'no great haemorrhage', we are wrong. But this is a rhetorical device. No sociologist has ever predicted haemorrhage; indeed, Bryan Wilson did not predict church membership decline at all. He referred to it as a sign of declining interest in religion, but the definition of the secularization that he was explaining was always put in terms of 'declining social significance' of religion—something quite compatible in the short term with continued church adherence.[25] Peter Berger's argument for the deleterious effect on commitment of diversity implies that the loss of interest in religion will be slow and generational.[26]

Finally it is important to appreciate exactly what Brown means by post-war revival. Some indices of church involvement increased after 1945, but not all did, none did much, and none came close to their Victorian or Edwardian peaks when expressed as percentages of the available population.

To summarize thus far: the decline in British church attendance began at or before the middle of the nineteenth century and the decline in membership began in the Edwardian years. At best what we see in the late 1950s and 1960s is a slight acceleration of a pattern first evident at least half a century earlier.

---

much that dip reflects a real change in the rate of disaffiliation and how much it is simply a pruning of deadwood from membership lists, as they were revised in the process of planning the rationalization of congregations.

[23] R. Currie, A. D. Gilbert, and L. Horsley, *Churches and Churchgoers: Patterns of Church Growth in the British Isles since 1700* (Oxford: Oxford University Press, 1977), table B3.

[24] D. Voas and A. D. Crockett, 'Religion in Britain: Neither Believing nor Belonging', *Sociology*, 39 (2005), 11–28.

[25] B. R. Wilson, *Religion in Secular Society* (London: C. A. Watts, 1966), p. xiiv.

[26] P. L. Berger, *The Heretical Imperative: Contemporary Possibilities of Religious Affirmation* (London: Collins, 1980).

## The Generational Roots of Decline

Churches decline because they lose members—by death or defection—faster than they recruit. The main source of compensating recruitment in the twentieth century is the socialization of children. As life expectancy has increased considerably and churchgoers generally lack the vices that hasten death, we can discount the possibility that shrinkage has been caused by an accelerating death toll.[27] Unfortunately, few churches record membership data in a way that allows us to distinguish clearly the relative weight of adult defection and non-recruitment of children, but we have enough information to suggest that the main problem is declining success in socializing the off-spring of members.

For long periods, Methodist churches reported members gained and lost in various ways every quarter. Clive Field has summarized the data for the period 1960–98: the largest part of the loss is not members who 'ceased to meet' but the relative decline in new recruitment, for which 'the teenage years still [are] far and away the most fertile soil'.[28] As a tradition that stresses an informed decision to join, we might expect the Baptists to be less reliant on childhood socialization, but, as David Hunt shows, the majority of those baptized in Scottish Baptist churches were children of regularly attending members and, taking a long view of Baptist data, there is a clear correlation between Sunday school enrolment in one decade and membership in the next.[29] Not all recruits to any one church are children of its members, but a large majority of new members have been raised

---

[27] In the first decade of the twentieth century, life expectancy was 49 for men and 52 for women. By 1991, it was 73 for men and 79 for women (A. H. Halsey and J. Webb, *Twentieth-Century British Social Trends* (London: Macmillan, 2000), 97).

[28] C. D. Field, 'Joining and Leaving British Methodism since the 1960s', in L. J. Francis and Y. J. Katz (eds), *Joining and Leaving Religion: Research Perspectives* (Leominster: Gracewing, 2000), 70. Sawkins makes the same point: 'the failure to recruit new members underpins overall membership decline' (J. Sawkins, 'Church Affiliation Statistics: Counting Methodist Sheep', *Soundings* (Mar. 1998), 17).

[29] D. Hunt, *Journeys to Faith: A Survey of People Baptised in Scottish Baptist Churches June 1996–May 1997* (self-published, 1997), 28; *Reflecting on our Past: A Statistical Look at Baptists in Scotland 1892–1997* (self-published, 1997), 15.

in some church. As the churches shrink, we might expect that proportion of outsiders recruited to rise (simply because there are more outsiders), but, even in recent studies, childhood socialization is key. A major 1992 survey of 'new Christians' showed that four-fifths came from a Christian family background and three-quarters had attended church-related organizations as children.[30] A second source of relevant data is surveys of the age of defection. The Scottish Social Attitudes survey asked those who had ever attended church regularly and no longer did when they stopped. The most popular ages were between 12 and 16. Well over half had stopped by the age of 20. A major study of English Catholics showed the most common age of ceasing to attend mass to be between 13 and 19.[31]

Clearly decisions about whether children should attend Sunday school, join or remain in church-related youth organizations, and then pass into adult membership must in good part reflect the preferences of parents and the effort they put into socializing their off-spring. Isolating parental influence from other sources of faith is difficult. As Voas and Storm[32] and Kelley and de Graaf[33] suggest, the ability of parents to pass on their spiritual capital is affected by the general levels of 'ambient religion' in the culture. That is, such aspects of the environment as religious socialization in schools, general cultural support for the churches, and the beliefs and attitudes of friends are important. But we do have considerable evidence that the chances of children following the faith of their parents are materially affected by intermarriage. Voas has boiled these observations down to a simple ratio that is a reasonable summary of the range of effects.[34] For the second half of the twentieth century, parents who had the same

[30] P. Hanley, *Finding Faith Today: The Technical Report* (London: Bible Society/Churches Together in England, 1992), 5.

[31] M. P. Hornsby-Smith, *Roman Catholics in England: Studies in Social Structure since the Second World War* (Cambridge: Cambridge University Press, 1987), 100.

[32] D. Voas and I. Storm, 'The Intergenerational Transmission of Churchgoing in England and Australia', unpublished paper, 2008.

[33] J. Kelley and N. D. de Graaf, 'National Context Parental Socialization, and Religious Belief: Results from 15 Nations', *American Sociological Review*, 62 (1997), 639–59.

[34] D. Voas, 'Intermarriage and the Demography of Secularization', *British Journal of Sociology*, 54 (2003), 83–108; Voas and Crockett, 'Religion in Britain'.

faith (Anglican and Anglican, for example) were likely to raise half of their children to be churchgoing when they reach adulthood.[35] This rate is halved if the parents are of different faiths (even when the differences are just Methodist–Anglican). Even if the parents agree on which faith they wish to pass on, the fact of disagreement makes the child aware that there are good people in other churches and introduces the relativism that weakens conviction.

If we accept that disaffiliation is substantially a generation effect, a major part of the explanation of any particular drop in enrolment will lie, not in the period where it is evident, but a generation earlier. If what is to be explained are missing new church members aged 20 in the period 1958–63, we should ask why the absentees did not start (or continue with) Sunday school, Band of Hope, or Boys Brigade between 1948 and 1953 or why their parents—who will have married a decade earlier, that is between 1938 and 1943—did not work harder to ensure their offspring followed in the faith. That logic suggests a probable cause of the acceleration of decline that Brown identifies in the late 1950s and 1960s. It seems highly likely that the social structures and patterns of interaction that helped reproduce religion from one generation to the next were severely disrupted by the war's impact on the extended family, the school, and the neighbourhood.

### The Dislocating Effect of the Second World War

Although excluded from combat during the Second World War, women were accepted into the armed services. About a quarter of a million women enlisted in the air force and navy and a similar number joined the Auxiliary Territorial Service (ATS). Some 12,000 joined the Queen Alexandra's nursing corps. The need to compensate for the loss of male agricultural workers to the military was met by the Women's Land Army and Women's Timber Corp, which enrolled

---

[35] There is a speculative leap in supposing that general patterns found even for the oldest respondents in recent surveys would have been found in the 1940s or earlier had such surveys been conducted then. However, the likely direction of difference, if there is one, runs in my favour rather than against. As all the major churches have become more, rather than less, ecumenical, the deleterious effects of religious intermarriage are likely to have been greater in the early parts of the century than in the later parts.

almost 90,000.[36] Women were active in the Civil Defence Rescue
Service: some 19,000 served full-time and ten times that served part-
time. Over 144,000 women served with the emergency casualty
services, while thousands more acted as fire-watchers at business
premises and factories. The Women's Voluntary Service, formed in
1938 to support Air Raid Precautions, had over one million members
by 1942.[37]

In addition, very large numbers of single women and married
women without children were conscripted for industrial production.
Not all the women involved in war work moved from their homes
and familiar surroundings. Especially in the cities, the main impact
was a change of occupation rather than a change of scenery. But even
this is likely to have considerably broadened the horizons of many
women as they were thrown into close contact with people from different class, ethnic, and religious backgrounds. In the forces, the
Land Army, or working in factories, very many women report excit-
ing social lives. One Land Girl in a remote part of Worcestershire
noted: 'Dumbleton village had no pub but once the local lads and
soldiers from the surrounding US army camps got to know the girls
better, they were taken further afield to other pubs, darts matches
and dances in the surrounding villages.' Another said of Romney
Marsh: 'There were troops everywhere. You could just take your
pick. You didn't know how many were married; you just had to
take their word for it....I had several boyfriends during the war....
It was a case of a broken heart one night and the next night a new
boyfriend.'[38]

Such mixing occurred in a novel atmosphere. Whether it was reaction to the proximity of death or simply the freedom from parental
and community control, the war years saw an increase in hedonism.
A contemporary critic of the Land Army wrote: 'I wonder whether
the value of all the tons of corn and potatoes brought in by the girls
does balance their really disgusting way of life.'[39] Such concern was

[36] A. Kramer, *Land Girls and their Impact* (Barnsley: Pen and Sword Books,
2008).
[37] C. Graves, *Women in Green: The Story of the WVS in Wartime* (London:
Heinemann, 1948).
[38] Kramer, *Land Girls*, 138–9.
[39] S. Hylton, *Their Darkest Hour: The Hidden History of the Home Front
1939–45* (Stroud: Sutton Publishing, 2001), 144.

not unfounded: women born between 1914 and 1924 were twice as likely to have had sex before marriage than those born ten years earlier.

By mid-1943 about 90 per cent of young adult single women were employed in the forces or in industry.[40] With vast numbers of young men in the armed forces being moved around the country, one way or another, the war gave almost all single British women an unprecedented opportunity to engage in pleasant and positive social interaction with people from very different social, regional, cultural, and religious backgrounds. For many of those whose children were to form the missing generation of church members in the 1960s, the war was a liberating experience.

We do not have statistical information about the extent of interreligious marriages and so we can only guess on the basis of biographies and anecdotal histories, but the guess hardly seems contentious. Simply as a matter of probabilities, the war changed the context in which young men and women met, married, and formed families. Without touching on the separate issue of whether the experience of war itself weakened religious beliefs, we can suppose that many more young people married outside their traditional pool of marriage partners and thus increased markedly the degree of religious intermarriage. Coupled with what we know of such marriages generally— that they are less likely than same-religion marriages to result in either parent's religion being passed on to the offspring—we have a source for a weakening of religious bonds twenty years before the time when church involvement takes a marked dip.

The above might seem a very long response to one local critique of the secularization paradigm, but it deserves attention because it represents an important challenge to the sociological approach. Brown wishes to replace the notion of a long-term and gradual generational decline in interest in religion with an abrupt and late 'period effect': the impact of the culture of the 1960s. I have presented two distinct reasons for thinking he is wrong. The first is that the pattern of declining church involvement does not support his dating. The second is that, to the small extent that decline accelerates in the late 1950s and 1960s, that owes much to a failure of

---

[40] C. Harris, *Women at War 1939–1945: The Home Front* (Stroud: Sutton Publishing, 2000), 11.

childhood socialization. That, in turn, must be partly explained by the attitudes of parents, which takes us back twenty years, where we find a probable cause. Religion, like any other cultural product, is best passed on in a stable environment. The young Catholic girl, daughter of immigrants from rural Ireland, growing up in the east end of Glasgow in 1930 was enmeshed in a Catholic web: her extended family, her school, her neighbours, the people who worked in the small factory at the end of the street, and at the heart of it, the church that provided social support and social events as well as religious instruction. A decade later, such girls were conscripted and sent to engineering factories in Coventry, where, free from community control, they worked and played alongside people of very different backgrounds, who did not require them to attend mass and who did not see them as carriers of an Irish Catholic identity that it would be disloyal to neglect.

## Conclusion

The argument over the dating of secularization in Britain is interesting, because it shows us the complexity of the dynamics of decline. We can have adult defection and a failure of child recruitment. The reasons why adults disaffiliate range from a conscious realization of disagreement over doctrine to a gradual and vague loss of interest. The contributors to the *Guardian*'s 'Comment is free' web discussion site are probably not representative even of *Guardian* readers, but a 2009 thread on how people lost their faith produced a fascinating range of responses.[41] Although many contributors could give an approximate age at which they stopped attending Sunday school or church, they found identifying the point when, let alone the reason why, they lost their faith much more difficult, because it was not the mirror image of the dramatic conversion; often it was the slow realization that they had never really believed but had been going through the motions, usually to placate a parent or grandparent. But more than half of the potted biographies referred to a lack of parental

---

[41] 'Losing faith' thread, Comment is free bulletin board, www.guardian.co.uk/commentisfree/andrewbrown (accessed 29 Aug. 2009).

reinforcement. One said: 'I don't think I thought much about [my loss of faith] for the next ten years until a brief but interesting conversation with my father at a funeral revealed that he'd been a lifelong atheist but didn't want to upset his mum by coming out of the closet.' Another wrote:

My departure from faith started at around 11 years old. My mother met my...stepfather. He was a very thoughtful and intelligent man with no religious baggage to speak of....He took me in a car to the closest RC church each week, waiting outside to take me home. After a few weeks he asked the question which made me think about my reasons for being an RC for the first time in my 11 years: 'Do you go because you want to go or because you're frightened not to?...

A third explained: 'My parent's solution to the clash of their respective religions was to raise my siblings and I with, essentially, no religion.'

From such sources, and from analyses of surveys, we know that a lack of parental support is a crucial element in the decision of children to drop a church connection as soon as they are allowed the choice and that one of the main reasons why parents do not effectively promote a particular religion is that they do not share a common faith. But noting the importance of intermarriage itself takes us further back, because young adults who are not strongly committed to a particular faith are more likely to marry out than are those for whom their church connection or religious heritage is an important part of their identity.

It is worth stressing that even the most mechanical sociological explanation would not expect to identify a simple correlation between the social forces that cause secularization and the decline of church adherence. The most Durkheimian of sociologists does not suppose that the population of even a small and culturally homogenous state is composed of identical people who respond in the same way to social forces. And, although small, Britain was not culturally homogenous during the period at issue. From the Civil War period, England, Wales, and Scotland have had very different religious establishments (Episcopalian in the first two cases; Presbyterian in the third) with very different relations to their subjects (with many in Wales viewing the Episcopalian church as a foreign imposition). In addition, all parts of Britain experienced significant waves of religious dissent but at different times. Add to that complexity the fact that relations between the three nations in Great Britain gave their respective religions differing roles in preserving national identity and representing it to the other parts. Then recognize that the secularization paradigm itself predicts that the putatively secularizing forces will impinge differently on groups defined by class, gender, occupation, and educational background.

We must then add interorganizational considerations. Periods of intense rivalry between competing denominations and sects, such as occurred in Scotland in the decade around the Free Church split in 1843 or in Wales during the rapid growth of Methodism in the second half of the nineteenth century, can produce an increase in church membership (as people are forced to take sides) without necessarily increasing the proportion of the people who are sufficiently committed to Christianity to attend church regularly.

And, as these examples show, different indices of religiosity may be out of sync with each other. Or, to cast the same point in a longer historical time frame, what is expected of Christians changes. In the Christendom model that the established churches tried to sustain well into the nineteenth century, the church did religion on behalf of the common people, who were expected to participate in rites of passage, financially support the church, attend major festivals, subscribe to core Christian beliefs, live a godly life, and accept the church's discipline when they fell short. The voluntary association model that spread from the dissenting sects into the established churches in the nineteenth century required adherents to be severally (rather than jointly) responsible for their salvation, active in pursuit of religious knowledge, and robust and mutually sanctioning in pursuit of the good life. This basic shift in expectations is precisely what the secularization paradigm asserts to be a consequence of modernization: it is an effect of the rise of individualism, the decline of deference, a new fluidity in social relations, and increasing levels of education. But its first effect is a *rise* in two measures of religiosity: church membership and frequency of attendance. Nonetheless, the same sociological paradigm argues that beneath that short-term rise in indices of displays of personal religiosity there is the more powerful current of long-term decline. By making religious affiliation a matter of personal preference, the rise of the voluntary association model undermines the taken-for-grantedness of religion, weakens its social presence, reduces the extent to which the state can promote a particular religion, separates religious rectitude from other vital forms of social being (such as extended kinship networks, citizenship, and national loyalty), and exposes the human origins of religion. In those senses, the voluntary model of the church relativizes religion and both reduces the need for faith to be successfully passed on to the next generation and weakens the structural supports for such transmission.

Further complexity is added by the fact that some social changes can reasonably be supposed to accelerate or retard changes in religious adherence even if they have no direct effect on the plausibility of religion. Migration forces people to reconsider their affiliations and commitments. In a climate where people are strongly religious, the need to create new social networks generally results in increased involvement in organized religion. Many Irish migrants to nineteenth-century Britain were more actively Catholic in Liverpool, Workington, and Glasgow than they had been in rural Ireland. The growth of the mining industry in County Durham in the nineteenth century was accompanied by the creation of vibrant new Primitive Methodist cultures. On the other side of the watershed, those who left the rural villages of north and mid-Wales in the 1950s abandoned their strong chapel culture and did not recreate it when they moved to English cities. This may come close to tautology, but it remains the case that the dislocation of religious people is accompanied by an intensification of religious commitment while the movement of people whose faith is weakening accelerates disaffiliation. And, as such movements of population were a regular but unevenly distributed phenomenon of the nineteenth century, we should expect patterns of church growth and decline to be distinctly lumpy.

These observations may seem to make the relationship between cause and effect in religious change so complex that we can sustain any claim about cause irrespective of what the evidence of supposed effect actually shows. That is, any explanation of secularization may in practice be untestable. However, I am not seeking to preserve a theory from empirical refutation nor am I recommending pessimistic resignation to agnosticism. My point is that so many complex considerations are involved in the apparently simple social phenomenon of popular involvement in organized Christianity that we cannot expect tests of competing explanations for changes in religious adherence to be easy.

However, some progress is possible. Brown is certainly right that his reading of the evidence challenges the conventional sociological treatments of secularization. His assertion that the major cause of church decline lies in the late 1950s and 1960s is best supported by church involvement remaining relatively stable until that period. The sociological account is most plausible if we can sustain an earlier dating for decline.

# 4

# Religion Outside the Churches

## Introduction

One way of challenging the secularization paradigm is to make it unnecessary. If we persuade ourselves that whatever point in the past we take as our start was less religious than we think and that the present is more religious than it appears, then we can believe that there has been no great change and hence there is nothing to explain.

A useful rhetorical device is to impute to your opponents an exaggeration of their views so that the reality seems like refutation. It used to be common for opponents of the secularization paradigm to assert that it required some 'Golden Age of Faith' (usually set in the Middle Ages) as the starting point for the described decline. Then a few examples of medieval impiety could be presented as proof that our ancestors were no more religious than we are.[1] There is so little merit to the argument that the religiosity of pre-modern Europe has been exaggerated that it is hardly worth mentioning. The cathedrals, the monasteries and convents, the sums left to religious causes in wills, Easter mass attendance, the popularity of shrines and the relics of the saints, and the constant reference to Christian themes in every form of literature and popular discourse are ample testimony to the

---

[1] For example, M. R. Goodridge, 'The Ages of Faith: Romance or Reality', *Sociological Review*, 23 (1975), 381–96.

prevalence of belief in the supernatural and of a largely Christian gloss to that belief.[2] The related claim that the extensive popular involvement in the church was merely social compliance cannot survive any sort of critical analysis. A few people may conform to widespread views they do not hold for fear of being ostracized, but, even in the most authoritarian societies, the majority of the people do not pretend for long. Some historians have added to our understanding of the religious culture of the pre-modern period by highlighting previously overlooked examples of religious deviance. Others have shown that Christian themes were often a thin veneer on top of an enduring pagan culture.[3] No serious historian has suggested that the people of pre-modern Europe were as likely as we are to be atheist, agnostic, rationalist, or religiously indifferent.

There is considerably more merit in revision at the other end of the process. To make the Middle Ages 'really' secular, we need to argue against the statements (made in stone as much as in words) of those people we are trying to understand. There is greater scope for suggesting that modern people are more religious than the secularization paradigm admits, because there are aspects of their behaviour that, with just a little misunderstanding, can be mistaken for enduring religious sentiment.

One version of this approach can be quickly dismissed. It is unfortunately common for people to work backwards from the consequences or characteristics of religion to a redescription of secular activities as religious. People take religion seriously, so anything that people take seriously is religious. Hence the fanaticism of some football supporters is taken as warrant for treating football support as religious.[4] Religious people often engage in collective acts of worship that temporarily take them 'out of themselves'. So, working backwards, we could say that, because it involves temporary release from the mundane, taking part in rave culture—that world of loud music,

[2] For a detailed restatement of the glaringly obvious, see S. Bruce, 'The Pervasive World-View: Religion in Pre-Modern Britain', *British Journal of Sociology*, 48 (1997), 667–80.

[3] E. Le Roy Ladurie, *Montaillou: Cathars and Catholics in a French Village, 1294–1324* (Harmondsworth: Penguin, 2002); K. Thomas, *Religion and the Decline of Magic* (Harmondsworth: Penguin, 1978).

[4] D. Hervieu-Leger, *Religion as a Chain of Memory*, trans. Simon Lee (New Brunswick, NJ: Rutgers University Press, 2000), 104.

drug-taking, and collective dancing—is religious.[5] There seems little point in renaming as religious secular activities that have some but not many features in common with religion. That young people are more likely to find ecstasy in a dance hall than in a church or invest more of their energy and wealth in following a football team than worshipping God seems pretty compelling evidence for, rather than refutation of, the secularization paradigm.

However, there are more serious versions of a critique that challenges the depiction of our world as largely secular, and this chapter will consider two bodies of work that share the argument that concentrating on such indices of formal involvement in institutional religion as church attendance causes us to overlook a mass of popular religiosity so large as to undermine the contrast between pre-modern and modern societies.

## Vicarious Religion

Grace Davie subtitled her book *Religion in Britain since 1945* 'believing without belonging'.[6] Although popular with church leaders looking for reasons to be cheerful, the idea that the churches declined because of an increasing unwillingness to form public associations, rather than because people lost faith, has not fared well under empirical scrutiny. Davie made her case by showing that apparently comparable activities (such as joining political parties and trade unions, or attending football matches and cinemas) had declined as fast as churchgoing and that some indices of religious interest (such as saying one believes in God) had remained high.[7] Hence the individualism

---

    [5] G. Beck and G. Lynch, '"We are all one, we are all gods": Negotiating Spirituality in the Conscious Partying Movement', *Journal of Contemporary Religion*, 24 (2009), 339–55. For a general discussion of the treatment of popular culture as religious, see S. McCloud, 'Popular Culture Fandoms, the Boundaries of Religious Studies, and the Project of the Self', *Culture and Religion*, 4 (2003), 187–206.

    [6] G. R. C. Davie, *Religion in Britain since 1945: Believing without Belonging* (Oxford: Blackwell, 1994).

    [7] A critique of Davie's use of the concept is presented in S. Bruce, 'Praying Alone? Church-Going in Britain and the Putnam Thesis', *Journal of Contemporary Religion*, 17 (2002), 317–28.

that plays such an important role in the secularization paradigm is redirected so that it is taken to undermine only the willingness to associate publicly. Faith, as such, has not declined.

The first point requires two different sorts of responses. Some once-communal activities became less popular because technological advance allowed us to achieve the same end better in other ways. That many people prefer to watch films on large televisions in the privacy and comfort of their own homes seems a good explanation for the decline of cinema-going that (unlike the decline in churchgoing) carries no implication for popularity of the core activity of film-watching. In some of Davie's other examples (the decline in political party membership, for example) the decline of the activity does seem to imply a loss of interest and thus supports the secularization interpretation of the collapse of the churches better than it supports Davie's rebuttal.

I have a third reservation about the attempt to separate church involvement from faith so that, if we can find non-belief-related explanations of the former, we can suppose the latter has not changed. It is certainly true that the expansion of secular leisure activities gave, for example, the people of 1930s Durham mining villages attractive alternatives to the social benefits of chapel membership. Sunday school outings, church choir performances, and brass band concerts drew fewer people as more could afford individual or family-based alternatives. But it is quite possible for people not to be seduced by the bright lights of secular leisure. Where the faith remained strong, the alternatives were rejected or ways were found to accommodate both. In Protestant Ulster and the highlands and islands of Scotland, the Sabbath long proved impervious to the work of the devil. In Catholic parts of Liverpool and Glasgow, many Catholics shifted their mass attendance so as to accommodate new secular forms of entertainment. While secular alternatives to churchgoing encouraged defection, we still need to explain why the faith was so weak that many succumbed to temptation.

We should also note that church involvement bears a very different relationship to being religious than cinema-going does to, say, being interested in the arts. As noted in Chapter 1, every strand of the Christian faith (and, for that matter, pretty well every major religious tradition) requires believers to engage in communal acts of worship. To describe oneself as Christian, though having no association with any organized expression of the Christian faith, is very different from asserting that one is interested in movies while never going to the pictures.

But in any case, rather than argue with its logic, we can address the believing-without-belonging thesis directly by testing how measures of church involvement and belief vary for an identifiable group of people. This was done by David Voas and Alasdair Crockett using a dataset of 5,750 respondents.[8] Voas and Crockett found that church attendance, religious belief, and religious identification had declined roughly in tandem. Far from belief remaining strong, it had actually declined slightly faster than belonging. Another major test, using European and World Values survey data, also failed to find any support for the believing-without-belonging notion.[9]

Davie has also promoted another version of the idea that apparently secular societies are more religious than they seem: 'vicarious religion'.[10] The phrase means 'the notion of religion performed by an active minority but on behalf of a much larger number, who (implicitly at least) not only understand, but, quite clearly, approve of what the minority is doing'.[11]

It is not hard to find vicarious religion in religious societies. Pre-Reformation Christianity, like most major world religions, allowed the transfer of religious merit. It was constructed on a clear division of religious labour: a small population of religious virtuosi glorified

---

[8] D. Voas and A. D. Crockett, 'Religion in Britain: Neither Believing nor Belonging', *Sociology*, 39 (2005), 11–28.

[9] O. Aarts, N. Need, M. Te Grotenhuis, and N. D. de Graaf, 'Does Belonging Accompany Believing? Correlations and Trends in Western Europe and North America between 1981 and 2000', *Review of Religious Research*, 50 (2008), 16–34. Using the pooled WVS dataset of over a quarter of a million respondents, Norris and Inglehart find that 'the strength of religious beliefs also predicts a country's level of religious participation with a fair degree of accuracy' (P. Norris and R. Inglehart, *Sacred and Secular: Religion and Politics Worldwide* (Cambridge: Cambridge University Press, 2004), 225).

[10] G. R. C. Davie, *Religion in Modern Europe: A Memory Mutates* (Oxford: Oxford University Press, 2000); 'Vicarious Religion: A Methodological Challenge', in N. T. Ammerman (ed.), *Everyday Religion: Observing Modern Religious Lives* (New York: Oxford University Press, 2006), 21–35; P. L. Berger, G. R. C. Davie, and E. Fokas, *Religious America, Secular Europe: A Theme and Variations* (Aldershot: Ashgate, 2008).

[11] Davie, 'Vicarious Religion', 22.

God on behalf of the entire people. The laity was not expected to show great piety (though many people did). Obedience to, and financial support of, the church and periodic attendance at the high services were sufficient. But this structure was made possible only by a theory that allowed one person to substitute for another (and 'vicarious' means precisely 'substitutionary'). Those who paid others to say masses on their behalf after death were indeed engaging in vicarious religion, because the prayers of chantry priests 'on behalf of' the testator were earning God's favour for the deceased. In July 1532, James Hadley, an affluent gentleman in Somerset, left in his will a shilling to every church and a shilling to every parish priest in a large part of the county, a shilling to every clergyman in the diocese of Bath and Wells who did not possesses a benefice, a shilling to every religious house, five shillings to the high altars of six named parish churches, and a shilling to every side altar in the same churches to have his name added to the rolls of those who were prayed for at them, £2 for the repair of the relic box in his own parish church, and money to pay for thousands of masses. Finally 'forasmuch as I have been negligent to visit holy places and going on pilgrimage' he left money to twelve shrines.[12]

But in addition to substitution, there is a further element implied in the notion of vicarious religion: the wish to be more properly religious oneself. Had a young James Hadley announced that he had no intention of trying to avoid sin but that he would buy his way out of trouble post-mortem, the church would have denounced him. The system retained plausibility only so long as it could be believed that the ungodly really wished to be different and were prevented only by human frailness or worldly responsibilities from maintaining a correct attitude to God. That is, it required those who benefited from the religious work of the virtuosi to subscribe to the virtuosi's belief system.

The important question for evaluating vicarious religion as a rebuttal of the secularization approach is 'How common is it?'. Davie finds a lot of it; I see very little. Davie's first example of how religion operates vicariously is that 'churches and church leaders

---

[12] 'Houses of Augustinian Canons: The Priory of Barlynch', *A History of the County of Somerset: Volume 2* (1911), 132–4, www.british-history.ac.uk/report. aspx?compid=40931 (accessed: 9 Dec. 2009).

perform ritual on behalf of others (notably the occasional offices)'.[13] Davie distinguishes two separate types of vicarious ritual: those in which the secular population relies on the church *in extremis* and those used by non-churchgoers to celebrate rites of passage. Consider her analysis of responses to the death of Princess Diana in August 1997:

In the week following the accident, significant numbers of British people were instinctively drawn to their churches. This happened in two ways: first the churches became an important, though not the only, gathering point for a whole range of individual gestures of mourning in which Christian and less Christian symbols became inextricably mixed, both materially (candles, playing cards, and Madonnas) and theologically (life after death was strongly affirmed, but with no notion of final judgment). More significant, however, was the awareness in the population as a whole that multiple and well-intentioned gestures of public mourning were inadequate in themselves to mark the end of this particular life, as indeed of any other. Hence, the need for public ritual or public liturgy (in other words a funeral), and where else but in the established church.[14]

This is hardly persuasive. First, as Davie notes, many people made secular gestures of mourning. Secondly, it is not clear that the Church of England was doing religion 'on behalf' of secular mourners. Religious organizations did religious things. Secular organizations did secular things. And some secular people attended religious events. Davie offers no evidence that non-religious people felt their mourning inadequate other than the fact that Diana was buried with much ado by the state church. As Diana was an occasional Anglican attender and the daughter-in-law of the Church's nominal head, her funeral would have been conducted by senior Anglican officials even if the population at large had not cared a hoot. And, as a test of the claim in the last sentence, we can ask whether people would have been disappointed had the state funeral been conducted by lay people (actors, perhaps) using suitably grave texts rather than by bishops. I doubt it. Even for churchgoers, the final phrase in her account is unlikely to be accurate. The Church of England is not the state church of Wales, Scotland, or Northern Ireland, nor is it the preferred church of most English Christians.

[13] Davie, in Berger et al, *Religious America*, 40.
[14] Davie, 'Vicarious Religion', 28.

The second type of vicariously religious activity—the occasional use by unreligious people of religious rites for secular purposes—hardly supports the case. The choice of a church wedding (or christening or funeral) by people who do not otherwise attend seems motivated less by an urge to be briefly religious than by a quest for solemnity, tinged with nostalgia. There is clear evidence for this in an interesting study of why avowedly non-religious couples chose a church wedding. John Walliss concludes that the motives were not 'almost religious' but quite secular.[15] Couples wanted to show that they were serious about their relationship and felt that an old ritual in an old building conferred more dignity and solemnity on the event than did a civil ceremony in the local council offices.

Nostalgia is an important element of outsider support for the Christian churches in Britain. In 2008 the *Daily Telegraph*, one of Britain's best-selling serious newspapers, mounted a campaign to save Britain's churches. As part of the case that the state should maintain ancient but underused (and hence decaying) churches, it offered social utility: despite tiny congregations, churches were apparently the centre of rural community life. It also made a strong appeal to heritage and nostalgia. The village church was, like the village green and the pub and the shop and the school, part of what, in this high Tory vision, made Britain great. That many of the paper's columnists happily declared that they were not personally religious suggests there was an element of vicariousness in this, but vicarious what? The campaign did not argue that tax income spent on repairing old churches would be good for the souls of tax-payers. Rather, it asserted that, because churches were an important part of the world that Conservative readers wish to see restored (no gays, no divorce, no working mothers, no migrants or asylum-seekers, poor people knowing their place, selective schooling, no poor people in universities, and the like), maintaining the institutional fabric of the Christian faith would be socially rather than religiously beneficial.

Although Davie is careful to allow that motives for visiting religious buildings may be mixed, she nonetheless presents church- and

[15] J. Walliss, ' "Loved the wedding, invite me to the marriage": The Secularisation of Weddings in Contemporary Britain', *Sociological Research Online*, 7 (2002), www.socresonline.org.uk/7/4/walliss.html. 2002.

cathedral-visiting as evidence of vicarious religion.[16] The Church of England quite explicitly links cathedral-visiting and implicit religion; according to a press release on its website:

The annual number of cathedral visitors has remained stable at approximately 10 million, but with the addition of Westminster Abbey and other Royal Peculiars this figure is closer to 12 million. Evidence released today also suggests that many of these 'tourists' use the opportunity of visiting these historic buildings for spiritual reflection: almost half (45 per cent) of those surveyed in a study by ORB said that they lit a candle or said a prayer during their visit.[17]

There are two bits of public-relations puffery in this. First, there is no attempt to estimate how many people visited more than one site or the same site more than once. Secondly, cathedral tourists are presented as a 'reserve army' that should be added to the total of regular churchgoers, when it is highly likely that many tourists were already churchgoers.

A 2005 survey showed that a quarter of visitors to St David's Cathedral, Pembrokeshire, were weekly church-attenders and a further 49 per cent attended church 'from time to time but less often than weekly'. Only 17 per cent never attended church.[18] Although the survey did not ask about motives for visiting, it did offer a variety of statements with which respondents could agree (or otherwise). The responses to questions about religious and spiritual experience were predictably and strongly correlated with churchgoing. For example, 77 per cent of the weekly attenders 'felt a sense of God's presence from my visit'—an experience shared by 50 per cent of the occasional attenders but only 18 per cent of the non-churchgoers. A similar range of responses was given to the statement 'I felt a sense of the spiritual from my visit': 72, 57, and 31 per cent respectively. We should appreciate the implication of those numbers. Of the 514 visitors who completed the survey, only 30 or so were non-churchgoers who had any sort of positive religious or spiritual response to their visit. In Davie's vision of vicarious religion, a large reserve army of

[16] Davie, *Religion in Modern Europe*, 156–60.
[17] Church of England, 'Cathedrals Inspire More People each Year', www.cofe. anglican.org/news/pr2807.html. press release 2007 (accessed 1 Nov. 2008).
[18] J. Garnett, M. Grimley, A. Harris, W. Whyte, and S. Williams, *Redefining Christian Britain* (London: SCM Press, 2006), 116.

quasi-believers is posited to augment the very small active minority. But, in this case, the bulk of that reserve army is actually the small active minority.

Religious organizations provide a variety of secular social services. Mother and toddler groups, crèches and nurseries, youth groups, badminton clubs, and the like routinely use churches and church halls. Religious organizations run schools and colleges, nursing homes and hospices. It is increasingly common for city churches to seek new uses for their buildings (while attracting potential members) by inserting a floor into the main auditorium, using the new first floor as a reduced worship space, and converting the ground floor into cafés and shops selling Fairtrade goods. Should secular people who use the coffee shop be counted as vicariously religious?

To summarize my difficulty with the idea of vicarious religion, what is missing from the above examples is evidence that the non-religious people who make secular use of the churches or wish them well do so because, in some vague way, they wish they were more religious or wish to gain religious benefits from the association.

## Trajectory

Davie argues that peripheral involvement in the churches is as important a measure of their strength as regular attendance or assent to statements of core Christian beliefs. Let us look at the trajectory of the three most popular forms of occasional participation: baptisms, weddings, and funerals.

Far from being enduringly popular, infant baptism has declined rapidly. In the 1930s the Church of England baptized three-quarters of all children born in the country. By 2006 the figure had fallen to 14 per cent. In the four years between 2002 and 2006 the number of births in England increased by 12 per cent; the number of Anglican infant baptisms fell by the same amount.[19]

The churches no longer officiate at the majority of British weddings. The proportion of marriages solemnized with a civil ceremony rose in Scotland from 17 per cent in 1950 to just over 50 per cent in

[19] D. Voas, 'Intermarriage and the Demography of Secularisation', *British Journal of Sociology*, 54 (2003), 83–108.

2006.[20] In 1851 almost all weddings in England were religious. By 1900, civil ceremonies accounted for 15 per cent and that proportion grew steadily until, by 2003, over two-thirds of marriages were civil.[21]

There are no good time-series data on forms of funerals, but there is no doubt that church involvement in disposal of the dead has declined since the start of the twentieth century. Cremations have become increasingly popular; in 2007 around seven out of ten bodies were cremated rather than buried. Although clergymen are often employed to officiate at crematoria, the religious input has declined markedly. According to a 2007 report from the National Association of Funeral Directors (which represents about 85 per cent of the industry), secular celebrations of a person's life, with poems and pop music, are replacing the conventional church service.[22] In 2009 Cooperative Funeralcare, which has a very large part of the British funeral business, reported that, while hymns had been the music of choice at 41 per cent of funerals in 2005, in 2009 they made up only 35 per cent of the requests. Pop music accounted for 58 per cent of requests, with Frank Sinatra's 'My Way' the most popular.[23] Even when the clergy do bury non-believers, there is generally so little religion involved in the ritual that it is hard to present such events as vicarious religion. A rural Anglican vicar told me of a recent invitation to bury an old man who had lived in the area. His children asked that the vicar 'leave out the religious stuff', because neither they nor the deceased were believers. They wanted him to officiate because he was experienced in handling such events and his presence would confer solemnity.

To summarize, vicarious religion is an important element of the religious life of societies in which a common religion pervades the

[20] General Registrar for Scotland, *Statistics on Marriage* (Edinburgh: GRS, 2007), table 7.7.

[21] Figures calculated from summaries of Office for National Statistics, *Marriage and Divorce Statistic: Historical Series*, FM2 vol. 16, table 3.8b, FM2 vol. 20, table 3.10 and vols 26–31, table 3.29b, available online at www.statistics.gov.uk/STATBASE/xsdataset.asp?vlnk=5284 (accessed 3 Mar. 2008).

[22] C. McLatchey, 'Rise of the Funerals that Leave out God', *Sunday Telegraph*, 4 Mar. 2007.

[23] Cooperative Funeralcare, 'Funeral Music 2009', www.co-operative.coop/funeralcare/about-us/news—community-events/Funeral-Music-2009 (accessed 3 Mar. 2010).

world view. When almost everyone shares a common set of beliefs about the supernatural and people differ only in degrees of commitment, a religious division of labour is common: the less godly pay the godly to placate God on their behalf. Davie's attempt to find a great deal of enduring religious sentiment in what others see as largely secular societies by dubbing peripheral and occasional involvement in organized religion as vicarious religion is unconvincing. Substitutionary religion is almost entirely absent from largely secular societies because only a strongly supernaturalistic culture can sustain the magical idea that some people can effectively do religious work on behalf of others.

## Popular or Folk Religion

A further rebuttal of the secularization paradigm that shares many features with Davie's approach concerns the extent and nature of popular or folk religion. Historians such as James Obelkevich, Jeffrey Cox, and Sarah Williams[24] have drawn our attention to the 'rich flora and fauna of religious beliefs and practices…profoundly shaped by an apparently seamless web of religiosity drawing on folk, superstitious and orthodox elements'[25] that exists beyond the world of churches and chapels. What is at issue in arguments over the secularization thesis is the relationship between institutional core and popular religion.

What is presented as popular or folk religion includes superstition that has varying degrees of connection with Christian ideas, popular appropriations of Christian themes and rituals, and occasional involvement with Christianity (for example, claiming a Christian identity, using religious offices for rites of passage and attending church for such major services as Harvest Festivals, Christmas, and

---

[24] J. Obelkevich, *Religion and Rural Society in South Lindsey, 1825–1875* (Oxford: Oxford University Press, 1976); Jeffrey Cox, *The English Churches in a Secular Society: Lambeth, 1870–1930* (Oxford: Oxford University Press, 1982); Sarah Williams, *Religious Belief and Popular Culture* (Oxford: Oxford University Press, 1999).

[25] Richard Sykes, 'Popular Religion in Decline: A Study from the Black Country', *Journal of Ecclesiastical History*, 56 (2005), 288.

Easter).[26] Williams defines popular religion as 'a generally shared understanding of religious meaning including both folk beliefs as well as formal and officially sanctioned practices and ideas, operating within a loosely bounded interpretative community'.[27]

Superstition will be discussed at length in Chapter 6. Here I will focus the enduring popularity (or otherwise) of occasional involvement with the churches. This is, after all, what mostly concerns those who use popular religion to rebut the secularization thesis. Williams, for example, presents her material under four chapter headings: urban folk religion, occasional conformity, the ideal of the true believer, and religion by deputy. The last three concern people's relationship to the churches, and the first is largely concerned with quasi-Christian beliefs and rituals.

Like Davie's believing-without-belonging, the popular religion refutation of the secularization thesis misses a vital element: there is little attention to change over time. Williams shows that there was a lot of religion beyond the churches in Southwark in her study period 1880 to 1939 and concludes that focusing on the decline of institutional religion is a mistake; so the secularization thesis, which is often illustrated with such evidence, is mistaken. And it is not only mistaken for Southwark in 1880–1939; it is mistaken *tout court*. To quote the final words of her book:

We need to understand how successive generations continued to construct, communicate, and adapt religious language if we are to appreciate popular religion as a distinctive system of belief in its own right, persisting not only beyond the advent of the modern industrial world but also into the postmodern era in which we find ourselves today.[28]

Unfortunately Williams does not show that popular religion persists. She shows that at one period, between 120 and 70 years in the past, there existed a vibrant popular appropriation of what was still then a persuasively powerful official religious culture. She does not track that culture for long enough (and for long enough after the decline of the churches) for us to be confident that successive generations continued to have any great interest in religion, popular or otherwise.

---

[26] Sykes, 'Popular Religion in Decline', 288.
[27] Williams, *Religious Belief and Popular Culture*, 11.
[28] Williams, *Religious Belief and Popular Culture*, 176.

Another work in this tradition—Timothy Jenkins's account of Whit Walks in the 1980s in the Kingswood area of Bristol—has the same weakness. He criticizes the secularization paradigm for being insensitive to the wider community roles of religion and discusses in detail one example of community religion.[29] What he does not do is tell us that the public parading of Sunday schools and church congregations at Whitsun is now so much less popular than it was in 1950 or 1920 that it is almost extinct.

The absence of time-series data leaves open an obvious riposte to the popular religion critique: popular religion has declined in tandem with institutional religion. Rather than being an enduring autonomous culture that shows that interest in religion (defined broadly) has not declined, popular religion may be inexorably tied to institutional religion. To explore this possibility, I want to discuss in detail one case study.

## Staithes and its Religious Institutions

David Clark's *Between Pulpit and Pew*, based on fieldwork carried out between 1974 and 1976, is a detailed study of the religious life of Staithes, a small fishing village in North Yorkshire. Over the twentieth century, the population of the Hinderwell parish (which contains Staithes) fluctuated with the fortunes of the local economy. Its peak was at 2,608 in 1920s; in 2006 it was estimated at 2,010, with about half resident in Staithes.[30] In the first part of the twentieth century, the main occupations were fishing and ironstone mining. The ironstone industry shrank in the 1940s and 1950s, and the last mines closed in the early 1960s, but they were replaced by potassium carbonate mining in the 1960s. During Clark's time over seventy villagers worked at the Boulby Potash mine. Others worked at the British Steel rolling mills at Skinningrove some seven miles away. There were ten teachers living in the village. Many women worked in offices and shops in Loftus and Middlesbrough to the north or Whitby to the south. By Clark's time there were few full-time fishermen.

---

[29] T. Jenkins, *Religion in English Everyday Life: An Ethnographic Approach* (Oxford: Berghahn Books, 1999), 25–31.

[30] North Yorkshire County Council, *Population Estimates 2007*, www.north yorks.gov.uk/index.aspx?articleid=5489&textonly=True (accessed 7 Jan. 2009).

The Anglican parish church base was two miles away in the village of Hinderwell and the Church was supported mainly by farmers. The lack of a church presence in the village left it open to dissenters. Congregational, Wesleyan, and Primitive Methodist chapels were opened in 1823, 1824, and 1838 respectively. The 1851 Census of Religious Worship gives us a good indicator of their strength. The total of attendances at the most popular services of the three chapels was 570: about 60 per cent of the population. And each chapel had over sixty children in its Sunday school.

The Church of England was slow to react to the growth of dissent. In 1874 it licensed its National School Room in the village for services, and the Hinderwell evening service was moved to what was dedicated as 'the Mission Church of St Peter the Fisherman'.[31] It never seriously competed with the three chapels and in the 1970s only a handful of villagers attended its services. Clark notes that there had been only eight Anglican baptisms in the previous century. In 1884 a Catholic church was built inland at the higher part of the village— Lane End—but it attracted few people from Staithes. Clark found only one Catholic family in the village.

One mark of chapel culture was the village's sabbatarianism. In the second half of the nineteenth century, Sunday was kept free of unnecessary work and public secular leisure. Fishermen got into harbour before midnight on Saturday and did not sail again until just after midnight on Sunday.[32] Another mark of evangelical religion was a change in boat names. Boats built in Staithes from 1755 to 1835 were named *Midsummer, Good Intent, Industrious Farmer, Adventure, Brotherly Love, Happy Returns, Two Brothers, Pomona, Friends Glory, Thomas and James, Flora, John and Elizabeth, Sophia Ann, Friends, Ceres, Endeavour Increase,* and *Ocean*.[33] A local historian lists the following late-nineteenth-century boats: *Simon Peter, Good Samaritan, Zoar, Rock of Ages, Rose of Sharon,* and *Star of Bethlehem*.[34]

[31] D. Clark, *Between Pulpit and Pew: Folk Religion in a North Yorkshire Fishing Village* (Cambridge: Cambridge University Press, 1982), 58.

[32] Clark, *Between Pulpit and Pew*, 61.

[33] Jean and Peter Eccleston, *A History and Geology of Staithes* (Staithes: Jean and Peter Eccleston, 1998), 118.

[34] John Howard, *Staithes: Chapters from the History of a Seafaring Town* (Scalby: John Howard, 2000), 201.

By the time Clark began his fieldwork in 1974, the chapels had shrunk. Most affected was Bethel. It had not had a resident minister since 1965 when it withdrew from the Congregational Union of England and Wales.[35] Its morning service attracted fewer then 10 people and its evening services attracted an average of only 30. The Wesleyans had 34 members and average attendances of 20 at the morning service and 30 in the evening. However the Sunday school remained popular, with 50 children on the roll and two-thirds attending regularly. The formerly Primitive Methodist High Street chapel had 32 members, with average attendances of 15 in the morning and 25 in the evening. But, as with the Wesleyan chapel, Sunday school was relatively more popular, with 40 scholars on the rolls.

### Popular Religion in Staithes

Clark follows his evidence of chapel decline by noting: 'this apparent institutional atrophy belies a persisting relevance in the community.'[36] That relevance for non-members included identifying with a chapel, attending church-based social events, sending children to Sunday school, occasionally attending services, singing hymns in a non-church context, keeping the Sabbath, and using religious offices for rites of passage.

Both Methodist chapels had a Bright Hour meeting, drawing support 'from a broad circle of women who consider themselves as either Wesleyans or Primitives, even though…this self-image may be rooted in the most limited ties to the chapel'.[37] Apart from opening and closing with prayer, the Bright Hour was mainly social. Like the meetings of the Women's Institute, the Bright Hour entertained and educated its attenders with handicraft displays, talks from visiting speakers, and the like. In addition to these weekly events, both chapels organized coffee mornings and other fund-raisers that were well supported by villagers who were not regular chapel attenders.

---

[35] According to *The Yorkshire Congregational Yearbook* (York: Yorkshire Congregational Union, 1952), in 1951 Bethel had 27 members and 30 Sunday scholars. *The Congregational Yearbook* (London: Congregational Union of England and Wales, 1966) for 1965 records 20 members and 50 Sunday scholars.

[36] Clark, *Between Pulpit and Pew*, 61.

[37] Clark, *Between Pulpit and Pew*, 63.

Almost all the village children were enrolled in Sunday school, and one of the highpoints of the chapel year was the Sunday school anniversary or 'Piece-saying Sunday'. All the children memorized a 'piece'—a song, a scripture text, or a poem—which they performed on Sunday and again on the Monday evening (when applause was permitted). Serious effort was put into preparation. The children were rehearsed on weekday evenings a couple of times a week in the month before the event. So that they were well turned out, the purchase or making of new clothes for the children was synchronized with the annual event.

One of the best-known elements of a popular religion culture in the village was hymn-singing. The revivalist songs of the Ira Sankey songbook were a great favourite. 'Old Singing Isaac' Verrill was the second of five generations of the same family to run the Primitive Methodist chapel. He gained his sobriquet from singing at the wake and at the graveside of every villager—a custom that others continued into the 1960s. On Sunday evenings in summer in the 1930s, large numbers of men gathered on the harbour front. Henry Verrill gave out the note, they struck up a hymn and marched up the road singing. As they passed each chapel, the men peeled off to their respective places of worship. One choir sang at London's Crystal Palace in 1900. In the 1940s Willie Verrill led a quintet that broadcast on the BBC a number of times.[38] That grew into a large choir that was proficient enough to perform in the Manchester Free Trade Hall.

Clark summarizes the links between chapel and popular religion as follows: 'for the majority of children, week by week involvement with the chapel ceases at the age of twelve or thirteen; henceforth attendance is usually restricted to the important events of the life and annual cycles. Despite its apparent arbitrariness, this form of chapel affiliation is likely to be lifelong.'[39] For adults, he adds:

nominal affiliation, grounded in the Sunday Schools, means attendance at the main events of the chapel year, such as Harvest festivals, and anniversaries...Undoubtedly it presupposes the baptism of one's children in the chapel and the expectation that one's funeral will eventually take place there. Nominal affiliation elicits support for coffee-mornings, bazaars, jumble sales and even, in some cases, extends to making commentary gifts

---

[38] Howard, *Staithes*, 207.     [39] Clark, *Between Pulpit and Pew*, 71.

to chapel funds in lieu of Sunday attendance. Above all, it signifies a deeply felt identification with the traditions of both village and chapel alike.[40]

Repeatedly Clark reports changes that are hard to describe in terms other than decline. His evocative description of funerals, for example, notes that villagers no longer sang hymns at the graveside or outside the home of the deceased. His account of the Sunday school anniversaries reports strategies the chapels used to disguise falling numbers. Nonetheless, he commits himself to a critique of the secularization paradigm based on the enduring nature of popular religion: 'The evidence from Staithes clearly points to [folk religion's] persistence and vitality.'[41]

### Staithes in 2009

In 2009 I visited Staithes on three occasions, consulted chapel records and local newspapers in the district archives, and interviewed a number of well-informed residents (including a long-serving Methodist minister).

Institutional religion in Staithes has all but collapsed. The Catholic Church continues to have occasional services, but these attract no more than the tiny numbers that attended in the 1970s. Although services are very occasionally scheduled there, the Anglican mission room is now a bookable community arts centre. Bethel closed sometime in the 1980s. Remarkably, its passing was so little mourned that, despite much effort, I failed to find anyone who had been a member.

The 1932 merger of Wesleyan and Primitive Methodism called into question the value of having two large chapels within a stone's throw of each other, but both societies repeatedly resisted merger until the situation resolved itself in 1981 when the former Primitive chapel could not produce enough members to fill the legally required offices and was closed. Its new status as sole chapel in the village did not help the Wesleyan Chapel. Membership continued to decline and in 2005 stood at 14, with a typical Sunday attendance of only 10 and no Sunday school.

What of popular religion? Sporadic attendance has ceased completely: no non-members attend the remaining chapel. There is no

---

[40] Clark, *Between Pulpit and Pew*, 76.
[41] Clark, *Between Pulpit and Pew*, 63.

active Sunday school for children of non-members to attend. Hence there is no piece-saying Sunday service to attract adult well-wishers. Not even Christmas attracts outsiders. In recent years, the nearest carol services were in Skinningrove, some seven miles away, and they were poorly attended. There are no longer any social activities organized by the chapels: no weekly Bright Hour meetings, no church bazaars, and no coffee mornings. Rites of passage are now very rarely celebrated in the remaining chapel: very few children are baptized there, very few marriages are celebrated in the chapel, and the few funerals are of existing members. More than a quarter of a century after Bethel and the High Street chapel closed, and with the Wesleyan chapel on its last legs, none of my informants thought that non-members identified with the chapel.

There is no longer any public singing of hymns, in the streets or by the graveside. The last of a series of choirs recruited from the chapels folded in 1980. Five years later some members formed 'The Men of Staithes' with a largely secular maritime repertoire. One member explained: 'When we revived the choir we sort of became secular, rather than sacred. The old choir was a sacred choir. Before they had the congregations. You've got to get people involved, to come to these concerts. That's why we like to do the secular stuff.'[42] This choir folded in 2005.

The wider influence of Christianity is more difficult to judge, but it is clear that sabbatarianism has completely died. There is nothing about the tenor of a Sunday in Staithes that distinguishes it from Sunday anywhere else. One final ironic note: when a young Strict Baptist tried to preach at the harbour in the late 1980s, he was reported to the police, who asked him to move on or be charged with breach of the peace.[43]

### Core and Periphery

The argument that concentrating on institutional religion leads commentators to exaggerate secularization implies that the sphere of popular religion is in some senses autonomous and enduring. Put

[42] D. Stradling, 'Staithes Men's Choir', www.mustrad.org.uk/articles/staithes.htm (accessed 3 Sept. 2008).
[43] Interview with Peter Meney, Hill Top, Eggleston 2008.

rather brutally, the conclusion of my restudy of Staithes is that, once there is no institutional religion, there is nothing to which people can occasionally conform. Once the chapels close, it is only a matter of time before the residual affiliations become erased.

But we can say something more than this, which returns us to my critique of vicarious religion. When a large majority shares a common religious world view, that many people only occasionally conform to the church's requirements is not a problem. Core and periphery collude. Core members think they are setting an example. People on the fringes pay lip service to the beliefs and values of the core and imply that, if only they were less busy, they too would attend regularly. As the core shrinks, such pretence becomes more transparent and tensions arise. There was a good example of this in attitudes to the Sunday school anniversaries. In the nineteenth century, when a much higher proportion of adults regularly attended church, the social aspects of the Sunday school could be appreciated as secondary benefits of a popular primary purpose: basic religious education. In the last third of the twentieth century, those chapel members sufficiently committed to teach in the Sunday school became increasingly resentful that their faith was being insulted by people who were interested only in seeing their children and grand-children do a turn.

In Chapter 6, I will consider the superstition element of folk religion. Thus far I have concentrated on peripheral involvement in organized religion. I now want to make a brief point about popular-ized Christian belief. What gave the sort of folk religion described by Williams in Southwark its cohesion was its borrowing of Christian themes, which brings me to perhaps the greatest weakness in the idea that a shared popular religion can survive the death of the churches. There can be Christian beliefs to be worked into local folk-lore only if the people are acquainted with basic Christian ideas, symbols, and rituals. With Christianity now largely absent from the mass media and from local schools (or presented there as only one of a number of equally persuasive alternatives) and with only a handful of villagers attending Christian services, there is no longer a common stock of religious knowledge to be popularized. In the 1920s children in the area skipped to the following rhyme: 'Tid, Mid, Mizzy, Ray, Carlin, Palm, Pace Egg Day'. Though few would have understood its origins, the words represented the six Sundays of Lent by borrowing words from the *te deum* prayer. 'Tid' was Te Deum, 'Mid' Me Deum, and Mizzy-Ray was Miserere. 'Carlin' was a reference to Carlin Sunday, a local custom of eating brown peas that was thought to have originated in the famine-relieving accident of a ship's cargo of such peas being washed ashore near South Shields. 'Palm' was Palm Sunday. Local children no longer skip to a chant that popularizes a major Christian festival. How could they, when none of them attends church?[44]

# Conclusion

The vicarious-religion and popular-religion critiques are important, because they go to the heart of the secularization story. To put the alternatives most starkly, the secularization paradigm assumes that the decline of the Christian churches is evidence of more than just a loss of interest in attending church. It is a sign that people have lost interest in the Christian faith, which, as Christianity has for centuries been the dominant form of religion in Europe, can be generalized as a loss of interest in religion. Both the vicarious and popular religion rebuttals wish to separate the fate of organized religion from some wider diffuse religious sentiment and argue that the loss of faith has been exaggerated by social scientists who ignore the continued existence of an autonomous enduring sphere of popular religious belief and interest. Both approaches suffer a common fault. They challenge a long-standing trend with data from single time periods. Davie offers a variety of weak marks of religious interest as a supposed counter-balance to the decline of the churches. Williams shows that there is considerable religion outside the churches at a specific time (incidentally, a time when the churches were still popular). Clark similarly shows that, when the chapels were popular, they exerted an influence beyond their core membership. This is not enough to make their case. What matters is the trajectory of change. For how long and to what extent does vicarious or popular religion survive the decline of the Christian churches? The answer is not long and not much.

---

[44] 'Sundays in Lent', *Dalesman* (Feb.1977), 896.

# 5

# Contemporary Spirituality

## Introduction

The idea that people should be free to choose their religion is novel. Most European states in the nineteenth century were dominated by a single church that expected the conformity of subjects and citizens. The governments of such states treated those who would not conform as a threat to national integrity: at best disloyal, at worst traitorous. Until 1813 it was a crime in Britain to deny the doctrine of the Trinity. Catholics were denied the vote until 1828 in England and 1829 in Scotland. Until 1871 only members of the Church of England could graduate from Oxford. In 1845 Norway allowed ordinary citizens (but not civil servants) to leave the Lutheran Church and then only to join an approved alternative. Sweden, now the beacon of liberality, did not allow complete religious freedom until 1951.

The gradual relaxation of the church–state bond and the weakening of the dominant church saw the penalties for religious innovation reduce from death to imprisonment to mild scorn. Modernization has been accompanied by a steady increase in the variety of religious expressions on offer. Initially the new religions were variants of Christianity. During the twentieth century innovators began to draw on the East for inspiration. As part of a general critique of Western civilization and economy, the counter-culture of the 1960s saw a flaring of interest in Hindu and Buddhist religion to augment those home-grown new religions that were 'spiritualized' forms of the secular psychotherapies inspired by Sigmund Freud and Carl Jung.[1] The relationship of these new faiths to secularization can be easiest seen if we divide them by their attitude to the everyday world. The most exotic ones such as Krishna Consciousness (aka Hare Krishna) and the Unification Church (aka the Moonies) were world rejecting: they attracted affluent young people who, temporarily at least, rejected the materialism of their parents to become full-time devotees of exotic sects. Others were world affirming: either they offered perspectives and therapies to help people become more successful or they promised to help people regain some of the authentic self they had lost in the struggle for advancement in the cold worlds of government bureaucracy and capitalist commerce.[2] Transcendental Meditation (aka TM), the cult of Shree Bhagwan Rajneesh, and Scientology helped people to do better and feel better in the material world. Instead of expecting monastic commitment, they stressed the ease with which their new revelations could be accommodated in a normal life. TM, for example, ran newspaper adverts that declared that meditating for 'just a few minutes everyday' would leave you 'feeling positive, alert and clear with the calmness and inner contentment to tackle life with enthusiasm'. In language reminiscent of dog-food adverts, it added that meditation 'helps to protect you from stress and future ill-health'.[3]

The new religions of the 1960s and 1970s got a great deal of press coverage and provided careers for a generation of sociologists of religion, but they attracted very few adherents. Looking at a source such as the glossy fat *New Religions: A Guide*,[4] it is easy to suppose that there is a vibrant world of novel religiosity out there and to miss the point that most of the listed movements had barely a hundred members in any European country. There were never more than a thousand Moonies in Britain at any one time. In the 2001 Census of

[1] For a good general account, see C. Campbell, 'The Easternization of the West', in B. R. Wilson and J. Cresswell (eds), *New Religious Movements: Challenge and Response* (London: Routledge, 1999), 35–48.

[2] R. Wallis, *The Elementary Forms of the New Religious Life* (London: Routledge and Kegan Paul, 1984).

[3] *Herald*, 17 Feb. 1995, 30.

[4] C. Partridge (ed.), *New Religions: A Guide: New Religious Movements, Sects and Alternative Spiritualities* (Oxford: Oxford University Press, 2004).

England and Wales only 1,781 people listed their religion as Scientology; in Scotland it was 58. Scotland could muster only 25 Hare Krishnas.[5] Although such movements are fascinating, they can hardly 'be viewed as a repudiation of conventional secularization and disenchantment perspectives'.[6]

Once the new religious movements had disappointed those who needed evidence that, despite the decline of the churches, people were enduringly religious, attention turned elsewhere. The prime candidate these days for refuting secularization is what is variously called New Age, alternative, or holistic spirituality.

As we will see, core features of the New Age movement make it hard to pin down. Even the word 'movement' exaggerates its cohesion. It is best thought of as a culture and a milieu. As a culture, it is a series of loosely interrelated themes that are now omnipresent in the mass media. As a milieu, it is a network of organizations, publishing houses, magazines, workshops, seminars and conferences, informal groups, websites, coffee houses, and shops bound together only by the overlapping interests of those who participate in it. And much of that participation is brief and segmental. As good a place as any to start is the definition given in *Wikipedia*.

The New Age...is a decentralized Western social and spiritual movement that seeks 'Universal Truth' and the attainment of the highest individual human potential. It includes aspects of cosmology, astrology, esotericism, alternative medicine, music, collectivism, sustainability, and nature. New Age spirituality is characterized by an individual approach to spiritual practices and philosophies, while rejecting religious doctrine and dogma.[7]

We can add Paul Heelas's definition of 'inner-life' spirituality:

---

[5] Figures supplied by the Registrar-General for Scotland. The totals may be artificially depressed by the fact that the census forms were completed on behalf of all members of a household by a single 'household reference person', usually the oldest male, who may have chosen to overlook a young family member's deviant religious identity. But, even if we doubled the numbers, they would remain trivial.

[6] T. Robbins and P. C. Lucas, 'From "Cults" to New Religious Movements', in J. A. Beckford and N. J. Demerath III (eds), *Sage Handbook of the Sociology of Religion* (London: Sage, 2007), 230.

[7] Wikipedia, http://en.wikipedia.org/wiki/New_Age (accessed 21 Sept. 2009).

Spiritualities of life today…typically take a holistic, life-affirming form. Whether it be yoga in Chennai or yoga in San Francisco, Aikido in Islamabad or Aikido in Birkenhead, one will encounter the theme that what matters is delving within oneself to experience the primary source of the sacred, namely that which emanates from the…depths of life in the here-and-now.[8]

Spirituality (as distinct from religion) generally has three features. Its ideological core is a belief in some sort of supernatural force or entity that differs from that of conventional religion in having no location outside the self, except in some all-pervasive notion of the cosmic consciousness. A phrase common in the New Age centre at Findhorn—'coming into your power'—nicely captures the sense that enlightenment, rather than accessing something external, makes you aware of what you already have. Its second component involves perception: becoming spiritual changes how one sees and feels about the world. Its third component is ethical: becoming aware of our spiritual nature should make us better people. These three features fit perfectly well with what Heelas and Woodhead mean by spirituality: 'subjective-life forms of the sacred, which emphasise inner sources of significance and authority and the cultivation or sacralisation of unique subjective-lives' and which they contrast with more conventionally religious conceptions 'which emphasise a transcendent source of significance and authority to which individuals must conform at the expense of the cultivation of their unique subjective-lives'.[9]

The secularization paradigm has no argument with the claim that there has been an increase in individualistic this-worldly religion. Indeed, the shift from authoritarian dogmatic religion predicated on an external creator God to individualistic forms of religion is a central part of the secularization thesis. What is at issue in evaluating the significance of holistic spirituality are first the scale and second the stability of this new way of being religious. Those who see secularization as 'change not decline' and offer holistic spirituality as evidence of enduring interest in religion broadly defined need to demonstrate

---

[8] P. Heelas, *Spiritualities of Life: New Age Romanticism and Consumptive Capitalism* (Oxford: Blackwell Publishing, 2008), 5.
[9] P. Heelas and L. Woodhead, *The Spiritual Revolution: Why Religion is Giving Way to Spirituality* (Oxford: Blackwell, 2004), 6.

that there is a lot of it about. And, as they usually compensate for small numbers by claiming strong growth rates, we need to consider what the nature of the current market for holistic spirituality tells us about its likely future.

The historical-expository approach to contemporary spirituality that we see in the works of J. Gordon Melton and Christopher Partridge is educational, but vague claims of vitality and growth do not help us evaluate the phenomenon.[10] Nor do detailed ethnographies. Close acquaintance with twenty-two people involved in meditation, Reiki healing, spiritualism, and the study of the occult in Nottingham allows Wood to make interesting observations about the New Age, but it does not allow us to estimate the popularity of such interests, and knowing that thirty people in Fife attended a fire-walking session is no help at all.[11] To assess the scale of the phenomenon we need representative sample surveys and extensive local area studies, and it is to these that I now turn.

I will confine this discussion to Britain, because it is one of the world's most secular societies. If the secularization paradigm is to be refuted by showing that the decline of shared institutional religion has been offset by the rise of individualized religion, then the British case should show ample evidence.

## Measuring Spirituality: Survey

In a 2001 survey, in addition to the conventional questions about religious beliefs and practices, Scots were asked a variety of questions designed to assess their involvement in a variety of alternative practices: consulting horoscopes in newspapers and magazines; fortune-telling, tarot or astrology; complementary or alternative medicines

[10] Partridge (ed.), *New Religions*; C. Partridge, *The Re-Enchantment of the West Vol. 1* (Edinburgh: T and T Clark, 2004); J. Gordon Melton, *Encyclopaedic Handbook of Cults in America* (New York: Garland, 1992).

[11] S. Sutcliffe, 'Unfinished Business: Devolving Scotland/Devolving Religion', in S. Coleman and P. Collins (eds.), *Religion, Identity and Change: Perspectives on Global Transformations* (Aldershot: Ashgate, 2004), 84–106; M. Wood, *Power, Possession and the New Age* (Aldershot: Ashgate, 2007).

and herbal remedies, homeopathy or aromatherapy; and yoga or meditation.[12]

Forty per cent of the sample had not been raised in a religion, did not identify with one, and had never regularly attended church services. A similar proportion had once regularly attended but had given up. Less than a quarter claimed to attend regularly. The sample was evenly divided between those who believed in a personal God, those who believed in a higher power or life force, those who agreed that 'there is something there', and those who believed none of these things.

A third of the sample described themselves as religious, 15 per cent described themselves as not religious but spiritual, and the rest declined to claim either label.[13] As I noted in Chapter 1, the problem with survey data is that talk is cheap. In discussing why working-class people of the 1930s would describe themselves as 'Christian' while avoiding any formal contact with the churches, Richard Hoggart explained that they took it to mean ethical, moral, honest, and respectable.[14] I suspect something similar of the fondness of celebrities for describing themselves as spiritual, only now the reputational work is concentrated on the sensitivity of the speaker's personality rather than on the decency of his or her behaviour. When best-selling author Dean Koontz explains his fondness for gardening by saying 'I'm a pretty spiritual person and I do feel that the natural world is a gift and we're meant to love it',[15] or when former pop star Victoria Beckham tells an interviewer that she is 'very spiritual' because she is 'very good at visualization...I lie in bed and think, what kind of look do I want to go for tomorrow',[16] we need to be wary of making too much of superficial claims.

To try to get beyond nominalism, the Scottish survey asked about activities and their importance (though, sadly, not about whether

[12] T. Glendinning and S. Bruce, 'New Ways of Believing or Belonging: Is Religion Giving Way to Spirituality?', *British Journal of Sociology*, 57 (2006), 399–413.

[13] Those who chose 'religious and spiritual' were classified as religious because it was clear from other characteristics that they were regular churchgoing Christians who interpreted 'spiritual' as the emotional side of being religious.

[14] R. Hoggart, *The Uses of Literacy* (London: Chatto and Windus, 1957), 97–9.

[15] Tony Horkins, 'Dean Koontz', *Observer Magazine*, 16 Aug. 2009, 26.

[16] *The Week*, 6 Dec. 2008.

people visualized their 'look' for the next day). The results can be summarized as follows. Casual experimentation was fairly common.[17] Forty-four per cent had tried various forms of alternative medicine. Thirty per cent had, 'aside from horoscopes', tried 'fortune-telling, tarot or astrology'. Twenty-two per cent had tried yoga or meditation. But more serious involvement was rare. When we add 'used this more than occasionally', the percentages fall to 21 for alternative medicine, 8 for forms of divination, and 11 for yoga or meditation. They fall further when respondents were asked 'and how important is this to you in living your life' (which sounds clunky but has been tried and tested in hundreds of polls). Only 20 per cent of those who had tried alternative medical therapies, 6 per cent of those who had tried divination, and only 9 per cent of those who had tried yoga or meditation thought it important.

Though interest in such things may be a mark of alternative spirituality, it is possible that the conventionally religious and the entirely secular have dabbled in meditation, aromatherapy, or astrology. To clearly identify a New Age set, we combined involvement in alternative practices with self-description as spiritual. Only 8 per cent of respondents said they had found some form of alternative practice important at some point in their lives and also saw themselves as a spiritual. Only 2 per cent of the sample had found alternative practices from the two interest groups of well-being and divination important in their lives and described themselves as spiritual.

Of course, one can raise all sorts of methodological problems with these data and their interpretation, but, until others produce better data, we have to make do with what we have and that can be summarized very simply. Familiarity with complementary medicine is widespread but of limited significance. Other things that might reasonably be described as evidence of holistic spirituality are sufficiently rare that even the kindest interpretation of the data will not support the idea that it is filling the gap left by the decline of the churches. Three-quarters of Scots are not conventionally religious (if one takes churchgoing as the mark). If we take belief in God as the mark, no more than half the sample could be described as conventionally religious and that is almost certainly an exaggeration.

[17] Glendinning and Bruce, 'New Ways'.

In either case, the non-religious are vastly more numerous than the 2–8 per cent we might sensibly describe as being involved in some activity or practice that could represent an 'individuated religion' or holistic spirituality.

Because it is relevant to the possible growth of alternative spirituality, we should note what sort of people are involved. Age, gender, education, and class are all implicated. Put succinctly, alternative spirituality is the preserve of middle-aged, middle-class women with university-level qualifications. Women with no educational qualifications do not engage with holistic practices centred on personal growth: they prefer horoscopes, fortune-telling, astrology, and tarot. Because this sort of finding is often misunderstood, it is important to stress that the evidence shows that most of those interested in things New Agey are middle-aged, middle-class women; this is not the same as saying that most middle-aged middle-class women are interested in the New Age.[18] They are not. Most people in every demographic category show no interest in alternative spirituality.

## Measuring Spirituality: Locale Study

A very different approach to measuring the extent of the holistic milieu is the locale study conducted in Kendal, a market town and local government centre in the north-west of England, between 2000 and 2002. Paul Heelas and Linda Woodhead of Lancaster University, and two full-time researchers, investigated the scale and variety of religious and spiritual practice. They compiled an inventory of all the churches and chapels, and of all the group activities and individual therapists that could be included within the broadest possible definition of holistic spirituality, and attempted to count the number of people involved in each category during a typical week. Finally, they

---

[18] For example, Woodhead explains female attraction to holistic spirituality (which is rare) by the 'double alienation' of women in modern society (which is presented as an almost universal condition) (L. Woodhead, 'Why So Many Women in Holistic Spirituality?', in K. Flanagan and P. Jupp (eds), *A Sociology of Spirituality* (Aldershot: Ashgate, 2008), 115–25).

surveyed participants and studied selected congregations and holistic spirituality groups in detail.[19]

With regard to the scale of the congregational domain, the conclusions were consistent with findings from national surveys: some 7.9 per cent of people were in church on any given Sunday, and that figure had been declining steadily over many years. They concluded that about 1.6 per cent of the population participated in one or more activities in the holistic spirituality milieu each week, and that the trend was up. Heelas and Woodhead maintain that alternative spirituality has been growing rapidly, that this growth can be expected to continue, and that we might reasonably expect the holistic milieu to overtake the congregational domain within the next thirty years or so.[20]

One may participate in the holistic milieu by attending a group (for yoga, tai chi, meditation, and the like) or by receiving personal attention from a practitioner (for example, of Reiki, homeopathy, aromatherapy, and so on). The researchers observed all group activities during one particular week and counted attenders. Counting the clients of therapists was more difficult, but the investigators estimated there were 840 acts of participation by, allowing for multiple involvement, some 600 people. For reasons given elsewhere, that estimate may be on the high side, but, as it is always best to criticize a case at its strongest, that figure can stand.[21]

It does not follow, of course, that the clients or participants viewed their activities as spiritual, and the listing of activities summarized in Table 5.1 does suggest the net has been spread too wide.[22]

More than half of involvement is in what most people would view as leisure or recreation: yoga, tai chi, dance, singing, art. Add in what women's magazines call 'pampering'—massage, bodywork—and we

---

[19] The methods and the findings are detailed in Heelas and Woodhead, *Spiritual Revolution*.

[20] Heelas and Woodhead, *Spiritual Revolution*, 48.

[21] For a detailed methodological critique of the Kendal Project, see D. Voas and S. Bruce, 'The Spiritual Revolution: Another False Dawn for the Sacred', in K. Flanagan and P. C. Jupp (eds), *A Sociology of Spirituality* (Aldershot: Ashgate, 2007), 43–62.

[22] I am indebted to David Voas for this table and for help in clarifying my criticisms.

Table 5.1. Acts of participation in the holistic milieu (%)

| | |
|---|---|
| Yoga and tai chi | 45.5 |
| Massage, bodywork | 13.9 |
| Healing and complementary health groups | 11.2 |
| Reiki or spiritual healing | 6.1 |
| Dancing, singing, art, and craft | 5.6 |
| Specialized spiritual/religious groups | 5.6 |
| Miscellaneous one-to-one | 5.0 |
| Homeopathy | 3.6 |
| Counselling | 3.5 |

have covered nearly two-thirds. Not all the 'healing and complementary health groups' are obviously spiritual or even unconventional; CancerCare, for example, which won the Queen's Jubilee Award for Voluntary Service in the Community, is one of the larger ones. Although some healing has a religious basis, a good proportion of the activities (homeopathy, for example) seem pseudo-scientific rather than spiritual.

Fortunately we do not have to decide just which activities should be classed as spiritual, because the respondents were asked that question. Just over half said 'not spiritual', and only a quarter chose 'spiritual growth' as the main reason for their involvement. Hence, in their own terms fewer than 1 per cent of the population of Kendal were involved in the world of holistic spirituality.[23]

If the holistic milieu spirituality is to compensate for the decline of the churches, it needs to be the right scale. The churchgoing population of Kendal is 7.9 per cent. If we increase that to 15 per cent to include all those who are at all interested in Christianity, we are left with 85 per cent of the population or almost 32,000 people who are not in the mainstream of religion and who are thus, in theory, available for recruitment to some alternative. Another way of estimating the potential market is to start with the proportion of people who attended church in 1851: 38 per cent.[24] If churchgoing in Kendal were

[23] Because a disproportionate number of the questionnaires were completed by practitioners rather than clients, this is almost certainly an overestimate.

[24] This figure is derived from the count of attendances adjusted as recommended by the late Alasdair Crockett, who was an expert on the interpretation of the 1851 census of Religious Worship.

as popular now as it was in 1851, there would be 14,500 churchgoers rather than the current 3,000. So the current performance of the churches in Kendal leaves more than 11,000 people unchurched. Set against that scale of decline, the 270 people involved in the holistic milieu for spiritual reasons seem a very small number indeed.

In order to preserve the claim that we are in the midst of *The Spiritual Revolution*, Heelas and Woodhead note the recent growth in the holistic spirituality milieu and engage in some questionable projection. Asked if their children shared their interest, two-thirds of respondents with offspring said 'no'. Heelas is impressed that 32 per cent said 'yes', but this level of transmission is disastrous.[25] In a society where parents have only two children on average, 100 per cent of them must be socialized into a practice for it to survive in the long term. Intergenerational transmission of Christian affiliation, attendance, and belief currently stands at about 50 per cent, which is widely regarded as a major problem for churches. Arguably holistic spirituality has an even higher mountain to climb, not least because women with spiritual interests are more likely than average to be childless. We also know that intergenerational transmission is halved again (that is, falls to 25 per cent) for the children of religiously mixed marriages (even when the mixing is just Anglican–Methodist). That around 80 per cent of the Kendal New Agers were female means that, in the vast majority of marriages involving a woman interested in holistic spirituality, her male partner does not share her interests. If the fate of the Christian churches over the twentieth century is any guide, the future for the New Age is decline, not growth.

It is strange that Heelas and Woodhead do not see the implication of their own age data. Only three respondents in the Kendal survey people were under the age of 30 and 83 per cent were aged 40 and over. As the New Age in Kendal has already failed to recruit young people, it is difficult to see why young people will be attracted in the future, and, unless they are, the milieu will contract, not grow, as its current inhabitants die out. It may be that people have sentiments or interests throughout their lives that they express only in activities (painting, for example) once their children have left home and they have free time. But, as yoga or meditation is no more time-consuming or

---

[25] P. Heelas and B. Seel, 'An Ageing New Age?', in G. Davie, P. Heelas, and L. Woodhead (eds), *Predicting Religion* (Aldershot: Ashgate, 2003), 234.

expensive than popular secular leisure activities, it is hard to see why an interest in these should be evidenced only late in life. It is even harder to think of obstacles to a 30-year-old saying he is spiritual, even if he is too busy yet to pursue that interest. Yet most people under the age of 40 describe themselves as neither religious nor spiritual.

Heelas and Woodhead's projections of growth may prove accurate, but the current evidence better supports the conclusion that holistic spirituality is a 'fashion' or 'period effect': a cultural product that appealed to a certain class of people who were adolescents in the 1960s and that will fade as they die out.

## An Aside on Expansive Definition

As we saw in the previous chapter when discussing vicarious and folk religion, it is always possible to inflate the numbers of people expressing some sort of spiritual interest by broadening our operational definition. For example, we could, as Heelas is, be impressed by the spread of the language of self-spirituality into schools, health service, and even commercial enterprises.[26] However, much of the commercial interest in 'empowering staff' and the like seems little more than shallow attempts to add the fairy dust of higher purpose to old-fashioned exploitation. Much of the apparent interest in the spirituality of health care seems driven by religious people (hospital chaplains, for example) struggling to find a new justification in largely secular or religiously diverse worlds.

As well as finding more spirituality by employing looser substantive definitions and by taking casual use of self-aggrandizing language at face value, we can find it by using functional definitions backwards. So we note that spirituality often involves temporarily transcending the mundane, believing in supernatural entities, or feeling a strong sense of communal bonding and then claiming for the spiritual secular activities that share those characteristics. So Stef

[26] D. Grant, K. O'Neil, and L. Stephens, 'Spirituality in the Workplace: New Empirical Directions in the Study of the Sacred', *Sociology of Religion*, 65 (2004), 265–83. P. Heelas, *The New Age Movement* (Oxford: Blackwell, 1996).

Aupers offers the popularity of role-playing computer games as proof of the importance of contemporary spirituality.[27]

It is, of course, important to explore the way new circumstances allow novel forms of expression of enduring sentiments, but such novelty confirms rather than refutes the secularization thesis. That people once found relief from their mundane lives through prayer, worship, and meditation and now find it through rave music and pretending to be someone else on the Internet seems like secularization.

## The Structural Weakness of Alternative Spirituality

There are many interesting things that can be said about alternative spirituality but I am concerned here only with what it tells us about secularization. The above is enough to answer those who want to use it as evidence of enduring religiosity and hence as support for the view that secularization is a change in the nature of religion rather than its decline. To put it starkly, the scale is wrong. Over the twentieth century the Christian churches in Britain lost the allegiance of at least 40 per cent of the population; at best the New Age might give us 2 per cent to balance that loss.

But there is a second reason for rejecting the 'change-not-decline' view of what has happened over the last 200 years: this new form of religion is itself a secularizing force. It is not an alternative to the secularization paradigm: it is a major component of secularization because it contains the seeds of its own destruction.

My previous observations on the New Age have sometimes been misunderstood as arguing either that the sort of individualistic this-worldly religion exemplified by the New Age is not 'really' religion or that it is superficial. The first claim is way off the mark. Durkheim and others of his generation regarded Christianity as the true religion, but modern sociologists practise 'methodological agnosticism'.[28]

[27] S. Aupers, *In de ban van moderniteit: De sacralisering van het zelf en computertechnologie* (Amsterdam: Aksant, 2004).

[28] E. Durkheim, 'Concerning the Definition of Religious Phenomena', in W. S. F. Pickering (ed.), *Durkheim on Religion* (London: Routledge and Kegan

We do not take sides, and I have no difficulty believing that people can take very seriously their interest in Rajneesh dynamic meditation, ley lines, and chakra points. My argument does not concern either the truth of, or the potential for serious engagement with, the ideas of the holistic spiritual milieu. It is an empirical argument about the consequences of 'epistemological individualism': the claim that every individual decides what is true for him or her. I will argue that, for structural reasons, individuated religion (and this applies as much to ultra-liberal Christianity as to holistic spirituality) is unlikely to engender the same levels of commitment as traditional religion.

The problem lies in the structural consequences of key ideas. Let us begin with the cardinal notion that the self is, or can become, divine. Traditionally, religions have generally assumed a division between God the Creator and the people he created. God was good, people were bad, and people became good by subjecting themselves to God's will and God's commandments. The New Age rejects that division. It supposes that we have within us the essence of holiness: the self is basically good. If we are bad, it is a result of our environment and circumstances. The aim of many New Age beliefs and therapies is to strip away the accumulated residues of our bad experiences and free the god or goddess within.

If the self is divine, there is no authority higher than the self. The final arbiter of truth is the enlightened self. Whether we should accept some revelation or therapy is framed in terms of whether it 'works for us'. One consequence of this is that New Agers generally do not argue. They synthesize apparently competing views at a more abstract level or they ignore disagreements. Findhorn, one of Europe's oldest New Age centres, requires that those who take part in its various forms of group work confine their talk to 'I statements'. Each participant has a right to say how he or she feels or thinks, but no one has a right to claim some extra-personal authority for his or her views.

Four things follow. There is no driver to coerce from an individual any more commitment than he or she initially wishes to make. There

Paul, 1975), 76. Far from arguing that alternative spirituality is not properly religious, I have suggested that it is a type of religion very well suited to modernity (S. Bruce, *Religion in the Modern World: From Cathedrals to Cults* (Oxford: Oxford University Press, 1966), ch. 8.

is no mechanism to produce consensus and sustain a shared life against the fissile tendencies of personal preference. There is no mechanism for maintaining cohesion and preventing ideas mutating. And there is little impetus to evangelize. Each of these will be addressed in turn.

## Commitment

Any ideological movement has to struggle to extract commitment from its adherents. The communist who should be selling the *Morning Star* outside the factory gates wants to stay in bed this wet Monday. The Pentecostalist would rather watch TV than attend another prayer meeting. The Catholic wants to use oral contraception. Within these ideologies there is an external power that the group can mobilize to press the weaker members to do what is right. Holistic spirituality lacks any levers to extract more commitment than the participant wants to give at any time. For example, a young woman who joined an informal meditation group after several years in Krishna Consciousness explained that she left it because the Krishna Consciousness leaders made her feel guilty about not being more committed.[29]

## Consensus

Getting people to agree is always difficult. Consensus is not the default position, even for people who inhabit similar social circumstances. It must be engineered. For any belief system to survive intact, there must be control mechanisms. These may be formal and bureaucratic, as they are in the Catholic Church, where officials deliberate slowly before announcing the Church's position. They may be informal and 'charismatic', as they are in many branches of Protestantism: the minister who preaches a gospel unacceptable to the audience finds himself without an audience. But in both cases there are controls. Institutional religion has the possibility of coercion. It is legitimated by the claim to have unique access to the will of God. As the elements of the cultic milieu do not claim a monopoly of salvational knowledge, they are severely constrained in what they can do to maintain discipline. Indeed, they often relish their freedom from such oppressive notions.

---

[29] Quoted in M. Wood, *Power, Possession and the New Age* (Aldershot: Ashgate, 2007), 133.

Of course New Agers share much in common. However, the consensus is greater the more abstract or procedural the proposition. Thus there is near unanimity on the principle of individual autonomy. There is considerable agreement on a variety of inclusive social principles: racism and sexism are bad, egalitarianism is good, everyone should be treated with dignity, and those principles should be extended to non-humans. However, when we get to specifics, we find little agreement, precisely because the things on which they agree encourage autonomy and diversity. The individual's freedom to choose competes with the power of the community. Stress the former and the latter is necessarily weakened. Insofar as New Agers are bound to each other at all (and many associate only in the sense of coincidentally consuming the same product), those bonds are weak because they are entirely voluntary and their voluntary nature is repeatedly asserted. The residents of the community at Findhorn can leave any time they find the company of their fellows uncongenial and their wills thwarted.[30] Indeed, New Agers pride themselves on constantly growing out of whatever 'school' or therapy they are presently exploring.

Without coerced consensus, a movement will always be less, not more, than the sum of its parts. A detailed ethnographic study of Glastonbury New Agers claimed that they 'sustain a mode of social organisation and a body of beliefs and ideas whose features in many crucial respects display striking similarities with the social and cultural forms of "original human society"—that is to say, human society in its evolutionary basic form'.[31] Hardly. New Agers may see themselves as having much in common with a romanticized vision of the primitive tribe, but it is not obvious why we should accept their self-understanding for our analytical purposes. The Glastonbury New Agers talked a good critique of the dehumanizing nature of modern work, the unsustainability of Western high maintenance lifestyles, and the virtues of self-sufficiency in a subsistence economy, but many were parasitic on the capitalist economy they effected to

---

[30] For an insider's account of New Age communities that provides many examples of limited commitment, see J. L. Boice, *At One with All Life: A Personal Journey in Gaian Communities* (Findhorn: Findhorn Foundation Press, 1989).

[31] R. Prince and D. Daiches, *The New Age in Glastonbury* (Oxford: Berghahn Books, 2000), p. xiii.

despise. Far from being the peasants *de nos jours*, they were recipients either of inherited wealth or of state welfare payments, or they lived by providing luxurious fripperies: candles, incense, soaps, magazines, and massages. Hardly an alternative to capitalism.

Despite the communitarian rhetoric, the Glastonbury New Agers found communal activity unusually difficult. A group of friends talked of forming a spiritual community 'that would meet on a regular basis, so that, in a stable environment, they might share their spiritual experiences'. The idea was discussed for several months before the first meeting, when 'it quickly became clear that those involved had very different expectations'. They disagreed over whether the group should be open or closed and whether it should involve children. The following week the group was smaller: the two couples with children had dropped out. The third week the conversation turned to the fact that 'nearly all the people there had been involved either in a new religious movement, or a more traditional one, or had closely followed the teachings of one particular teacher'. What they had in common was the experience of feeling 'too confined...their individuality had been threatened'. The group continued to meet for several weeks, getting smaller all the time, until it petered out.[32] The one attempt to create an alternative school was hardly more successful. The parents fell out with the original trustees and with each other and the school closed after a year.[33]

## Cohesion

The absence of any consensually accepted external authority means that the world of holistic spirituality is almost infinitely eclectic. Fragments of other cultures can readily be brought into the milieu. There is a general preference for the 'ancient' and the 'traditional', though, as in the case of Wicca and Druidism, the supposed ancient is often a modern invention.[34] But beyond that there are few limits to inventiveness. Like low levels of commitment, the lack of cohesion has the benefit of permitting elements of the movement to spread

---

[32] Prince and Daiches, *The New Age*, 176–7.
[33] Prince and Daiches, *The New Age*, 166–8.
[34] R. Hutton, *The Triumph of the Moon: A History of Modern Pagan Witchcraft* (Oxford: Oxford University Press, 1999).

rapidly. There can be real spread, as in the case of the Body Shop chain promoting a line of Ayur Vedic products. There can also be rapid spread by definitional incorporation when already popular activities and ideas, such as osteopathy, chiropractic, and Alexander technique, are claimed for the milieu (either by New Agers themselves or by commentators keen to inflate the phenomenon).

However, the lack of cohesion has the disadvantage that elements can readily be sampled, trivialized, and co-opted by people whose interest in the spiritual hinterland of some practice is slight. In China, Feng Sui is a form of geomancy: a serious matter of relating to the souls of the dead, especially one's ancestors. In the West it has been stripped of its spiritual content and, like the resolutely plain Shaker furniture, reduced to just another interior decorating style. In its original home in Hinduism and Buddhism, meditation is a physical and psychological discipline intended to have spiritual consequences, but, once it was no longer embedded in its original religious traditions, it quickly changed. Some practitioners use it as a spiritual exercise; many more use it simply as a form of relaxation. Yoga has become so thoroughly removed from its roots that my farming neighbour could attend a course of classes and have no idea that it had anything to do with Hinduism. To her it was just an alternative to the Jane Fonda workout video and the Pilates course.

## Evangelism

Coherent ideologies can be transmitted intact, but the diffuse ideology of a milieu must always be reinvented. Evangelism is inappropriate, which is fortunate, because it is also impossible. Evangelism is inappropriate because enlightenment comes from within, and each of us is the best judge of what is true for us. Like the friend who tells you about a great new restaurant, the beneficiary of a course in Rajneesh's dynamic meditation may want to share that information with others but there is nothing like the impetus to spread the word one finds in conversionist sects such as the Mormons and the Witnesses. In particular, there is little concerted effort to socialize children into the basic principles. A conservative Protestant will work hard to convert his children because he believes that, unless they have the true faith, he will not see them in heaven. Even the most committed habitué of the holistic spirituality milieu will share the liberal Christian's view that the best thing you can do for your children is to teach them to think for themselves, even if the predictable consequence is that some of them will think differently.

But, even if the psychological dynamic to evangelize were not missing, the structural prerequisite is. As with liberal Christianity, holistic spirituality lacks agreement except on principles so general that no firm rules can be derived from them. A conservative Catholic can tell you the ten things you must believe to be saved. No ten members of the Findhorn Foundation could agree on a list of essential teachings.

The model of agreeing about big principles and agreeing to differ about details has some advantages. New Agers can cooperate in joint marketing, as in London's long-running festival of Mind–Body–Spirit, where hundreds of purveyors of various forms of cultic religion rent stalls in a large hall and mount a week-long programme of New Age events. They can provide a general location for the promotion of New Age ideas. These may range from the large and internationally known (for example, the Osho Multiversity in Holland and the Findhorn Foundation) to the very small (for example, the Beacon Centre at Cutteridge Farm, where Wendy and Basil Webber run a 'transformational centre for personal, inter-personal and planetary healing'). They can organize regular presentations on the model of adult education evening classes. But, in each of these sites for reproduction, a wide variety of revelations and therapies, which can be reconciled only at a high level of abstraction, is presented. The appeal or persuasive force of any one approach is not reinforced by its coincidence with another. Cultists cannot add momentum to their persuasive efforts, because their diffuse beliefs prevent them from agreeing in sufficient detail on what is to be promoted.

Those who know the holistic spirituality milieu well may find the above argument pointless: of course the world of alternative spirituality is utterly unlike that of a conversionist sect such as the Mormons. I have laboured the differences only because they are relevant to the projections that Heelas and Woodhead and others make for the future of the phenomenon. The presently available evidence suggests that serious interest in alternative spirituality is largely confined to a narrow social group, limited by race, age, class, and cultural background. We should not dismiss growth projections out of hand, but we can evaluate them in the light of what we know about current adherents. The point of the above is that the same structural features that have allowed a shallow form of the movement to spread far and wide deny it the advantages that explain the success of conversionist new religions such as the Mormons and the Witnesses.

## Conclusion

This chapter is neither a comprehensive description of the world of alternative spirituality nor a judgement of its intrinsic merits. It is concerned only with the implications of the holistic spirituality milieu for the secularization paradigm. The issue is simple. Some critics of the secularization approach to religious change argue that what we have seen in the West is not the decline of religion as such but only the decline of the institutional form of religion. Inspired by Thomas Luckmann's *The Invisible Religion*,[35] they accept entirely the argument that various features of modernization undermine the plausibility of authoritarian dogmatic religion but insist that people's enduring need for religion will find new individualized forms of expression. Hence, secularization should be seen not as decline but as change. Alternative, contemporary, or holistic spirituality is presented as proof of our enduring religiosity. Those who wish to make that case have to demonstrate that there is a lot of it about. The evidence reviewed in this chapter suggests otherwise.[36]

Far from refuting the secularization paradigm, both the nature and the extent of alternative spirituality offer strong support for a key element of the paradigm: individualism undermines religion.

[35] T. Luckmann, *The Invisible Religion: The Problem of Religion in Modern Society* (New York: Macmillan, 1967).

[36] For a test of Luckmann's approach that uses large-scale survey data from Germany and concludes that he is mistaken, see D. Pollack and G. Pickel, 'Religious Individualization or Secularization', in D. Pollack and D. V. A. Olson (eds), *The Role of Religion in Modern Societies* (New York: Routledge, 2007), 191–200.

# 6

# Superstition

## Introduction

The Grill at London's Savoy Hotel avoids seating a table of thirteen for dinner by setting an extra place for a wooden effigy of a cat. District nurses in the mining areas of County Durham are instructed not to set out on their rounds until the shift is underground, because any miner who sees a nurse on his way to work will go home and skip his shift. A hospital avoids having an operating theatre 13 by numbering it 12a.

Superstition is important to the secularization paradigm because it helps clarify just what change is being explained. To recap the discussion so far, we know that the power, popularity, and prestige of institutional religion has declined across Western Europe. The secularization paradigm assumes that this is a symptom of a deeper loss of interest in religion. Critics argue that religious sentiments remain popular and that the collapse of the churches is better explained by two analytically separate phenomena: we no longer like collective activity and we are disinclined to do what we are told. Hence, institutional religion is unpopular, but there is still vicarious religion, folk religion, and alternative spirituality. The previous chapters have, I believe, answered those challenges to the secularization paradigm and restored the plausibility of the original assumption: that the decline of the churches is a symptom of a wider loss of interest in the supernatural.

We can now return to the element of folk religion that I passed over in Chapter 4. This chapter offers a preliminary sketch of a secularization treatment of superstition. As the subject has rarely been treated in this way, this essay is more a statement of what needs to be researched than a summary of reliable research findings. Nonetheless, this seems a useful task. I will identify the key characteristics of superstition and assess its popularity and importance. Having given some good reasons for thinking superstition is now less popular than it was in the pre-modern world, I will explain its decline by showing how the causes of secularization identified in Chapter 2 have impacted on the world of folk cures, omens, lucky charms, and divination. Finally I will consider what conclusions we should draw from the evidence of residual supernaturalism for the overall plausibility of the secularization paradigm.

## What is Superstition?

The category of 'superstition' is broad. Generally it refers to supernatural influences on our fortunes and the rituals adopted either to harness or to deflect such influences. The supernatural forces imagined in superstition differ from those of religions in lacking a consistent ethical thrust. The fates periodically intervene in our lives in ways for which the wise would do well to prepare. For example, presumptuously counting your chickens before they hatch invites disappointment, but the unfortunate who spills salt deserves to be punished only in the sense that he failed to perform the appropriate preventative act of throwing salt over his shoulder. Superstition also differs from religion in being chaotic and inconsistent. It is an accumulation of diverse elements rather than the product of ideological work by religious leaders and organizations. Superstition sometimes comes close to magic in the sense that one can engineer good fortune by performing certain ritual acts, but it is rarely as directed and specific as, for example, the inflicting of injury on an enemy by sticking pins in a wax effigy. Much superstition is concerned with divination or foresight. It may be knowledge of a fate that we cannot avoid, as in the belief that a rich crop of berries on certain trees and bushes is a sign that the coming winter will be unusually hard. It may be knowledge that should spur us to act, as in the case of an astrologer telling us which days are 'well starred' for certain acts.

Superstition is often dismissed as the cosmology of those who know no better, but a more sympathetic explanation was presented in Bronislaw Malinowski's anthropological classic *Argonauts of the Western Pacific*.[1] The Trobriand Islanders he studied fished in two very different contexts. When they fished in the lagoon, the men never resorted to fishing magic because the waters were relatively calm and safe. But, before fishing in the potentially treacherous open seas, they performed various rituals as protection against hazards over which they have no more practical control.

Typically superstitions are associated with activities or areas of life that are hazardous in unpredictable and unmanageable ways—hence the deserved reputation of coal miners and deep-sea fishermen for superstition and the vast lore that surrounded pregnancy and child-birth. It is also strongly associated with activities that involve chance: gambling, playing the lottery, playing bingo, and the like.

## Measuring Superstition

It is expensive and time-consuming to do it well, but in principle it is not difficult to measure the popularity, power, and prestige of religion. All religions have specific ritual or worship requirements, and involve-ment in these can be measured. We can compare how many people attended Christian churches in 1851 and 2008. We can estimate quite accurately the financial support for religious activities. We can ask people what they believe and compare responses over time and place.

Superstition is considerably more difficult to assess. There is no doubt that the people of the Middle Ages were superstitious. Although the basic elements of a Christian world view pervaded all areas of life, there was also a strong belief in witchcraft and beyond that a vast repertoire of superstitious beliefs and practices.[2] By the nineteenth

---

[1] B. Malinowski, *The Argonauts of the Western Pacific* (New York: E. P. Dutton, 1961).

[2] K. Thomas, *Religion and the Decline of Magic* (Harmondsworth: Penguin, 1978).

century, blaming misfortune on witches had mostly died out, but a general notion that there was good and bad fortune that could be attracted and avoided, respectively, by the possession of charms and the performance of small ritual acts was still widespread, as was the notion that the future was knowable by supernatural means. Nineteenth-century commentators of an antiquarian bent often regretted the loss of 'the old saws...which once formed a sort of supplement to the national faith',[3] and there is no reason to doubt their judgement, but it is unfortunate that we cannot create measures that would allow us to trace a trajectory of decline before the post-war era.

## Surveys

From the middle of the twentieth century we have a great deal of survey data, but much of it is dubious quality. The diffuse and ambiguous nature of superstitious belief means that the usual survey trade-off—you can have good questions or a large and representative sample but not both—is particularly crippling.[4] A second problem is the lack of any obvious ordering to superstitious beliefs. Because they are relatively well organized and maintained by organizations, religious beliefs tend to cohere in packages and have a degree of stability, so that evidence about one part of the package—church attendance, for example—can often be taken to stand for much of the rest. The wide range of beliefs and attitudes that find expression in superstitions hinder us from making reliable inferences from apparent changes in the popularity of this or that superstition. Apparent stability is as difficult to interpret. When believing in lucky numbers could mean using such numbers to choose a spouse or using them only to make choices that are necessarily arbitrary (in doing the lottery, for example), it is difficult to know what we should make of the fact that surveys in 1950 and 1968 show very similar figures (24 and 22 per cent) in response to a lucky-number question.[5] A further limitation is

---

[3] Mary Russell Mitford, writing in 1830; quoted in I. Opie and M. Tatem, *A Dictionary of Superstition* (Oxford: Oxford University Press, 1989).

[4] Web-based surveys are popular and attract large numbers of respondents, but are representative only of Web-surfers interested in the topic.

[5] G. Gorer, *Exploring English Character: A Study of the Morals and Behavior of the English People* (New York: Criterion Books, 1955), 267, and N. Abercrombie, J. Baker, S. Brett, and J. Foster, 'Superstition and Religion: The God of the Gaps',

that questionnaires are not good at picking up innovations. Repeatedly asking about the same thing may allow us to track changes in that particular field, but, unless the survey has opened-ended questions of the type 'Name your three main superstitions', it will not pick up new superstitions. And open-ended questions have their own problems: quickly given answers may reflect the general popularity or cultural presence of some practice rather than its particular importance to the respondent. Finally we can note compliance effects. Geoffrey Gorer's 1950 survey asked the same questions in an anonymous postal questionnaire and in face-to-face interviews and found that those interviewed in person seemed markedly less superstitious than those who responded by post. This he explains as a result of respondents not wishing to appear foolish in the eyes of the interviewer.[6]

With all those reservations in mind, we can look at some data from the better surveys on divination: a strand of superstition that is still sufficiently widespread for us to be confident that responses are at least vaguely concerned with the same thing. In 1950, 42 per cent of respondents in an interview survey said they read their horoscopes in newspapers regularly, but only 16 per cent thought there was 'something in it' and only 4 per cent took the advice given.[7] In 1968, a third of respondents read their horoscopes regularly and 9 per cent said 'they took account of what the stars said in their everyday life'.[8] In 2007, the 'reading-regularly' figure was 23 per cent, and 6 per cent said that horoscopes 'accurately predict events' in their lives.[9] As it involves more action and expense, visiting a fortune-teller might be a more rigorous test of interest in divination. In 1950, 44 per cent of the population had consulted a fortune-teller, but only 7 per cent had had more than two consultations.[10] In 1968, only 18 per cent had 'visited a palmist, fortune-teller or astrologer'.[11] In 2007, the comparable figure

*A Sociological Yearbook of Religion*, 3 (1970), 93–129. This survey has only 238 respondents, but the thoroughness of the execution and the detail of the material make it better than most.

   [6] Gorer, *Exploring English Character*, 317.
   [7] Gorer, *Exploring English Character*, 277.
   [8] Abercrombie et al., 'Superstition', 101.
   [9] Ipsos MORI, 'Survey on Beliefs', 31 Oct.2007, www.ipsos-mori.com/research publications/researcharchive (accessed 4 Oct. 2009).
   [10] Gorer, *Exploring English Character*, 266.
   [11] Abercrombie et al., 'Superstition', 102.

was 24 per cent. In Scotland in 2001, 30 per cent had, 'aside from horoscopes', tried 'fortune-telling, tarot or astrology', but only 8 per cent had tried forms of divination 'more than once'.[12]

These and comparable data could be read as showing a decline in the popularity of divination, but it is probably safer to conclude first that surveys are not very helpful for this kind of belief and, secondly, that the major change that interests the secularization paradigm had occurred before the advent of modern surveys. We know that the Greeks and Romans consulted oracles frequently and took omens and portents very seriously. We know that Britons of the Middle Ages took divination extremely seriously. Gorer is almost certainly right to note that many of his respondents saw a visit to the palmist or the crystal-ball gazer (especially at the seaside) as an entertainment, a bit of a laugh.[13]

## Content Analysis

Opie and Tatem's *A Dictionary of Superstitions* contains almost two thousand entries, most illustrated with more than one example of use. The illustrations are dated, so we can gauge some idea of when the superstition was current. In many cases the date of the illustration is that at which a collection of folklore was published, and many entries hint at the near-extinction of the custom. For example, a Manx source adds 'it is still occasionally done even in Peel or Douglas', which implies both that the superstition is dying out and that superstition is generally confined to rural areas outside the Isle of Man's two metropoles.[14] Other illustrations show the personal source dismissing the superstition as outdated. For example, a 60-year-old woman is recorded as saying in 1988: 'In County Durham we used to say if you dreamed of a baby you would hear of a death.'[15] Because the speakers in the illustrations may be referring to their childhood or the views of their parents or even grandparents, my method of counting may disguise a degree of obsolescence, but that

[12] T. Glendinning and S. Bruce, 'New Ways of Believing or Belonging: Is Religion Giving Way to Spirituality?', *British Journal of Sociology*, 57 (2006), 399–413.

[13] Gorer, *Exploring English Character*, 266.

[14] Opie and Tatem, *Dictionary*, 76.     [15] Opie and Tatem, *Dictionary*, 71.

is fine, because it means I am slanting the evidence against, rather than in favour of, my case.

To illustrate the age of various superstitions, I created four time periods: pre-1800, the nineteenth century, 1901–50, and post-1950. Sampling the 400 or so entries under the initial letters S and C shows that 3 per cent are pre-1800, 30 per cent are nineteenth century, 37 per cent are from 1901–50, and 28 per cent date from 1950 onwards.

The impression created by my first count is misleading for two reasons. That so few illustrations date pre-1800 does not tell us about usage; it tells us only that folklorists rely on published sources, and most of what we know about ancient folklore comes from works published more recently. It is also misleading, in that many superstitions with a relatively modern example also had examples of much older usage. If we count only those for which the *first* illustration comes from after 1900, we find only 14 per cent, and if we narrow it further to just those post-1950, we find only 5 per cent.

The antiquity of most superstitions is clear from their content. Very few concern a modern object or activity. This is a list of the topics under C with the number of entries for each if it is more than one: cabbage stalk; calendar; candle (13); cards (2); cats (24); cat or dog (2); caterpillar (2); cattle (4); caul (2); cave; chain-letter; chair (7); chamber pot; champagne cork; charms in food; Childermas Day; children (2); chime child; chimney; chimney sweep (2); christening (9); Christmas (14); church (13); churching (4); cigarette (2); cinders; clergy (4); clock (11); clothes (6); clover (4); coal (6); cock/hen (4); coffins (4); coin (4); comet; communion (3); confirmation; conversation; cooking; coral; cork; corn dollies; corner house; corpse (19); counting (3); cows (3); cradle (2); cramp (2); cricket (2); cripple; crockery; crooked things (4); cross (5); crossed fingers or legs (3); crown; crows/ravens (2); cuckoo (10); cutlery (2). Only two of these involve objects or actions extant only after 1900: cigarettes and chain-letters. We can raise that count to three by adding that one of the chimney entries refers to a man who held his football coupon up to the chimney for good luck.

The same point can be made by listing those topics that have generated the largest number of entries. Those with five or more entries are candles, chairs, Christenings, Christmas, church, clocks, clothes, coal, corpses, crosses, and cuckoos—all common or important objects in pre-industrial societies. We can also clearly see a strong link between superstition and institutional religion. Of the eleven topics with five or more entries, four directly concern Christian rituals or the church.

Beyond counting, we can see clear evidence of the decline of superstition in the difference in tone between nineteenth- and twentieth-century illustrations. The former tend to be confident statements of fact and practice. The latter tend to be hesitant and to distance the speaker from the superstition being noted. For example, a 1950s entry had a middle-aged London woman saying: 'It's superstition really. It's supposed to be unlucky if you go out before you're churched.'[16] A 1950 illustration of the use of 'clergy' in divination has a Forfar women saying: 'If you counted all the ministers you saw up to 100, the next man you spoke to would be your future husband. We used to haunt the Lour Road, where most ministers lived.'[17] The use of the word 'haunt' in the second sentence's confession of cheating the outcome suggests a lack of faith in that particular oracle. Another speaker cited a superstition but denied it: 'I know corner houses are supposed to be unlucky but we haven't done too badly in this one.'[18]

## Expert Judgement

Writers on folklore can be divided roughly into two camps. The casual writers of popular books tend to go to one extreme or the other: either modern people are quite unlike their foolish and ill-informed ancestors or people are every bit as anxious and as susceptible to irrational belief and actions as ever they were.[19] The serious folklorists seem agreed that 'we, as a society, are much less superstitious than we were a hundred, or even fifty years ago'.[20] Their grounds are twofold. First, there is a clear loss of knowledge: 'in the present day the real significance of many of the superstitions has been forgotten.... the serious ritual of throwing wheat over a bride "in tokenyng of plentie and fruitfulnesse" has degenerated into a frolicsome

---

[16] Opie and Tatem, *Dictionary*, 81.    [17] Opie and Tatem, *Dictionary*, 84.

[18] Opie and Tatem, *Dictionary*, 97.

[19] As an example of the former, see C. Chaundler, *Everyman's Book of Superstitions* (London: A. R. Mowbray, 1970); for an example of the latter, see E. Maple, *Superstition and the Superstitious* (London: W. H. Allen, 1971).

[20] S. Roud, *A Pocket Guide to the Superstitions of the British Isles* (London: Penguin Books, 2004), p. ix.

throwing of paper rose petals.'[21] Secondly, there is a loss of serious-ness: however superstitious people may think themselves, 'few act on them in the way that previous generations did'.[22]

## Opportunity or Motive?

We cannot immediately take the disappearance of particular super-stitions as evidence of a change in attitude, because it may reflect only a loss of opportunity. The vast body of lore about fires and hearths could not have survived the disappearance of open fires from most homes. The Opie and Tatem collection contains hundreds of super-stitions connected with clothing. Maple cites the following 1960s example: 'If the first time you wear a dress you win a new boyfriend the dress is a lucky one and you always wear it again when you want to win another boy.'[23] Clothing is now so cheap and so subject to fashion that few clothes are kept long enough to become the object of superstitious beliefs and rituals: my daughters are more likely to think that anyone who wears the same dress twice does not deserve a boyfriend. However, the disappearance of a particular body of lore is significant if there is not corresponding innovation elsewhere. Previ-ous chapters have repeatedly made the point that, if we want to assert that people are enduringly religious, we need evidence that some new expression is popular enough to fill the gap left by the decline of church involvement. So too with superstition. Maple, for example, supposes that the total amount of superstition will be stable: 'there is no reason to suppose that the mind of man has changed at all within measurable time and that, therefore, our behaviour in crisis can be regarded as an unvarying expression of a common inheritance, an implanted pattern.'[24] Unfortunately he provides only one example of a modern superstition: telephone-related lore. If Maple is right, we should be generating new superstitions that relate to iPods, IVF treatment, computers, Facebook pages, Scandinavian stoves, cars, occupational pension schemes, and cappuccino-makers. And new high-risk occupations such as investment portfolio manager, oil-rig worker, and deep-sea diver should be generating new bodies of folklore into which novices are initiated as they learn the technical

---

[21] Opie and Tatem, *Dictionary*, p. xiii.   [22] Roud, *Pocket Guide*, p. ix.
[23] Maple, *Superstition*, 17.   [24] Maple, *Superstition* 8.

components of their trade. To date this possibility has not been seriously researched (which itself is probably a partial answer to the question), but the indications mentioned below are largely negative.

For analytical completeness, I should also add that, while the loss of a large body of superstitious lore may initially reflect a loss of opportunity rather than a change in attitude, the first often causes the second. When people stopped walking long distances because cheap motor transport offered a faster alternative, the change initially told us nothing about attitudes to walking. But people got out of the habit. It is reasonable to suppose that, if a sufficiently large body of folklore is lost, the whole style of thinking and acting is endangered.

## Applying the Secularization Paradigm

Rather than work through every element of the model outlined in Chapter 2, I will describe and explain the secularization of superstition under three general themes: use value, plausibility structure, and privatization. As we will see, these divisions are something of a writer's convenience: whether people find something useful is partly a matter of learning and social persuasion.

### Use Value

In Chapter 2, I argued against giving too great a role in the decline of religion to the discoveries of natural science. Particular bits of new knowledge periodically cause problems for some groups of believers (for example, US fundamentalists still denounce Darwin), but the major world religions have generally proved adept at reconciling their teachings with new knowledge. After all, God created science too. And the ethical and salvational aspects of Christianity or Islam are relatively untouched. New opportunities create new issues to debate. (should Christians accept blood transfusions, for example), and changes in cosmology force some of the details of salvation to be adjusted (few now think heaven is above us), but the key idea of a creator God with powers of moral judgement can remain relatively intact. Science poses a greater threat to superstition, because it makes very obviously redundant those elements of folklore that are concerned with practical matters. As it is easier to have warts frozen by the nurse at the local health centre than it is to identify an adulterous male and surreptitiously to rub your hand against his leg, it is easy to see why the citizens of Banff now prefer the former to the latter remedy.

Until the twentieth century, the death of infants in Britain was common. In 1921 there were thirty-five deaths of children in the first four weeks per thousand live births. By 1999 the figure had fallen to only four.[25] The prospects for the mother are also much improved. Giving birth is no longer risky. Hence there is no surprise that most of the folklore associated with pregnancy and birth has disappeared.[26] The point can be extended to health generally. Until the twentieth century there was little effective medical science and health care, which explains why so many of the superstitions listed by Opie and Tatem are what would now be called complementary or alternative medicine. Except that in 1800 they were not alternative therapies: they were pretty much all the therapy there was. And they did not work very well.

As an aside, it is worth countering a common misunderstanding. There is an unfortunate imperialism in social science that takes a truth and turns it into a falsehood by exaggeration. Since Peter Berger and Thomas Luckmann's *The Social Construction of Reality* popularized the phrase, social construction has become the unruly ivy in the garden of modern thought.[27] It is true that, in understanding behaviour, what people make of the world is often more important than some underlying objective reality. It is also true that in trying to comprehend the world we impose upon it shared meanings. However, it does not follow either that there is no objective reality or that in every case our social constructions make much difference. It certainly helps to appreciate that the role requirements that are set for men and women differ enormously from culture to culture and thus

[25] Office of National Statistics, Childhood, Infant and Perinatal Mortality: Stillbirth and Infant Death Rates by Age at Death 1921–1999', www.statistics.gov.uk/StatBase/xsdataset.asp?More=Y&vlnk=3209&All=Y&B2.x=66&B2.y=6 (accessed 1 Oct. 2009).

[26] Maple, *Superstition*, 67.

[27] P. L. Berger and T. Luckmann, *The Social Construction of Reality* (Harmondsworth: Penguin, 1973).

cannot be explained entirely by the biological differences between men and women. However, biological differences are real enough and in some aspects and on some occasions they constrain what role expectations can be 'socially constructed'. The metric and imperial systems for measuring length are competing social constructions, but length is, for all practical purposes, an objective reality that is independent of which system we use to measure it. I raise the point because, especially under the influence of Michel Foucault's distinctive approach to the history of science and medicine, a concern with changes in social perceptions can often blind us to the simple point that there have been real advances in medical science and therapy that are not reducible to changes in the method of social control.[28] The historian of medicine may be interested in the role of various professional interests in the development of the category of 'infant mortality', but that is tangential to the substantial change in the real world. In 1921 there were eighty-three deaths under the age of 1 per thousand live births; by the end of the century it had fallen to just six.[29] The local 'wise woman' who provided folk remedies to the working class of Southwark may have been ushered off the stage by imperialist male medical professionals, but her fate was already determined by improvements in diet, in working and housing conditions, and in medical knowledge. The creation in 1948 of the National Health Service, with treatment free at the point of delivery, relegated folk remedies to the status of optional extras.

Science and technology also removed much of the risk-related superstition found in dangerous industries. Before they disappeared altogether, British deep-mine collieries saw their safety record vastly improve. Over the eighty years from 1873 to 1953, the number of people employed in mining rose from around 580,000 to just over 700,000, but the number of fatalities fell from 1,173 to 392—a drop of almost two-thirds.[30] Though it takes me to the second theme of

[28] M. Foucault, *The Birth of the Clinic* (London: Routledge, 1994).

[29] Office for National Statistics, 'Childhood, Infant and Perinatal Mortality: Stillbirth and Infant Death Rates by Age at Death 1921–1999', www.statistics.gov. uk/StatBase/xsdataset.asp?More=Y&vlnk=3209&All=Y&B2.x=66&B2.y=6 (accessed 9 Jan. 2009).

[30] According to data helpfully supplied by the Director of the National Coal Mining Museum, the annual fatalities rate fell from a peak in 1877 of 2.63 deaths per thousand people employed in the industry to 0.55 in 1953 and 0.1 in 1983.

plausibility structures, I should add that two important social changes also weakened the power of mining superstition. First, increasing affluence allowed workers greater choice in where they lived and thus weakened the communities in which shared folklore was reproduced. Secondly, as part of a general increase in social mobility, mining families broadened their occupational base and brought into the home, the street, and the pit village new ideas and perspectives.

The same point can be made about the impact of agricultural science and technology. Not only was much farming folklore made redundant by effective technologies, but the standing of custom and tradition was itself undermined by the success of the new knowledge. In the nineteenth century, Buchan farm servants on graduating from being an Orra Loon (general dogsbody) to Horseman were inducted into the Society of the Horseman's Word—that 'word' being a secret formula for pacifying and managing working horses. Farm workers are now trained in colleges, their status is marked by certificates and membership of the Young Farmers or the Transport and General Workers Union, and there are no longer any magical words.

At an even higher level of abstraction, we can see the impact of technology on the fundamental approach of superstition. Maple presents, as a now rare practice, the example of some 1960s Cornish housewives who believed that they should not try to clean fruit stains from a fabric until that fruit was in season. This, according to Maple, is a continuation of 'one of the most venerable precepts of magic, the doctrine that there is an interconnection between an object and its parts no matter how distantly separated they might be'.[31] That holistic principle is challenged by the whole ethos of modern technology, which supposes that, far from possessing an enduring unity, complex objects can be broken down into infinitely replaceable components.

Finally under this theme of decreasing usefulness, we can note the impact of what Martin called 'increased mastery over fate'.[32] Luck, good and bad, is what we have when we lack understanding and control. The importance of luck (and the rituals to change it) varies with the matter in hand, but it also varies with our general sense of empowerment and importance. The more we feel we understand the

---

[31] Maple, *Superstition*, 27.
[32] D. Martin, *The Religious and the Secular* (London: Routledge and Kegan Paul, 1969), 118.

forces that shape our lives and can manage them, the less likely we are to be superstitious. As noted in the previous chapter, of the relatively few people seriously interested in things New Age, middle-age university-educated professional women tended to be involved in activities that promote psychological and physical well-being (and that have some putatively rational connection to the desired end), while young working-class women favour astrology, horoscopes, palmistry, and the like. At the risk of labouring the point, we must stress that most people are not much interested in either New Age well-being therapies or attempts magically to predict the future, but, of those who are, the class pattern roughly fits what we would expect in terms of a general sense of empowerment and control over one's life.

As a final comment on use value, it is probable that superstition is much more vulnerable to secularization on this point than conventional religion because its lack of an overarching supernatural agent with the power of moral judgement (a God, if you like) means that, when material functions are replaced by secular alternatives, there is nothing left.

### Plausibility Structures

Belief is not just a response to the objective value of some activity. There is always an element of social construction, which is why large parts of Chapters 2 and 5 were concerned with those features of the social structure that make it easier or harder for particular kinds of belief system to be reproduced and maintained.

Consider what Bryan Wilson called 'societalization'. The process of rationalization often takes the form of local particularities being overridden by bodies that are informed by national and international considerations.[33] In his description of new variants on old superstitions, Maple mentions the reluctance of air crew and motorists to tempt fate by using words such as 'crash' and 'accident' or by talking about their lack of accidents to date: 'there is always a

---

[33] I am assuming that, the larger the number of people involved, and the more diverse the sources of knowledge, the more rational the thinking. The idiosyncratic gets lost in the mix, and what is likely to survive is the calculable and the well evidenced.

reluctance to boast of an accident-free record, for this represents an open invitation to the devils of disorder to strike the motorist down.'[34] That was perhaps true of the early 1960s, but insurance companies now require us to boast of our years of no claims if we want affordable insurance, car-hire companies require similar boasting, and the international mechanisms for reporting and recording air accidents and near-accidents ignore our supposed sensitivities. Far from being avoided, 'accident' now appears in the name of the British government body responsible for air safety: the Air Traffic Accident Investigation Board.

Fishing communities were rife with superstitions. The modern occupation closest to deep-sea fishing in terms of risk, environment, and working conditions is oil-rig worker, and it is relative free of superstition, for reasons that are hardly obscure. First, the workforce is drawn from a very wide variety of backgrounds, cultural and geographical, and, away from the rig itself, there is no tight residential community that can sustain a shared culture. Secondly, any cultural preference that threatens the productivity of rigs is overruled by the multinational companies that own and manage them. As well as seeking efficiency, those companies abide by the law. Although few women work offshore, this is a reflection of the general shortage of women in engineering and the difficulties of combining offshore work with child-rearing; it is not because rigs workers have taken on the old fishermen's view that women at sea were bad luck. My number of respondents is small ($n = 22$) and is a result of snowball-sampling (that is, I asked my friends), but none of the North Sea rig workers I asked could think of any rig-related superstitions.

It is instructive to consider the fate of domestic folklore. A very large number of the examples in the Opie and Tatem collection and in local area studies concern housework. Household objects such as furniture, food, cutlery, and clothing and activities such as cleaning and cooking were enmeshed in complex webs of folklore. And those beliefs were passed from mothers to daughters. Social change has reduced the importance of mothers in the domestic-science education of their daughters. Over the twentieth century, the proportion of women staying in full-time education increased, as did the proportion working outside the home and the immediate neighbourhood.

---

[34] Maple, *Superstition*, 33.

Of women aged 35 to 44 only 10 per cent were economically active in 1911; by 1991 the proportion had risen to almost three-quarters.[35] Families became smaller. People became more socially and geographical mobile. More and more household tasks were mechanized, outsourced, and brought under the control of large-scale commercial enterprise. The speed of innovation meant that generations no longer shared common needs or experiences. For centuries, the broom was a vital piece of domestic equipment, and it changed very little. Hence broom-related folklore (and there was a lot of it) could pass from generation to generation. Not only has it now been replaced by the vacuum cleaner, but types of powered cleaning device change so rapidly that there is not time for folklore to develop around them.

One way in which the local cultures that carry superstitions are overridden is through the increased commercialization of life. Much pre-industrial superstition was calendrical—agricultural seasons and the festivals of the Christian Church being accompanied by an array of timely superstitious rituals—and it was local. Holidays are now set by national governments, local authorities, and large-scale commercial enterprises. The end of the Christmas festivities is marked, not by Twelfth Night and its associated superstitions, but by whatever date the major agencies deem allows a suitable length of time off. How we spend our holidays is largely determined, not by local folklore, but by national mass media and multinational supermarket strategies. Residues of superstitions can survive, but they are stripped of distinctive content and meaning. So the four major British supermarket chains heavily promote Halloween but in its US form, with 'trick-or-treat' replacing 'guising' and imported pumpkins (much easier to carve into lanterns) taking the places of turnips.

Previous chapters have stressed the importance of the weight of opinion, felt through interaction, in the successful transmission of religious beliefs across generations. When everyone is socialized into the same culture, the beliefs acquired have the strength of taken-for-grantedness. When one is aware that decent people see and do things differently, it becomes difficult to remain as sure of one's own faith. Superstition is more vulnerable than conventional religion to the disconfirming effects of diversity because its contents are almost

---

[35] D. Gallie, 'The Labour Force', in A. H. Halsey and J. Webb (eds), *Twentieth-Century British Social Trends* (London: Macmillan, 2000), 292.

arbitrary and hence more variable. We can identify major themes or concerns of folklore—the start to the day or a major change of life, portents of death, not presuming on good fortune—but, as the following examples show, the details associated with such general themes are largely arbitrary.

It is common for certain playing cards to be unlucky, either for the card game or for life, but there is no consensus as to which ones, beyond them being black. Black cats may be lucky or unlucky. Cats are frequently claimed as forecasters of wet weather, but the activity that portends rain is variously lying with its forehead to the ground (cat on brain/it's going to rain), sitting with its back to the fire, 'going mad', and washing behind its ears, though this may also mean that there will soon be visitors.[36] Folklore about the buying of bees was commonplace and widespread, but in some areas it was held that bees could be exchanged only for other goods and never for money; in others, that bees should be bought only with a gold coin; and, in yet others, that bees could be bought only with silver. Unfortunately we have no direct evidence of this, but it seems highly likely that, by increasing mobility and improving communication, industrialization brought the conflicting superstitions into contact and thus conflict. With competing religions, the disconfirming effects of diversity can be resolved by claiming an underlying unity (hence the shift towards more liberal and ecumenical versions of the faith), but there is no equivalent with superstition and we have to suppose that, the more people become familiar with alternative versions of their superstitions, the less likely they are to remain sufficiently committed to their own to pass them on to their children.

The above can be briefly summarized. First, modernization has reduced the need and scope for folklore. Improvements in the treatment of illness and disease, the greater use of efficient technology in once-risky occupations such as mining and fishing, and the increased rationalization of areas of work such as the construction industry have either removed the problem that superstition addressed or provided a more effective solution. Secondly, social changes have weakened the frameworks that sustained shared superstitious beliefs. The replacement of the community, where work, family, and education are intertwined, by the dormitory from which people with widely

[36] Opie and Tatem, *Dictionary*, various cat entries.

differing standards of living, experiences, and life chances commute to very different occupations, undermines the social preconditions for the reproduction of distinctive local cultures. As an illustration, we can note that half of the Staithes villagers described in Chapter 4 commute more than 6 miles, in various directions, to their varied places of work.[37] These changes do not make superstition impossible, but they make it increasingly optional and increasingly a matter of personal preference. The author may not have given much thought to the term, but it is revealing that a 2007 survey used the word 'foibles' for a variety of superstitious beliefs that had in the Middle Ages been extremely important.[38]

## Privatization

Often prior to and then alongside the decline in commitment to religious belief systems, secularization shows itself in the increasing privatization of religion. People no longer expect the nation state to impose a single religion on all its citizens. Religion becomes less a matter of public performance of socially agreed rituals and roles and more a matter of private consolation or encouragement. The realm of superstition shows a similar change. There is certainly a clear difference between ancient and contemporary astrology. The Babylonians read the stars for information about the fate of peoples and kingdoms. Although some New Agers use star charts and readings as the basis for social commentary, the vast bulk of astrology is now concerned with the fate of the individual: charts are drawn to advise people on employment and marital prospects. In a 1968 survey, the most popular reasons respondents gave for their interest in horoscopes were to 'understand what kind of people they were' and to see if they were likely to form relationships with certain other people.[39]

---

[37] Calculated from the 2001 Census data available on the Office of National Statistics NOMIS website (www.nomisweb.co.uk).
[38] Ipsos MORI/Schott's Almanac, 'Survey on Beliefs', Oct. 2007, www.times online.co.uk/multimedia/archive/00227/Schott_beliefX_227035a.pdf (accessed 10 Mar. 2010).
[39] Abercrombie et al., 'Superstition', 101.

While shared communal superstitions have declined, what has remained common is the individual ritual of reassurance. Students take mascots and charms into examinations. Sportsmen often have elaborate rituals that help them prepare for matches. Paul Nicholls, a successful horse trainer, admitted:

I have a lucky shirt that I call my Kauto Star shirt because every time I wear it, he wins—except for the time Denman [another Nicholls-trained horse] beat him but that was still lucky.... I don't usually keep shirts very long but that shirt is five years old and its not allowed to be thrown out.[40]

Even people in dull and serious occupations may admit to using charms. In 2009, Harriet Harman, British deputy prime minister, told a newspaper: 'I wear my lucky jacket on overwhelming occasions, such as when I went to Manchester to get the result of the deputy leadership election or did prime minister's questions the first time.'[41]

It is unfortunately rare for people to be pressed on what they think is the causal mechanism behind some personal ritual or reassurance, but it seems likely that there has been a process of secularization that parallels the 'psychologization' of religious beliefs described in Chapter 2. If pressed to explain why she wears her lucky jacket for particularly stressful events, Harriet Harman is unlikely to assert that it offers her access to objectively extant supernatural power. Instead she will talk about it reminding her of past successes and thus building her confidence.

One way of describing change in mainstream religion since the late nineteenth century is to say that it has become more optimistic. It is noticeable that the bad bits disappeared first: belief in hell declined faster than belief in heaven. T. S. Eliot responded to the discovery that a Catholic friend did not believe in hell by asking 'is your God some kind of Santa Claus?'[42] This shift was partly due to the sense of 'increased mastery over fate' produced by technology, improved health, increased longevity, and increased prosperity. It is also partly driven by privatization. It seems plausible to suppose that, when people are free to select from a cultural repertoire, rather than

[40] Daily Telegraph Magazine, 17 Oct. 2009.    [41] Guardian, 24 Sept. 2008.
[42] Quoted in M. Wood, 'A Lot of Travail', London Review of Books, 3 Dec. 2009.

being socialized into a complete world view, they will pick the bits they like best and, though some depressives might concentrate on the dark side of life, in the realm of superstition this takes the form of continuing with the positive while dropping the negative. Much preindustrial folklore was concerned with protecting oneself against 'all perils and dangers of this night', to quote from the final part of the Church of England's evensong service. That which survives is much more likely to concentrate only on the upside of the possible outcomes. In the 1950s almost a quarter of Britons claimed they believed in lucky and unlucky numbers, but, while 18 per cent had a lucky number, only 3 per cent had an unlucky number, and a further 3 per cent had both. Similarly for lucky days: 9 per cent had a lucky day, but only 5 per cent had an unlucky day.[43] Pre-modern astrologers were often doom-sayers; modern horoscopes are resolutely positive.

A final element of the secularization of superstition is the disappearance of the originally supernatural basis. Consider wedding rituals. Guests scatter confetti. The bride throws her bouquet and whoever catches it will be the next married. The groom should not see the bride fully dressed for the ceremony until the ceremony itself. The bride wears something old, something new, something borrowed, something blue. It seems clear that such rituals are no longer treated as powerful devices for gaining knowledge about the future or ensuring a propitious one; they survive because they give some structure to the event. Like those maps of interesting walks provided for tourists, they offer a range of pleasant and amusing activities that pass the time. I recently watched my son construct some luck business for his first serious school examinations. After experimenting with a few, he settled on a particular kind of felt tip as his 'lucky exam' pen. When I suggested buying a box of ten, in a slightly teasing voice that showed he recognized that he was inventing a game, he replied: 'Oh, no. Your lucky exam pen has got to be unique!' The next day he declined to use that pen for homework, because 'Your lucky exam pen can't be used for ordinary stuff'. Pagan cultures had many instances—some very bloodthirsty—of burying objects in the floors and walls of new buildings to ensure the prosperity and good fortune of those who lived in them. Now we bury time capsules containing

---

[43] Gorer, *Exploring English Character*, 265.

local newspapers and objects emblematic of our times to entertain and inform future generations. The activity may seem similar; the meaning is very different.

## Conclusion

The theme of superstition is useful, because it allows me to clarify what the secularization paradigm requires to remain plausible. The unhelpful caricature is that secularizationists expected all or most modern people to be materialists and rationalists who reject all notions of the supernatural and confine their cast of causal agents to mundane this-worldly individuals and organizations. This is not what the secularization paradigm expects. It expects a decline in the prevalence of shared beliefs about the supernatural. It expects that, as such beliefs become more diffuse, any individual's particular collection will become more idiosyncratic and 'odd' in the statistical sense. Because they lack social confirmation and reinforcement, such beliefs will lose power and significance. In contrast to those of the Trobriand Islanders, who knew exactly what they were doing and why, modern superstitions are, according to Colin Campbell, 'barely articulated, have virtually no coherent structure and are only partially accepted by those who carry out the associated practices'.[44]

Effectively to rebut the secularization paradigm, modern superstition should minimally be as popular and as powerful as ever it was. This is not the case. An even more effective rebuttal would be to show that superstition has become more popular and powerful to take up the slack left by the decline of interest in the supernatural represented by the decline of institutional religion. That is so far from being the case that no serious scholar makes it.

[44] Quoted in D. Newnham, 'Hostages to Fortune', *Guardian*, 14 Dec. 2002.

# 7

# The Supply-Side Alternative

## Introduction

Thus far we have been considering a number of fairly limited criticisms of the secularization paradigm, most of them arguing that it exaggerates or misunderstands the apparent signs of decline because it fails to give sufficient weight to signs of religious or spiritual sentiment beyond the churches. This chapter considers an altogether more radical challenge. Since the early 1990s, a number of US scholars have tried to reshape the sociology of religion by applying the principles of economics.[1] Inspired by Nobel prize-winning economist Gary Becker's imperialist vision of an economics of everything, Rodney Stark, Roger Finke, and Laurence Iannaccone have produced a large body of work that seeks to explain both large-scale social patterns (such as why some societies are more religious than others) and micro-decision-making (such as shifting between denominations) by considerations of market structure and cost–benefit calculations.

---

[1] For good summaries, see T. Jelen (ed.), *Sacred Markets, Sacred Canopies: Essays on Religious Markets and Religious Pluralism* (Lanham, MD: Rowan and Littlefield, 2002) and L. A. Young (ed.), *Rational Choice Theory and Religion* (London: Routledge, 1997). For a general critique see J. M. Bryant, 'Cost-Benefit Accounting and the Piety Business: Is Homo Religiosus, at Bottom, a Homo Economicus?', *Method and Theory in the Study of Religion*, 12 (2001), 520–48.

As it is fundamental to understanding his supply-side model of religious change, it is worth noting that Stark, with William Bainbridge, had previously developed a theory of religion that pretty well ruled out secularization. That theory started from the proposition that people seek rewards.[2] When they cannot get the desired rewards, they accept compensators. Compensators, somewhat confusingly, can be either explanations of why the rewards are not forthcoming or promises of the rewards at some future date. Because religions can make promises about the afterlife, they can offer bigger compensators than secular alternatives. If only because our desires are fuelled rather than dimmed by being satisfied, people are perpetually short of rewards. So they are perpetually in need of compensators, and religion is better than anything else at providing them. So demand for religion will be stable and high.

If the demand for religion is relatively unchanging, we need a new explanation for the all-too-apparent fluctuations in the popularity of expressions of religious sentiment. Why are Lutherans of German background more religiously observant in the USA than they (or their ancestors) were in Germany? Why is church attendance so much higher in Ireland than in Britain? Stark finds the answer in features of religious markets that influence the supply of religious products.

This chapter will briefly consider the applications and success of the supply-side approach. It will then consider the basic elements of the economistic approach to human behaviour and argue that the foundational idea—that we can explain people's behaviour as attempts to maximize utility—does not work for religion because the conditions for rational choice are absent. Finally, I will argue that the economist's version of rational choice (which, we should remember, involves a very narrow notion of rationality) will work for religion only in largely secular societies. Far from refuting the secularization paradigm, the rational-choice approach is viable only in the circumstances that Stark and his colleagues are determined to persuade us cannot exist.

[2] R. Stark and W. S. Bainbridge, *A Theory of Religion* (New York: Peter Lang, 1987). This is considered at length in S. Bruce, *Choice and Religion: A Critique of Rational Choice* (Oxford: Oxford University Press, 1999).

## The Supply-Side Approach

Taking as his inspiration the supposed superiority of an unregulated free market over the regulated economy in meeting and stimulating needs for such consumer goods as cars, Stark argues that differences in religious vitality, usually measured by church membership or church attendance, can be explained by structural features of religious economies. A free and competitive market creates a vibrant religious culture. Religious monopolies or hegemonies, especially if they are supported by the state, suppress innate demand and depress the religious culture.[3]

At first reading, many detailed propositions apparently derived from the general approach seem plausible. There is something intuitively appealing about the idea that, the greater the variety of religion on offer, the more people will find something they like. You want hierarchy, incense, dressing up, and ritual? You can attend Catholic, Orthodox, or 'high' Anglican churches. You want spontaneous worship? You can join a Pentecostal church.

The claim that state church clergy, because they are paid from public taxes, work less hard to win and retain the support of a congregation than do entrepreneurial clerics in a free market also rings true. Any fan of Jane Austen or Anthony Trollope will be familiar with the upper-class Church of England cleric who takes the income from a number of 'livings', winters in Italy, and pays a fraction of his wealth to curates to do his work for him. And, where clergy careers depended on toadying to the wealthy landowners who controlled appointments rather than on serving well one's parishioners, it was always likely that the Church would periodically become remote from its people.

---

[3] R. Finke, 'An Unsecular America', in S. Bruce (ed.), *Religion and Modernization: Sociologists and Historians Debate the Secularization Thesis* (Oxford: Oxford University Press, 1992), 145–69; R. Finke and L. A. Iannaccone, 'Supply-Side Explanations for Religious Change', *Annals of the American Academy of Political and Social Science*, 527 (1993), 27–39; R. Finke and R. Stark, *The Churching of America, 1776–1990: Winners and Losers in Our Religious Economy* (New Brunswick, NJ: Rutgers University Press, 1992); L. A. Iannaccone, 'The Consequences of Religious Market Structure', *Rationality and Society*, 3 (1991), 156–77.

However, intuitive plausibility is not enough, because, without much effort, we can think of examples that run counter to the rational-choice expectations. For example, Stark says of German Lutheran clergy that, as their salaries are independent of the size of their congregations, they will prefer to be unpopular. However, we do not have to look hard for a counter-example. The salaries of most senior academics are very largely independent of the numbers of students who take their courses, and they could avoid work by teaching badly, but most of them (possibly even Stark) prefer to attract students, because they take a pride in their work and believe that what they teach is important.[4]

As illustrations can readily be found to support or challenge the supply-side approach, we need to move to systematic testing. Working in various combinations, Stark, Finke, and Iannaccone, not surprisingly, found much evidence to support their theory, mostly in contemporaneous correlations of religiosity in parts of the USA with differing degrees of religious diversity. The more diverse an area, the greater the level of religiosity. Attempts by others to replicate such research have usually failed.[5] The arguments are often technical. For example, Finke and Stark claim to find a strong link between church membership and religious diversity in the 150 largest towns and cities of the United States using the 1906 US Census of Religious Bodies.[6] However, Finke and Stark's own statistics show the link to be very strongly negative: the more diverse places had the lower rates of church membership. There was a very strong link between the proportion of Catholics and church membership (but that may well have been because all baptized Catholics were counted as 'members'). Finke and Stark managed to produce statistics that suit their case only by controlling for the percentage Catholic in their regression equations. The experts will understand the problem of multi-colinearity.[7] The rest of us can simply note that the procedures may come

[4] R. Stark, 'German and German–American Religiousness', *Journal for the Scientific Study of Religion*, 36 (1997), 182–93.

[5] Bruce, *Choice and Religion*.

[6] R. Finke and R. Stark, 'Religious Economies and Sacred Canopies', *American Sociological Review*, 53 (1988), 41–9.

[7] D. V. A. Olson, 'Religious Pluralism in Contemporary US Counties', *American Sociological Review*, 63 (1998), 757–61; 'Religious Pluralism and US Church Membership: A Reassessment', *Sociology of Religion*, 60/2 (1999), 149–73.

close to cooking the books. When others tried to replicate Finke and Stark's work, they failed. Land and colleagues analysed US county-level data for over 700 counties and for a subset of counties that contained the 150 cities studied by Finke and Stark.[8] In both cases they came to the opposite conclusion. For the large sample, diversity was associated with low rates of church adherence, even when the percentage Catholic was figured into the regression equation. On the smaller sample of just the counties containing the big cities, they found that the direct effect of diversity was negative, until they entered the percentage Catholic into the equation, when it became positive but only very weakly so. When they added data from the 1920s and 1930s so that they could see the effects of diversity on church membership over time, they found that the negative effect of diversity was even greater. Only for a small sample containing the big cities could anything like the relationship posited by Finke and Stark be found and that was so weak as to be statistically insignificant. As the team put it: 'Our conclusion is that religious monopoly—not diversity—fuels religious expansion... [and] ethnic homogeneity is also conducive to religious expansion.'[9]

In subsequent exchanges, the supply-siders have tried to answer these criticisms, but they have failed to satisfy other scholars that the statistical manipulation of the data that produced their confirming results was justified. Without such sleight of hand, studies of the relationship between pluralism and religious vitality in the United States have found either no connection or the negative effect the secularization paradigm would expect. Rather than going through all the contested studies, I will defer to Chaves and Gorski, who evaluated twenty-six published articles or chapters that analyse the links between religious pluralism and religious participation. Ten of those (seven of them authored by some combination of Stark, Finke, and Iannaccone) found a positive relationship. Eleven found a negative relationship. Five found null effects. Within these publications, Chaves and Gorski found a total of 193 separate analyses and of these

    [8] K. C. Land, G. Deane, and J. R. Blau, 'Religious Pluralism and Church Membership', *American Sociological Review*, 56 (1991), 237–49.
    [9] J. R. Blau, K. C. Land, and K. Rudding, 'The Expansion of Religious Affiliation: An Explanation of the Growth in Church Participation in the United States, 1850–1930', *Social Science Research*, 21 (1991), 329.

only 24 (12 per cent) yielded results that appear to support the new paradigm. After painstaking secondary analysis, Chaves and Gorski conclude: 'The empirical evidence contradicts the claim that religious pluralism is positively associated with religious participation in any general sense.'[10]

Fortunately the supply-side model can be assessed without getting mired too deep in technical argument by focusing on big differences between nation states and large changes over time. Here the model fails comprehensively. When we compare diversity and religiosity at the nation-state level, the relationship almost always runs the wrong way. In the Western world, the generally more homogenous Catholic and Orthodox societies (Spain, Portugal, Italy, Greece, Ireland) are more religious than the diverse Protestant ones (such as Britain). Even when we take states that are in many ways very similar, we find that the more diverse ones are the least religious. The three Baltic states of Latvia, Lithuania, and Estonia have had very similar political histories. Of the three, Lithuania is by far the most religious. In 1996 'at least weekly' church attendances were as follows: Lithuania 31 per cent; Latvia 16 per cent, and Estonia 9 per cent. It was also the most religiously homogenous. Three-quarters of Lithuanians are Catholic, but Latvians are divided fairly evenly between Catholic, Lutheran, and Orthodox, and Estonians are evenly divided between Orthodox and Lutheran churches. I might add, in further support for the secularization paradigm, that the least religious of the three Baltic states—Estonia—is also the most economically developed.[11]

The supply-side story also fails the test of comparison over time. However diverse Britain is compared to the USA, it had a much freer and more diverse religious market in 2000 than it had in 1851. Over that time period, weekly church attendance fell from at least 50 per cent to less than 10 per cent. Boundary changes caused by two world wars and some sub-state conflicts have slightly altered the religious composition of some European states. The extermination or expulsion of Jews slightly reduced the religious diversity of some countries. Intermarriage and voluntary departure reduced the Protestant population of the Irish Free State (later the Irish Republic) from about

---

[10] M. Chaves and P. Gorski, 'Religious Pluralism and Religious Participation', *Annual Review of Sociology*, 27 (2001): 261–81.

[11] Bruce, *Choice and Religion*, 100–4.

10 per cent in 1891 to 3 per cent in 2000.[12] But such examples of increased homogeneity are too rare and small in overall impact to change the basic fact that over the twentieth century all modern industrial democracies became markedly more diverse as they experienced migration from Africa, the Middle East, and Asia, and they all relaxed their regimes of religious control. As the variety of religions on offer went up and government restrictions went down, religion should have become more popular. As we saw in Chapter 1, the opposite is the case. As Norris and Inglehart conclude from their study of the massive WVS dataset: 'In the world as a whole the most homogenous religious cultures and the societies with the greatest state regulation of religion, have the greatest religious participation and the strongest faith in God.'[13]

## Individual Religious Behaviour

As well as providing a radical challenge to the secularization paradigm on the big issue of overall levels of religiosity, the economistic version of rational-choice theory has been applied to a range of smaller problems in the sociology of religion. In trying to evaluate this body of work, our difficulty is not that rational-choice theory is wrong (though it usually is); the greater problem is that, beneath the brittle veneer of hypotheses and equations, there is a sea of vagueness that allows almost any outcome to be claimed as support for rational choice. This can be demonstrated by considering Iannaccone's 'human-capital' approach to denominational mobility, the typical age of converts, the typical pattern of inter-religious marriage, and the levels of participation found in different sorts of marriages.[14]

Iannaccone used the metaphor of 'investment' to explain why most Americans stay in the churches in which they were raised,

[12] The data from various censuses are summarized on www.wesleyjohnston. com/users/ireland/past/protestants_1861_1991.html.

[13] P. Norris and R. Inglehart, *Sacred and Secular: Religion and Politics Worldwide* (Cambridge: Cambridge University Press, 2004).

[14] L. A. Iannaccone, 'Religious Practice: A Human Capital Approach', *Journal for the Scientific Study of Religion*, 29 (1990), 297–314.

return to those churches if they have drifted away, and, if they move, ideologically travel only short distances. Typically, Southern Baptists stay Southern Baptists; if they change it is to something very similar, such as the American Baptist Church. This is explained, Iannaccone believes, by the fact that, once we have invested a certain amount of human capital (that is time and effort to non-economists) in acquiring the beliefs of one tradition and mastering its liturgical or ritual procedures, we are reluctant to waste that investment. It is miserliness that explains why few Baptists become Catholics.

However, we can account for the same pattern by supposing that beliefs sediment so as to shape our receptivity to future alternatives. That you have held for some time a Baptist view of religion may not stop you ceasing to be religious but makes it likely that, if you remain religious or wish to return to a supernatural faith at some later stage of your life, you will find most plausible those beliefs that accord with the residues of your previous faith. By considering what makes beliefs more and less plausible, we can understand the pattern demonstrated by Iannaccone perfectly well without recourse to his dubious investment metaphor.

Iannaccone believes that data on the typical age at which people experience religious conversion also support his model:

The human capital model predicts that religious switching, like job changing, will tend to occur early in the life cycle as people search for the best match between their skills and the context in which they produce religious commodities. Across time, the gains from further switching will diminish as the potential improvement in matches diminishes and the remaining years in which to capitalize on that improvement decrease.[15]

Again, the presented data fit the prediction but they also fit the more conventional explanation: the longer we hold a particular set of beliefs, pleasantly interact with like-minded people, and find that those beliefs produce a satisfactory understanding of the world and our place in it, the more convincing those beliefs become.[16] It is not the knowledge that they have few years left to profit from their new investment that discourages 50-year old Scottish Presbyterians from

[15] Iannaccone, 'Religious Practice', 297.
[16] That is, being religious and being religious in a certain way is what Elster calls an 'adaptive preference' (J. Elster, *Sour Grapes: Studies in the Subversion of Rationality* (Cambridge: Cambridge University Press, 1983) ).

becoming Scientologists. It is that a long, and (one has to assume, because otherwise it would have been ended earlier) rewarding, involvement with Presbyterianism makes them ill disposed to believe L. Ron Hubbard or Tom Cruise.

To sustain the investment metaphor, Iannaccone has to assume that religious ideas and liturgical practices are hard to learn. The religious virtuoso who wishes to master the entire Shorter Catechism may be discouraged by the thought of the effort, but most Christian churches are similar and, as researching sociologists regularly prove, their rituals can be picked up easily by imitating the person in the pew in front or following the words helpfully provided on the overhead projector. Furthermore, Iannaccone regards learning as a cost, which misses the point that it can also be an enjoyable challenge. After all, knowing that they do not have enough life left to become another Picasso or Constable does not prevent many old people taking up painting.

The explanation of data on the effects of inter-religious marriages is hardly more persuasive. We know from a variety of sources that, where a couple belong to the same church or religious tradition, they are more likely than 'mixed' marriages to be regular church attenders, to give money to religious work, to raise their children in the faith, and so on. Iannaccone supplies the explanation:

A household can produce religious commodities more efficiently when both husband and wife share the same religion. Single-faith households benefit from 'economies of scale': the same car drives everyone to church; there is no question as to how time and money contributions will be allocated to different religions; it is not necessary to debate the religion in which one's children will be reared.[17]

No doubt marital disagreement about religious affiliation can be painful, and hence there is no surprise in the data Iannaccone presents to show that people tend to marry within the same denomination. People can imagine the disputes and act to avoid them. But a much simpler explanation of the pattern is that churches provide an excellent venue for meeting young people who are similar not only in religion but in social class, culture, and ethnic background.

Better evidence for Iannaccone's model is in data that show that same-faith marriages have higher rates of church attendance than

[17] Iannaccone, 'Religious Practice', 301.

interdenominational marriages, but, again, nothing in this tests the claim that the pattern arises because 'partners of the same religion can produce religious commodities more efficiently'. The obvious alternative is airily dismissed when he says that 'a shared faith should have only indirect effects on individual beliefs'.[18] Let us reintroduce the idea of strength of beliefs. An axiom of sociology is that reality is socially constructed, maintained, and changed. To add to one's own internalized faith a wife or husband who reinforces such beliefs will have a profound impact on the strength of one's faith and hence on the enthusiasm with which one participates in collective expressions of such beliefs.

## First Principles and General Problems

Becker believes that 'the economic approach is a comprehensive one that is applicable to all human behavior, be it behavior involving money prices or imputed shadow prices, repeated or infrequent decisions, large or minor decisions, emotional or mechanical ends'.[19] Reasons for doubting the value of such imperialism can best be explained by briefly working through Becker's succinct summary of the assumptions underlying the economist's model of human action. It assumes first that people engage in maximizing or economizing behaviour: if we can buy an identical product in two shops at different prices, we will buy the cheaper. Secondly, there are 'markets that with varying degrees of efficiency co-ordinate the actions of different participants…so that their behavior becomes mutually consistent'. Thirdly, 'prices and other market instruments allocate the scarce resources within a society'.[20]

A basic requirement for maximizing utility is that alternatives be comparable. With some commodities, comparing value is easy. Washing powders now show on the side of the box how many typical washes that box will do. For more refined calculations, we can subscribe to the reports of a consumer association that tests products for us.

[18] Iannaccone, 'Religious Practice', 303.
[19] G. Becker, 'The Economic Approach to Human Behaviour', in J. Elster (ed.), *Rational Choice* (Oxford: Basil Blackwell, 1986), 108–22.
[20] Becker, 'The Economic Approach', 112.

But how can we compare the value of being a Baptist or a Buddhist? The truth of the competing core claims made by religions can be known only after death, on the Day of Judgement, or when the Messiah returns. As of now, we have no way of knowing which, if any, is correct and, without knowing that, their other differences are trivial. Secondary aspects or 'latent functions' of faith can be tested against other religious or secular alternatives. We could certainly research the relative success of churchgoing and concert-going as ways of making new friends. We might even be able to test the evangelist's assertion that 'getting right with Jesus' or getting 'clear' with Scientology will have greater benefits for mental health than would buying sessions of secular psychotherapy or just ignoring the problem. But even here comparison is difficult because the psychological benefits of religious conviction are, I presume, enjoyed only by the converted. I cannot pretend to get right with Jesus to see if I feel better. So, even with peripheral aspects of religious behaviour, one of the conditions for maximizing utility is absent.

And it is certainly absent for the core business of religion. Until death we cannot be sure whether any religion is correct. Or, to put it another way, we cannot hedge our bets. We can manage soap-powder uncertainty by buying some of each of rival brands; we cannot diversify our religious portfolios as a hedge against choosing the wrong God. This, of course, is why Pascal was wrong to argue that, in the absence of certainty about the existence of God, we should 'wager' that He exists; Pascal assumes there is only one God.

The key difference between soap powder and religion can be seen clearly if we consider the power of ideology to shift perceptions fundamentally: the radical switch at the point of conversion. When we change soap powders, we do not renounce or denounce our previous brand. Although many religious adherents can be polite about other religions and one faith may grudgingly admit that another has an incomplete vision of the truth, most conventionally require that the claims of competitors be rejected. There is no God but Allah; my God is a jealous God.

Comparing the benefits of rival products is one condition for maximizing utility; comparing costs is another. My supermarket prevents me from being hoodwinked by unusual jar sizes and shapes by telling me on a tag below each jar of coffee the price of that jar and the price per kilo. I can thus accurately compare the cost of competing brands.

But to talk of the price of religious involvement is stretching a metaphor too far. Scientology may sell enlightenment, but the major religious traditions do not. The metaphor is not saved from shipwreck by substituting the 'shadow price' of time for money. How costly is time spent on some activity depends on the extent to which we find that passage of time rewarding. As an impatient agnostic with a bad back, I find a two-hour prayer meeting 'costly', but clearly the believers among whom I sit find it a great pleasure.

In brief, the economistic model of human action requires that we be able to assess costs and returns from some neutral or consensually agreed standpoint before we make a commitment to one religion rather than another. But the nature of religion does not allow such comparisons and measurements.

Becker also lists as a precondition for maximizing utility the existence of a market. One of the weaknesses of the supply-side explanation of levels of religiosity is that its concentration on interference in the market (for example, by the state supporting one church) blinds it to far more pervasive social obstacles to shopping around. Maximizing is constrained by our culture and its embodiment in our relationships. Religious affiliation is often so closely tied to other forms of identity that most people are not free to switch. In Sarajevo, Baghdad, or Kabul, religious affiliation is a matter of communal identity, not a personal preference to be altered at will. Those who switch may well find themselves ostracized or worse. People are not executed for changing car brands; in many countries they are shunned, expelled, or killed for switching religion. Even in the USA, social identities constrain religious choices. Very few congregations are racially mixed, and few white Americans attend black churches or vice versa. American churches remain so racially divided that George Gallup entitled an article on the subject 'The Most Segregated Hour'.[21]

The same point can be made about the producers of religious commodities: officials of religious organizations are even more constrained than consumers. Their position is quite unlike that of producers of secular commodities and services. My local Ford car dealer switched his franchise to Honda and then gave up cars altogether when he found that he could make more money building houses on

---

[21] G. H. Gallup Jr, 'The Most Segregated Hour', *The Gallup Report*, 9 July 2002, www.gallup.com/poll/6367/most-segregated-hour.aspx.

his car lot. Churches, sects, denominations, and cults do sometimes change, but the change has to be very slow, because too obvious an alteration betrays the human origins of what is supposed to be the inspiration of a divine source. The radical difference between religious ideologies and consumer products is clear in the way their producers respond to failure. Churches sometimes borrow the language of marketing and fret about how to make their 'product' more attractive to potential congregants. Supermarkets never borrow from religious organizations a dogged determination to press on regardless. When sales fall, the directors do not say 'Well, that just proves our clothes are too good for ordinary people' and proudly carry on. In the world of consumer products, the customer is by definition right. There is no other authority. Religious organizations wish to be popular and may adjust at the margins, but in the end it is not the customer who is right: it is God.

To summarize, rational-choice models of behaviour depend on the actors in question knowing what is the rational choice. Becker has helpfully told us that the economic model of human action assumes an attitude and two conditions. Personally, I do not find the language of 'maximizing utility' helpful for understanding most of what people do, but we can let that stand because the whole unwieldy metaphorical edifice is undermined by the two conditions. Whatever the formal structure of the market, most people are not free to choose, because religious affiliation is rarely just a personal preference. And the basic elements of pricing—the calculation and comparison of costs and rewards—are absent. As Jon Elster said of rational-choice theory in general: 'To the extent that we cannot tell, or cannot tell uniquely, what the rational choice would be, the theory fails.'[22]

## Secularization and Maximizing

The supply-side explanation of religious vitality is presented by its adherents as a comprehensive alternative to the secularization paradigm. I would argue that religion is such a profoundly social cultural

[22] J. Elster, 'Introduction', in J. Elster (ed.), *Rational Choice* (Oxford: Basil Blackwell, 1986), 17.

product that the theories of Stark, Finke, and Iannaccone will become persuasive only when societies become largely secular. The model of the maximizing individual works best for something like the motor industry: where there is widespread and general demand for a product; where costs and values can be assessed from a neutral or consensual standpoint that does not change fundamentally at the point of choice; and where choice is free from enduring and powerful social identities. And that is pretty much what religion is like in largely secular societies.

It is worth remembering that the secularization paradigm is not solely concerned with the decline of religion. As both cause and symptom of decline we see the following changes: the supernatural diminishes as core beliefs are rationalized and psychologized; this-worldly rewards become more important than the afterlife; the therapeutic benefits of religion displace the glorification of God as the primary purpose; external authority is either replaced by the choosing individual (as in the New Age) or becomes severely attenuated (as in liberal Christianity); major religions cease to claim sole access to the will of God and become increasingly ecumenical; states give up enforcing religious conformity; religion becomes free from other major social identities; religious requirements bear on ever smaller areas of life (as spheres such as the economy and the polity are released from the control of religion) and on ever fewer people (so that others are not required to follow the religious laws that bind me); people distinguish the morality that God requires from the law that the state can be expected to enforce; an ever-greater variety of religions is tolerated; religion becomes a matter for the private life of the individual; and, as religion shrinks in importance, people become increasing indifferent to the particularities of religion while generally remaining vaguely benevolent to religion in the abstract.

If we are looking for a sphere of religious activity that at all resembles the free market of diverse providers competing for the attention of the free-floating consumer, we find it in the world of New Age spirituality. The cultic milieu of alternative spirituality is a marketplace of competing providers. Thoughtful (that is, maximizing) consumers can try Bachian flower remedies and aromatherapy, take a yoga course, attend workshops on Tibetan overtone chanting, fire-walking, or Bhagwan Rajneesh's dynamic meditation, and experiment with Hopi ear candles and Sufi dancing. From a now-truly-global cafeteria of spiritual practices, Westerners can (with little fear of being stigmatized as dangerous deviants) construct their own idiosyncratic faith packages. Something like rational choice is possible in this milieu, because the value of the product is knowable: the promised benefit is mundane and therapeutic and attained in this life. You can know if dynamic meditation works for you and you know some of what it costs you. However much some may wish otherwise, the providers in the New Age milieu cannot demand total loyalty. Interests do not form the basis for enduring communities with constraining shared identities. Yoga practitioners do not form a closed community. They do not refuse to marry people who do not do yoga. In most of the respects discussed above, the cultic milieu does not throw up obstacles to rational choice. But what makes the cultic milieu possible and underpins it is the novel epistemological principle that the believer is the final arbiter of what is true 'for her' (and it usually is a woman); or, as they say in secular trade: the consumer is always right. This is, of course, a very long way from the epistemological foundation of the major world religions, which assume that there is a God or Gods, whose will is knowable through clear but limited channels controlled by the properly appointed officials.

One way of summarizing the secularization thesis is to note that the complex pattern of social changes we gloss as 'modernization' has been accompanied by an increase in individual liberty. For some, that liberty has taken the form of abandoning organized religion altogether; for others, it is expressed in a highly selective attitude to the precepts of once-hegemonic faiths. That has been visible in the liberal wings of the major Christian churches since the late nineteenth century, and since the 1960s even conservative churches in the West have had to compromise much of their behavioural distinctiveness—Puritanism is rare, even amongst fundamentalists—and become less dogmatic and authoritarian. While the sovereign consumerism of the New Age may be extreme, it is part of a general trend in the religious culture of the Western world.

## Conclusion

Before I conclude, I want to make clear the limited nature of my criticism of rational choice. None of the above should be read as meaning that people are fundamentally irrational. On the contrary, if human action was not minimally rational (in the sense of following from understandable interests and beliefs reasonably applied to the actor's perception of the situation), we would not be able to understand it at all. My point is that the very narrow notion of rationality used in the economist's 'maximizing-utility' model of human behaviour applies only in a narrow range of circumstances. It does not work well in cultures that take their religion very seriously. When the world at large becomes as secular as the metropolitan centres of the West, then and only then will the economistic imperialism of Gary Becker offer a plausible approach to religion.

This simplifies his case, but Wilson's contrasting treatment of European and US religion can be summarized by saying that secularization took two forms.[23] In Europe, the churches became less popular; in the United States, the churches became less religious. That contrast explains the very narrow appeal of the work of the supply-side theorists, which has been largely ignored by sociologists outside the USA. While still hardly convincing, viewing religion as a sphere for maximizing utility is more plausible in the USA than in the rest of the world because many Americans do treat religion as a consumer commodity.

[23] B. R. Wilson, *Religion in Secular Society* (London: C. A. Watts, 1966), ch. 6.

# 8

# Unexceptional America

## Introduction

The association between modernization and secularization is not slight, it is not brief, and it is not narrowly confined. David Voas, summarizing a very large body of survey data, wrote: 'Of the 20 most modern nations in the world...19 are becoming increasingly secular. These countries have very different histories, speak 11 different languages and are located on four different continents.'[1] The exception is the United States of America. Americans are more likely than Europeans to claim a religious identity, to go to church, and to pray. To sustain the claim that there is some general causal connection between modernization and secularization, we must show either that there is evidence of religion in the USA declining in power, popularity, and prestige, or that American exceptionalism can be explained by principles consistent with the secularization, or both.

This chapter will make four points. First, there is clear evidence of Christianity in the USA losing power, prestige, and popularity. Secondly, there is also clear evidence that Christianity in the USA has become increasingly secular. Thirdly, despite the recent influence of the Christian Right in public life, there has been no significant

[1] D. Voas, 'The Continuing Secular Transition', in D. Pollack and D. V. A. Olson (eds), *The Role of Religion in Modern Societies* (New York: Routledge, 2008), 29.

reversal of the major trend of religion becoming marginal to the operation of the social system. Finally, to the extent that the USA does differ from Europe, those differences can largely be explained in ways that fit the secularization paradigm.

## Patterns of Church Adherence

Though indices of popular church involvement are higher in the USA than in most European countries, those indices now show decline. In 1948 only 2 per cent of those polled said they had no religion; sixty years later the figure was between 12 and 16 per cent.[2]

For decades, US social scientists were happy to accept at face value poll data that showed around 40 per cent of Americans claiming to have attended church 'in the last seven days'.[3] In the early 1990s, C. Kirk Hadaway, a sociologist employed by one of the major denominations, became aware that the rates of church attendance claimed in social surveys were incompatible with what the churches knew about their own congregations.[4] The Gallup Organization's own data contained an enigma: although the headline figure for weekly church attendance remained the same, the number saying they attend 'less frequently' has always been greater than that of those who now attend 'more frequently'.[5]

To test their suspicion that self-reported rates of church attendance were inflated, Hadaway and his colleagues went to painstaking

---

[2] The 1948 data and the 12 per cent for 2008 figures come from F. Newport, 'This Easter, Smaller Percentage of Americans are Christian', 10 Apr. 2009, www.gallup.com//poll/117409/Easter-Smaller-Percentage-Americans-Christian (accessed 10 Aug. 2009). The 16% for 2007 comes from the Pew Forum on Religion and Public Life, *Faith in Flux: Changes in Religious Affiliation in the US*, www.pewforum.org (accessed 15 July 2008). See also J. G. Condran and J. B. Tamney, 'Religious "Nones" 1957–1982', *Sociological Analysis*, 46 (1985), 415–23.

[3] A. Greeley, *Religious Change in America* (Cambridge, Mass.: Harvard University Press, 1989), 56.

[4] C. K. Hadaway, P. L. Marler, and M. Chaves, 'What the Polls don't Show: A Closer Look at US Church Attendance', *American Sociological Review*, 58 (1993), 741–52.

[5] R. Bezilla, *Religion in America 1992–93* (Princeton: Princeton Religion Research Centre, 1993), 44.

lengths to estimate accurately attendance at all known churches in Ashtabula County, Ohio. They took lists of congregations from registers and church yearbooks and also searched the county for unlisted churches. Where they could not get the clergy to promise an estimate of attendance, they counted cars in the car parks during services and adjusted the figure for the probable number of passengers. Having constructed a reasonable estimate of how many people attended services from the clergy returns and from their own counts, the researchers used a standard telephone survey to ask a sample of Ashtabulans if they went to church. They discovered that the observance claimed by their respondents was 83 per cent higher than their best estimates of actual attendance.

Hadaway and Marler then repeated the study with one particular congregation: a Baptist church in a metropolitan area of Alabama. They found that 984 people (about 40 per cent of the membership) were at worship on a particular Sunday. During the following week a sample of 300 adult members of the congregation were interviewed about various matters, including their church attendance in the previous week: 70 per cent said they had attended. If that were generalized to the whole membership, there should have been 1,710 people in church: almost twice as many as actually were!

Even more compelling evidence of overclaiming was produced by comparing actual attendance at the adult Sunday school (where the names of those present were recorded) with what members said when asked in a telephone poll the following week. 'Sunday school attendance at this church was over-reported by 58.8%.'[6]

Although the initial response to the research was remarkably hostile, its general thrust has now been widely accepted, and a consensus has emerged around the figure for typical weekly attendance of 20 per cent. A similar proportion now say they never attend.[7] That is, while US churches remain more popular than their European counterparts, church adherence in the USA has declined markedly since the 1950s.

---

[6] P. L. Marler and C. K. Hadaway, 'Testing the Attendance Gap in A Conservative Church', *Sociology of Religion*, 60 (1997), 182.

[7] P. Norris and R. Inglehart, *Sacred and Secular: Religion and Politics Worldwide* (Cambridge: Cambridge University Press, 2004), 92.

## Changes in the Nature of US Religion

In 1996, Bryan Wilson drew a contrast that has turned out to be remarkably accurate. He suggested that, while Europeans secularized by abandoning the churches, Americans secularized their churches.[8] Describing the faith of millions of people over a century clearly requires considerable simplification. I will begin with some illustrative data from social surveys and then consider the recent history of US Christianity.

Although the change has been nowhere near as great as in Britain or Australia, there has been a decline in commitment to what were once orthodox Christian beliefs. For example, the percentage of those who believed that the Bible is 'literally true' has fallen from 65 per cent in 1964 to 37 per cent in 1984 to 26 per cent in 2009.[9] In 2007 the Pew Forum reported that 74 per cent of Americans believed in heaven but only 59 believed in hell. It also found that, while 92 per cent of Americans said they believed in God, almost a third preferred the 'impersonal force' formulation to that of 'personal God'.[10]

One crucial indicator of change is the age correlates of various practices and beliefs. In 2007, 57 per cent of those aged 65 and over said they have absolutely certain belief in a personal God, but only 45 per cent of those aged 18–29 said the same. A steeper gradient was visible in claiming to have attended a place of worship weekly: 54 per cent of those 65 and over, but only 33 per cent of those under 29. Those who say they pray daily outside of religious services ranged from 68 per cent for those 65 and over to 48 per cent of those under 29.[11]

---

[8] B. R. Wilson, *Religion in Secular Society* (London: C. A. Watts, 1966), 122.

[9] The first two figures are from R. Wuthnow, *The Restructuring of American Religion* (Princeton: Princeton University Press, 1988), 165. The third is from www.barna.org/barna-update/article/12-faithspirituality/317-new-research-explores-how-different-generations-view-and-use-the-bible (accessed 1 Nov. 2009).

[10] Pew Forum on Religion and Public Life, *US Religious Landscape Survey*, http://religions.pewforum.org/pdf/report2religious-landscape-study-chapter1.pdf, 5 (accessed 5 Sept. 2009).

[11] Pew Forum on Religion and Public Life, *US Religious Landscape Survey*, http://religions.pewforum.org/pdf/report2religious-landscape-study-chapter1.pdf, 29, 38 and 46 (accessed 5 Sept. 2009).

The simplest way of describing the changes in content of much American religion is to say that the supernatural has been diminished and it has been psychologized or subjectivized. Religion used to be about the divine and our relationship to it. God was a real person; the Bible was his revealed word; miracles actually occurred; Christ really was the son of God and he did actually die to atone for our sins; heaven and hell were real places. And the primary purpose of religion was to serve and glorify God. Over the twentieth century much of mainstream Christianity shifted to a rather different version of the faith. God was no longer an actual person but some sort of vague power or, in the final reduction, our own consciences. The Bible was no longer the revealed word of God but a gradually accumulated collection of useful ethical and moral guidelines for living. Miracles were explained as myths or misunderstandings. Christ was not actually God's son but an exemplary prophet and teacher. Heaven and hell were not real destinations but psychological states.

Harry Fosdick Emerson, a leading liberal Protestant clergyman of the 1930s, said that the starting point of Christianity was not an objective faith but faith in human personality. The consequence of increasing irreligion was not that people were going to go to hell but that 'multitudes of people are living not bad but frittered lives—split, scattered, uncoordinated'. The solution was a religion that would 'furnish an inward spiritual dynamic for radiant and triumphant living'.[12] Religion was no longer about glorifying God but about personal growth. This fundamental shift in mainline Christianity began in the 1930s and reached its zenith in the popularity of Norman Vincent Peale. Peale was a liberal Presbyterian minister, pastor of one of the biggest churches in New York and the originator of what he called 'the power of positive thinking'.[13] In the first two years after its publication, the book of the same name sold over two million copies. For Peale the Christian message was reduced to a battle between good and evil, but these were no longer realities external to us. Evil was a lack of self-confidence; good was positive thinking. Those people who think positively (while conforming to the norms of

---

[12] S. Bruce, *Pray TV: Televangelism in America* (London: Routledge, 1990), 84.
[13] C. V. R. George, *God's Salesman: Norman Vincent Peale and the Power of Positive Thinking* (New York: Oxford University Press, 1994).

suburban middle class 1950s America) will be successful; this is salvation. Those who do not will be damned. That is, they will be unhappy.

At the same time as the faith was being stripped of its traditional supernaturalism, it was also losing its behavioural distinctiveness. Asceticism was out. Churchgoers no longer gave up smoking, drinking, dancing, or going to the theatre. They wore the same clothes as other people, lived in the same kinds of houses, and had the same increasingly liberal moral and ethical standards. For example, they got divorced.

When Wilson first presented his 'internal secularization' argument, he had in mind the mainstream churches. The conservative wing of Protestantism seemed relatively immune. Indeed, evangelicals and fundamentalists defined themselves by their refusal to modernize their faith. In part they were able to resist new ideas and attitudes because they did not benefit so immediately from the prosperity that encouraged the innovations. They remained poor, and their puritanism helped reconcile them to their poverty. Television was unacceptable, because it carried Satanic messages, but then most fundamentalists could not afford a television anyway. When the prosperity of industrial America began to seep down to the communities in which fundamentalism and Pentecostalism were strong, puritanism waned. As more could afford televisions, the injunction against watching TV weakened. Fancy clothes and personal adornment were sinful until Pentecostalists could afford them, and then the lines shifted. Tammy Faye Bakker (later Messner), who became one of the leading figures in television evangelism in the late 1970s, wrote movingly about the troubles she had as a teenager in the 1950s squaring her interest in fashion and make-up with her church's teachings.[14] In 1988, the General Assembly of the Church of God, the USA's oldest Pentecostal sect, reconciled itself to the status quo and voted to change elements of its moral code: 'It is not displeasing to God for us to dress well and be well-groomed.'[15] So long as Pentecostalists were so poor that the break-up of the family would have pushed them into destitution, divorce was entirely unacceptable. As they

---

[14] T. F. Messner, *Tammy: Telling it my Way* (New York: Villard, 1996).
[15] J. B. Tamney and S. D. Johnson, 'The Popularity of Strict Churches', *Review of Religious Research*, 39 (1998), 219.

became better off, that line was moved: a 2000 survey showed that 'born-again' adults were more likely than others to have divorced.[16]

The decline of puritanism is ably illustrated in a 1982 survey of young evangelicals that repeated questions first asked in the 1950s and again in the 1960s.[17] In 1951, almost all those asked thought that social dancing (tangos, waltzes, and the like) was 'morally wrong all the time' and that folk dancing was hardly more acceptable. In 1982, no one objected to either. Almost all the 1950s cohort regarded drinking alcohol as sinful; in 1982, only 17 per cent thought it morally wrong. In 1951, almost half thought watching 'Hollywood-type' movies was morally wrong; in 1982, none did. The responses to questions about sex are interesting. The evangelical consensus against 'petting' and sexual intercourse was so strong in 1951 that the questions were not asked. In the early 1960s, 81 per cent of evangelicals thought 'heavy petting' morally wrong all the time. Twenty years later, less than half took that view. There has been no recent update with precisely the same questions, but the Barna Organization, which regularly polls on religious and moral issues, finds considerable evidence of further relaxation. In 2003, almost half of born-again Christians thought that 'living with someone of the opposite sex without being married' was morally acceptable. Oddly, a smaller proportion (but still high at 35 per cent) thought that extramarital sex was acceptable.[18] Unless they imagined celibate co-habitees, we must presume the respondents took extramarital to mean cheating on a spouse.

The decline of puritanism was accompanied by a more positive valuation of the self that had clear echoes of Peale's positive thinking. Conservatives had been bitterly critical of liberals for turning salvation from an other-worldly goal into this-worldly personal therapy. Yet, two generations later, evangelicals were rewriting the gospel in the same way. The frequent references to Jesus and the Bible and, in

[16] G. Barna, 'The Year's Most Intriguing Findings', *Barna Research Online* (2000), 3.

[17] J. D. Hunter, *Evangelicalism: The Coming Generation* (Chicago: University of Chicago Press, 1987), 59.

[18] Barna Organization, 'Morality Continues to Decay', www.barna.org/barna-update/article/5-barna-update/129-morality-continues-to-decay (accessed 1 Nov. 2009).

the charismatic movement, the popularity of speaking in tongues, rather blinded observers to the fact that a large part of conservative Protestantism was becoming world-affirming.[19] Hunter makes the point economically by listing the titles of best-selling evangelical books of the 1980s: *You Can Become the Person You Want to Be, How to Become your own Best Self,* and *Self-Esteem: The New Reformation.*[20] Among the best-sellers on the 2009 lists of Zondervan, the biggest evangelical publishing house in the USA, is *Pure Pleasure: Why Do Christians Feel so Bad about Feeling Good?*[21]

Chapter 2's explanation of secularization drew attention to the growth of practical relativism. A common feature of religion in culturally diverse democracies is a shortening of reach: injunctions that were once binding on all God's creation are now thought to apply only to those who voluntarily accept them. There are clear signs of such relativism becoming common among American Christians. In the 1920s, Robert and Helen Lynd studied life in a small American city they called *Middletown.* Numerous Middletown restudies allow us to track changes. In 1924, the Lynds asked for responses to the statement that 'Christianity is the one true religion and all people should be converted to it'.[22] Ninety-four per cent of those asked—that is, nearly everyone—agreed. When the same question was put in 1977 to a sample of *churchgoing* young people, only 41 per cent agreed. The restudy concluded: 'half of Middletown's adolescents who belong to and attend church and who believe in Jesus, the Bible and the hereafter do not claim any universal validity for the Christian beliefs they hold and have no zeal for the conversion of non-Christians.'[23] Hunter's study of young evangelicals suggested similar changes in even that

[19] The change is ably documented in R. Quebedeaux, *The Worldly Evangelicals* (New York: HarperCollins, 1980) and M. A. Shibley, *Resurgent Evangelicalism in the United States* (Columbia, SC: University of South Carolina Press, 1996) and 'Contemporary Evangelicals: Born-Again and World-Affirming', *Annals of the American Academy of Politics and Social Science,* 558 (1998), 67–93.

[20] Hunter, *Evangelicalism,* 69–70.

[21] www.zondervan.com/Cultures/en-US/Product/Book/Index.htm?Query StringSite=Zondervan (accessed 1 Nov. 2009).

[22] R. S. Lynd and H. J. Lynd, *Middletown: A Study of Contemporary American Culture* (New York: Harcourt, Brace and Co., 1929), 316.

[23] T. Caplow, H. M. Bahr, and B. A. Chadwick, *All Faithful People: Change and Continuity in Middletown's Religion* (Minneapolis: University of Minnesota Press, 1983), 98.

constituency. While their views on what *they* had to do and believe in order to attain salvation remained orthodox, they had softened considerably their views of other people's chances of being saved. In 2008, 70 per cent of Americans who claimed a religious identity agreed that 'many religions can lead to eternal life'; more remarkably, almost half of white evangelicals agreed.[24] There was no longer the sectarian certainty that there was only one way to heaven.

One Middletown restudy contained a fascinating observation that accords well with Wilson's view that there has been a significant change in the reasons for church adherence. The Lynds asked why people went to church, and the most popular answer was that obedience to God required it. In a 1977 restudy, the most popular reason given for church-going was 'pleasure'.[25]

To summarize thus far, Wilson's belief that the enduring popularity of churchgoing in the USA may well reflect important changes in the substance of American religion now seems prescient. When the lead singer of the Pussycat Dolls (a girl group famous for sexually provocative dance) writes in the sleeve liner notes of their first CD 'First and foremost I would like to thank my Lord and Savior for granting me the voice, humility, strength, guidance and grace to live my dream', and a member of Megadeth (as the name suggests, a leather-and-studs heavy metal band) says 'My faith is behind why I'm playing so good now and how I got rid of my demons', it is easy to be misled by the continued popularity of religious rhetoric and suppose that Americans are as religious as ever they were.[26] In addition to the evidence of church decline, we need to appreciate the extent to which the content of American Christianity has been secularized. Wade Clark Roof, who spent thirty years documenting shifts in American religious life, concluded a wide-ranging survey of changes since the 1960s by noting: 'the religious stance today is more internal

---

[24] Pew Forum on Religion and Public Life, 'Many Americans Say Other Faiths Can Lead to Eternal Life', 18 Oct. 2008; http://pewforum.org/docs/?DocID=380 (accessed 1 Mar. 2008).

[25] T. Caplow, H. M. Bahr, and B. A. Chadwick, *All Faithful People: Change and Continuity in Middletown's Religion* (Minneapolis: University of Minnesota Press, 1983).

[26] Pussycat Dolls, *PCD*, A&M Records, 2005; 'Welcome back Megadeth', *Classic Rock* (Oct. 2009), 12.

than external, more individual than institutional, more experiential than cerebral, more private than public.'[27]

## The Constraints on Fundamentalism

One feature of American religious life that strikes Europeans as unusual is the role that religion plays in politics. Religiously derived moral arguments are politicized to an extent unknown in contemporary Europe, and pressure groups inspired by Christian values enjoy an unusual degree of influence on the Republican Party. I have no wish to minimize what Hunter called 'culture wars',[28] but, before we too readily accept them as proof of excessive piety, we need to appreciate both the unusual features of American public life that encourage them and the limits that American culture imposes on theocracy. There are parallels in the underlying causes of US Protestant fundamentalism and its Islamic counterpart, but there are far greater differences in their goals and how they attempt to achieve them.[29]

### Opportunity Structure

What one makes of any phenomenon depends rather on what one expects. Some of the more extravagant assessments of the Christian Right result from failing to appreciate just how open the US political system is to well-organized minorities. Socio-moral issues are more contentious in the USA than in, say, Britain or Australia, because America has more conservative Christians. But they are also more contentious, because the political structure of the USA makes it considerably easier for conservative Christians to have a public impact.

First, far more offices are filled by election than by appointment. Voters are often asked 'to elect half a dozen state officers apart from

[27] W. C. Roof, 'God is in the Details: Reflections on Religion's Public Presence in the United States in the Mid-1990s', *Sociology of Religion*, 57 (1996), 153.

[28] J. D. Hunter, *Culture Wars: The Struggle to Define America* (New York: Basic Books, 1992).

[29] See M. Riesebrodt, *Pious Passion: The Emergence of Modern Fundamentalism in the United States and Iran* (Chicago: University of Chicago Press, 1993), and S. Bruce, *Fundamentalism* (Cambridge: Polity Press, 2008).

the governor, to elect state commissioners and judges, state treasurer and state attorney, as well as their mayor, their councillors, the members of the local school board, the city court judges, their tax collectors and many more'.[30] When the turnout for the Congressional elections that fall between the four-yearly presidential elections is often as low as 35 per cent, there is ample opportunity for any committed interest group either to win seats or to exercise influence on those running for office.

Secondly, US politics are unusual in the lack of party cohesion. Although most elections are nominally fought by Republicans and Democrats, party is rarely the force it is in Europe. In the UK, the party selects candidates, meets their election expenses, determines policy, sets the legislative agenda, and controls how elected representatives vote. Party domination is recognized by the electorate, which votes for the party rather than for the individual. In the USA, candidates need not even be loyal members of the party they purport to represent. They are chosen by those members of the electorate who wish to register as Republican or Democrat, and who are willing to turn out for a caucus or a primary election.

Consequently, the decision as to who is—and hence what is—a Republican... has been taken from the hands of the party bosses, whether at local or at state level or at federal level, and vested in local population: and this means that Democratic or Republican means just what this or that locality, in this or that year or set of circumstances, has decided they shall mean. And that varies all over the country from election to election.[31]

At local, state, and federal level, US politicians have considerable opportunities to initiate legislation. Though bills will become law only if widely supported, the ability to table proposals and ensure votes on them allows zealots to publicize their issues and to force others to take a position on them. Come the next election, legislators who refuse to support some ill-drafted piece of pet legislation can be depicted as voting against God and the family.

Although widely seen as an irritant by party managers, conservative Christian pressure groups have been courted by Republicans

[30] S. E. Finer, *Comparative Government* (Harmondsworth: Penguin, 1982), 227–8.

[31] Finer, *Comparative Government*, 228–9.

because their networks can deliver the time and money of millions of 'small people'. They are the Right's equivalent of trade unions and ethnic interest groups. The Christian Right also allowed a new way of recruiting the common people. As overt racism became unacceptable as a base for popular conservatism, socio-moral issues offered both an alternative and, to some extent, a cover. The legacy of the 1861–5 Civil War left the USA with an unusual party alignment. Though southern whites had little in common with left-wing, labourist, and ethnic-minority northern Democrats, they supported the Democratic Party because it was not the Republican Party of Abraham Lincoln. Southern dislike for the Republicans gradually waned. By the 1960s, signs of realignment were visible, and the mobilization of socio-moral conservatives by Christian Right organizations helped push that process. Because conservative Protestantism was strong in those parts of the USA that had traditionally supported the racist wing of the Democratic Party, promoting family values and attacking minority privileges were a convenient form of dog-whistle politics: sending coded messages that formally met the requirements of polite discourse while nonetheless being correctly heard by the target audience.

## Mobilized by Impotence

In taking the public presence of the Christian Right as evidence of the power of conservative religion, we may miss the more important point about protest movements: winners do not protest. The Christian Right groups of the 1940s and 1950s were tiny and insignificant, because few people saw the need for them.[32] The Moral Majority, founded by television evangelist Jerry Falwell in 1978, and the host of similar organizations came to prominence because conservative Christians were losing the arguments. Women were becoming increasingly independent. Sexual mores were becoming increasingly liberal. Christian domination of the public sphere was being eroded by the proliferation of new religious movements and by the growth of non-Christian religions, and it was being challenged by court

---

[32] S. M. Lipset and E. Raab, *The Politics of Unreason: Right-Wing Extremism in America 1790–1977* (Chicago: University of Chicago Press, 1978).

judgments that enforced the separation of church and state. Homo-sexuality was becoming acceptable; divorce commonplace. Hedonism and promiscuity were not invented by the hippies of the 1960s, but post-war affluence seriously weakened public hypocrisy.

There are two senses in which the emergence of the Christian Right represented growing strength: its support base was growing wealthier and relatively more numerous. From the 1960s, the liberal denominations declined and the conservative ones grew. This was not, as some people imagined, a matter of relative appeal. Few Epis-copalians and even fewer Congregationalists became Southern Baptists. The differences were primarily demographic: conservatives had larger families.[33] Conservative Protestants prospered with a major shift in the economic base of the USA: the rise of new industries and service enterprises in the south and west and the decline of the old metal-beating industries of the north. As they grew, they prolifer-ated schools, colleges, universities, and forms of mass media. And they lost much of their sense of cultural inferiority. That combination of American culture becoming more liberal and conservative Protes-tants becoming more self-confident was the basis for the rise of the Christian Right.

While it has strengthened the conservative wing of the Republican Party, the Christian Right has signally failed to achieve any of its spe-cific goals. Administrative action and court judgments have made abortions more difficult to obtain, but abortion has not been banned nor made unconstitutional. Far from making the lives of homosexu-als more difficult, all the legislative and judicial decisions since the founding of the Moral Majority in 1978 have been in the liberal direc-tion. In 2003, the US Supreme Court struck down a Texas law that criminalized sodomy and explicitly overruled an earlier decision that had found no general constitutional protection for sexual privacy.[34] The 2003 judgment held that intimate consensual sexual conduct was part of the liberty protected by substantive due process under the

[33] M. A. Hout, A. Greeley, and M. J. Wilde, 'The Demographic Imperative in Religious Change in the US', *American Journal of Sociology*, 107 (2001), 468–500. The debate about the sources of conservative growth is ably summarized in J. A. Mathisen, 'Tell me again: Why do Churches Grow?', *Books and Culture: A Christian Review* (2004), www.ctlibrary.com/12135/2005 (accessed 9 July 2008).

[34] Lawrence v. Texas, 539 US 558 (2003).

Fourteenth Amendment and effectively invalidated similar laws throughout the United States that criminalized sodomy between consenting same-sex adults acting in private.

There has been no significant change in the various church–state arguments that excite the Christian Right. Despite regularly changing the grounds on which the case is made (and the name: from Creationism to Creation Science to Intelligent Design), the Christian Right has failed to make it a requirement that the teaching of evolution be balanced by the Genesis version of the origin of species. Equally telling is the fate of Judge Roy Moore, the Chief Justice of the Supreme Court of Alabama and his courtroom monument of the Ten Commandments. His refusal to obey a federal court instruction to remove the monument eventually led to him being sacked in 2003 by a unanimous decision of the Court of Judiciary. The monument was removed to a separate room, where the Commandments could be read by any Christian with a poor memory.

More telling than the failure of the legislative agenda is the failure to reverse the preferences of ordinary Americans. Since 1978 the proportion of mothers of young children working full-time outside the home has gone up, not down. Divorce has become more commonplace and 'living in sin' is so common that the phrase is now passé. Women have become more, not less, prominent in public life. We may argue about the extent of patriarchy, now or in 1978, but we can be sure there is less now than there was then. There has been a slight decline in abortion, but this is almost certainly due to an improvement in contraception rather than a decline in sexual activity or conversion to the 'pro-life' position. And, far from being forced back into the closet, homosexuals are now sufficiently well accepted that popular TV series can feature gay men and women in positive roles, voters can elect gay politicians, and openly gay clergy can be elected bishops of the Episcopalian Church. Gay marriage may be some way off, but most major corporations and government bodies now extend spousal rights to gay partners.

In brief, the culture wars tell us that Americans are more polarized on these issues than Europeans and that the diffuse structure of US politics offers considerable opportunity for interest groups to promote their agendas, but those battles are ending in the same way as the less dramatic European versions.

## Secular Rules of Engagement

Finally we should note an important feature of the way in which the culture wars are being fought. Critics of the secularization paradigm sometimes point to the Christian Right as evidence that social differentiation has not marginalized religion. I draw the opposite conclusion from the same data. Perhaps the most compelling evidence that theocracy is not an option in a liberal democracy is the fact that Christian Right organizations now present their causes in secular language. They cannot say that Creation should be taught in schools because God requires it. They have to accept the primacy of secular science and argue that the Genesis account of the origins of species is as consistent with the scientific evidence as any other explanation. They cannot assert that their God dislikes divorce. They have to argue that divorce is socially dysfunctional. Legal battles over abortion are fought on the entirely secular principle that abortion infringes the universal right to life. Most conservative Christians accept that they cannot demand a privileged position for their culture on the ground that God is on their side. Instead they argue for their rights as a legitimate minority.

Some of this rhetoric may be cynical, but that such dishonesty is required is strong evidence for the marginalization of religion. With varying degrees of consciousness, most Americans seem to appreciate the practical benefits of liberalism and toleration. Some have a conscious commitment to the separation of church and state. Frank Buono is a conservative Catholic who has been pursuing through the American courts the issue of a cross on the Mojave Preserve in southern California (land managed by the National Parks service):

I want the cross on every Catholic church. I want the cross in my home. But I don't want the cross to be permanently placed on federal government public lands...It matters to me that the lands that are held in common by the United States do not become the venues for sectarian religious expressions, even of my own religious expressions.[35]

Buono is unusual in his pursuit of his principles, but many Americans have a vague sense that the separation of church and state is

---

[35] Public Broadcasting Service, 'Mojave Cross', *Religion and Ethics News Weekly*, 2 Oct. 2009, www.pbs.org/wnet/religionandethics/episodes/october-2-2009/mojave-cross/4424 (accessed 10 Oct. 2009).

useful. We see this in responses to opinion polling on the propriety of religious leaders being politically active. Surveys regularly show 66–70 per cent opposing churches endorsing candidates in elections. Ironically, given all the attention on the Christian Right, it is Black Protestants, who traditionally support the Democrats, who are most in favour of churches backing candidates. Among white Protestants, evangelicals at 68 per cent opposed are not far behind mainline Protestants at 73 per cent, and that opposition is steady across all levels of religious commitment.[36] When asked what they thought of faith-based charities receiving government funding for welfare programmes, 44 per cent were in favour, but a quarter of the sample thought it a good idea only if such programmes stayed away from religious messages. Nearly a third thought it a bad idea for the state to fund religious organizations for any purpose. Most telling were the responses to questions about public prayer in schools. Only 12 per cent of evangelicals thought that such prayers should be specifically Christian and 53 per cent of evangelicals (the same as for the general public) thought that a moment of shared silence was the best solution to the problem.[37]

## Why the USA is Different

Even allowing for the corrections suggested above, it is clearly the case that the USA is more religious than other industrial societies. If the secularization paradigm is to stand, it must be able to explain that difference in ways that are consistent with the way it explains decline elsewhere. I think it can.

### Migrants and Cultural Transition

One obvious cause of US religious vitality is mentioned surprisingly rarely: large-scale migration from non-industrial countries with

---

[36] Pew Forum on Religion and Public Life, 'Americans Wary of Church Involvement in Partisan Politics', http://pewforum.org/docs/?DocID=358 (accessed 7 June 2009).

[37] Pew Forum on Religion and Public Life, 'It's wrong to base voting on religion, say most Americans' (2001), www.pewtrusts.com (accessed 8 July 2002).

powerful conservative religious traditions. In 1998, it was estimated that one in ten of the population had been born outside the USA. Since the 1970s the most common places of origin have been Mexico, the Caribbean, and Asia.[38] Very few migrants were from Europe. Unless the migrants were untypical of their native religious cultures, they would be considerably more devout than the typical US-born American. The impact of immigration is not limited to the transfer of existing religious 'capital'. As noted in Chapter 2, one of the important social functions of organized religion is to aid migrants to make the transition from old to new world. Churches form important linkage points in allowing migrants to retain contact with elements of their old culture—their religion and their language—while allowing them to mix with earlier migrants who are better established in the new territory. Churches also gain from the role religion may play in lessening the anomie or sense of loss that many migrants suffer. To complete the comparison with the UK and Europe, we need note only that most European societies have seen little immigration and such as they have experienced has been of Muslims and Hindus, who, while they add religious capital in the sense described above, weaken rather than strengthen the local religious tradition.

## Local Consensus and National Diversity

The second major difference between the USA and other industrial democracies has already been mentioned: the federal and diffuse structure of its polity. In order to cope with its size and internal diversity, the United States has evolved systems of regulation for such matters as education and public broadcasting—two fields that are vital to the preservation of a minority world view—that are considerably more open and diffuse than the heavily centralized structures of the United Kingdom or France. In the USA it is relatively easy and inexpensive for people to start their own schools. Private schools may teach pretty much what they like, and even state schools have considerable autonomy. With the exception of the schools run by the Catholic Church and the Church of England (and the latter

[38] S. A. Camarota, 'Immigrants in the United States 1999: A Snapshot of America's Foreign-Born Population' (Center for Immigration Studies, 1999), www.cis.org (accessed 4 May 2001).

are not numerous at the secondary level), the United Kingdom has only a very small and expensive elite private-school sector. Moreover, teachers are trained in secular public universities, accredited by public agencies and paid at national wage rates. State-funded schools (which includes the church-managed ones) are constrained by a national curriculum, and even private schools are kept similar by the common class and educational background of their staff and the requirements of the examination boards that validate their qualifications.

The ability to control information and ideas is vital to the preservation of any distinctive world view and way of life. Until the invention of satellite television and the liberalization introduced by the Conservative government from 1979 to 1994, the British mass media were heavily constrained. There were only four national radio channels, all controlled by the state British Broadcasting Corporation (BBC). Until 1982, when a fourth was licensed, Britain had only three television channels, two of them run by the BBC. Even the commercial channels were heavily controlled. Individuals and organizations could not buy air time to show their own programmes, and ideological advertising was not permitted. The BBC and the commercial companies were required to provide religious broadcasting, but its content was heavily regulated so that it encompassed the broad consensus of Christian churches. As Britain has become more culturally diverse, that consensus has been broadened. Opportunities to broadcast on the BBC Radio Four's *Thought for the Day* or *Songs of Praise*, for example, are rotated around the varying religious organizations and traditions roughly in proportion to their presence in the population at large, and there is a very clear understanding that spokesmen will not provoke, criticize, or proselytize. Since the 1970s, the space given to religion has diminished, and the broadcasters now fulfil their statutory obligation to produce religious programming by having secular programme-makers make programmes *about* religion. To summarize, for most of the twentieth century British television and radio produced common-denominator religious programmes of an essentially ecumenical character. What they did not do was allow particular religious organizations or communities to produce programmes that represented their views.

We can see the importance of these different regulatory regimes if we consider the ability of US sectarians to construct their own world.

The following is a composite sketch of a fundamentalist family in Lynchburg, Virginia, constructed by mixing together three such families that I got to know well in the early 1980s. Call them Fred and Wilma. Fred was an assistant pastor in Jerry Falwell's Liberty Baptist Church; Wilma taught in the Church's independent Christian school. Their two children attended that school. On graduation one child went to Falwell's Liberty University; the other went to another religious institution, Oral Roberts University in Tulsa, Oklahoma. During the holidays the students of Liberty University helped run a fundamentalist summer camp. The church also supported a maternity home and adoption agency for unmarried mothers, a programme for reformed alcoholics, and a prison-visiting programme. Wilma's mother had an apartment in a church-run complex for 'Senior Saints', who helped out with the church bookstore and with the mailing operation that raised funds to televise Falwell's *The Old Time Gospel Hour*. The family watched Christian programmes on evangelical cable networks. The kids listened to Christian rock and country music. The family did not take a secular newspaper but subscribed to a range of weekly and monthly Christian magazines. Fred had a publication called *Christian Yellow Pages* that allowed him to make sure he purchased goods and services from like-minded fundamentalists. The family typically holidayed at a leisure complex on the South Carolina coast run by fundamentalists.

What struck me about this life was not that committed Christians spent a lot of time in church-related activities. It was that even mundane activities such as watersports were done in a fundamentalist environment. Fundamentalists in Lynchburg could inhabit a world that was fundamentalist nearly to the extent that England in the Middle Ages was Christian. They constructed a culturally homogenous society to support their fundamentalist subculture. They ensured that the outside world was seen only through a fundamentalist lens. They provided themselves with fundamentalist alternatives to secular institutions. And they had almost no positive interaction with people who were not fundamentalists.

This is the paradox that is overlooked by the rational-choice theorists discussed in the previous chapter. Diversity, if it produces a pluralistic structure for public administration and government, allows people considerable freedom to *avoid* diversity. While British Christians are offered an almost unavoidable diet of programming that openly challenges or insidiously undermines their faith, US evangelicals have been able to create a system that allows them to avoid what they do not like and produce what they do like. The parallel world of US fundamentalist institutions allows a young fundamentalist to study law at a good-quality conservative Protestant institution. The Scottish evangelical who wishes a career in law will be taught by unbelievers in a secular institution.

## Conclusion

The United States is secular in the Wilsonian sense of religion playing little part in the core operations of the social system: 'neither individuals nor institutions operate primarily to attain supernatural ends.'[39] We can go further and say that the USA is also showing signs of religion losing popularity. And within the churches there is clear evidence of the secularization of Christianity. In the style pioneered by Peale's power of positive thinking, key beliefs have been abandoned or subjectivized. The focus of faith has shifted from the next world to this one and from the glorification of God to the satisfaction of human needs. Authoritarian dogmatic beliefs have given way to a softer relativism that no longer condemns the infidel to hell. Casually describing the Christian Right as fundamentalist misses the most significant point: that it is no longer possible to promote any agenda on the grounds that God demands it be so. Those Christians who regret the secularization of their culture have no choice but to accept secular rules of political engagement and public argument.

Were it the case that the USA had become more religious over the twentieth century, we would have cause to doubt the secularization paradigm. However, we need only to explain why religion in America has been slower than its European counterparts to show signs of secularization, and we can do that in terms that are perfectly compatible with the basic themes of the secularization approach.

[39] B. R. Wilson, 'Secularization: The Inherited Model', in P. E. Hammond (ed.), *The Sacred in a Secular Age* (Berkeley and Los Angeles: University of California Press, 1985), 19.

# 9

# Secularization Elsewhere

## Introduction

The secularization paradigm in its original European setting is contentious enough. Its application elsewhere is more so because the arguments are more about the future than the past. They are more politics than history, and highly partisan politics at that. Conceptual clarity is not promoted by the frequent confusion of the political agenda of secularism and the social processes of secularization. For example, one scholar blames Western social science for the damage done to Ethiopia by the Marxist Derg, which ruled from 1974 to 1991. The leaders of the Derg justified their oppressive actions on the secularist grounds that 'the process of modernization requires a dismissal of any traditional religious commitments that do not comport with a scientific, naturalistic, enlightened worldview'; therefore the secularization paradigm is to blame.[1]

Anthropologist Talal Asad has a more sophisticated reason for slipping between secularism as a project and secularization as an often inadvertent process.[2] He challenges the scientific neutrality of

---

[1] W. N. Brisett, 'Secularization in the Global South: The Case of Ethiopia', *Hedgehog Review* (Spring/Summer 2006), 147–51.

[2] T. Asad, *Genealogies of Religion: Discipline and Reasons of Power in Christianity and Islam* (Baltimore: Johns Hopkins University Press, 1993). For sympathetic commentaries, see D. Scott and C. Hirschkind (eds), *Powers of the Secular Modern: Talal Asad and his Interlocutors* (Stanford: Stanford University Press, 2006).

the secularization paradigm by imputing to the process as a whole the motives of some key agents of change. Michel Foucault pioneered a curiously popular way of discovering the meaning to social phenomena.[3] First, like the genealogy snob who claims the one aristocratic ancestor while overlooking the thousand non-noble predecessors, Foucault constructs a very selective history of some idea. Then he assumes that, like original sin, whatever motivates the initial action or idea must pervade any current expression of it. Thus for Asad secularization is an anti-religious French Revolution ideal (that is, it is really secularism) and all current expressions of secularization, even if motivated by quite different concerns, share in the original offence. As he denies the possibility of non-normative social science, what should be an argument about the accuracy of the descriptions and explanations involved in the secularization paradigm is sidetracked into a partisan argument about the desirability of particular social arrangements.[4] Chapter 2 should have made clear the differences between secularism and the sociological account of secularization. That secularism played some, often small, part in secularization does not mean they are the same.

Paul Collier, an Oxford economist who has worked for the World Bank, divides the world into three blocs. One is the billion or so people in the developed world. The remaining five billion people in the world divide between four billion or so in countries such as China, Brazil, and India that are experiencing growth and prosperity and *The Bottom Billion*: the inhabitants of some fifty or so failing states whose circumstances worsen.[5] This chapter is concerned with what the second and third of Collier's blocs can tell us about the plausibility of the social-scientific hypothesis that modernization erodes the power, prestige, and popularity of religion.

---

[3] M. Foucault, *The Birth of the Clinic* (London: Routledge, 1994); *Discipline and Punish* (Harmondsworth: Penguin, 1991).

[4] Similar views can be found in the contributions to G. B. Levey and T. Modood (eds), *Secularism, Religion and Multicultural Citizenship* (Cambridge: Cambridge University Press, 2009).

[5] P. Collier, *The Bottom Billion: Why the Poorest Countries are Failing and What Can Be Done about It* (Oxford: Oxford University Press, 2007).

## Applying the Paradigm

If modernization caused the secularization of the West in the sense that heating a metal caused its expansion, we should see the process repeating. We take each of the countries of Central and Latin America or Africa and assess to what extent they have become modern and to what extent they have become secular. Unfortunately the social world is not the physicist's laboratory. Demerath neatly delineates the problem by distinguishing four different types of secularization, based on the interaction of two principles: the extent to which secularization is internal or external, and directed or non-directed.[6] First there is what Demerath calls *emergent* secularization. This is the series of changes that occurred in the West and is described in Chapter 2: internally produced, largely unintended, and very slow to occur. Secularization may also be internal but, in the second case, *directed* or imposed. Good examples are provided by Turkey under Kemal Atatürk, the Soviet Union after the 1917 Revolution, and China after the victory of Mao's communists. Atatürk's Hat Law of 1925, which banned the wearing of the fez because of its association with the defunct Ottoman Empire, was a small but potent symbol of his determination to create a modern secular democracy by imposing the structural differentiation and privatization of religion that he took to be one of the causes of the West's success.

Demerath's third and fourth types of secularization are external in origin. As the name suggests, *imperialist* secularization is deliberately imposed while *diffused* secularization is the result of imitation and emulation. As one of its measures to weaken Japan after the August 1945 surrender, the USA, as the imperial occupying power, deliberately reduced the power of state Shinto, stripped the Emperor of his divine status, and introduced a secular constitution. In the countries of the Warsaw Pact, the Soviet Union 'encouraged' its partner communist parties to marginalize the churches and to create alternatives to religious rituals and ceremonies. Demerath's fourth

---

[6] N. J. Demerath III, 'Secularization and Sacralization Deconstructed and Reconstructed', in J. A. Beckford and N. J. Demerath III (eds), *The Sage Handbook of the Sociology of Religion* (London: Sage, 2007), 57–80.

type of secularization involves diffusion: the spread of innovations from one society to another by emulation. Even when more secular countries take no part in the affairs of less secular ones, they can still, as the West did for Atatürk, act as a model.

Designations of changes as external or internal, and imposed or enthusiastically sought, are often contentious because key actors use the explanation in promoting or resisting it. For example, it suits the Iranian fundamentalists who campaign against 'occidentosis' to present any change as externally imposed. They can then portray political reformers (no matter what their inspiration) as traitors guilty of treason.[7]

Demerath's distinctions are artificially simple. The coercive secularization of the communist USSR or China was internally imposed, but it was inspired by Marxism: a secularist ideology created in the West. The spread of the language of human rights, with its guarantee of religious liberty, may be read as an example of diffused secularization, but there is an imperial element to it in that the Western powers have made at-least-rhetorical acceptance of such language a prerequisite for international acceptance. Nonetheless, the distinctions are useful because they remind us of the crucial difference between what is discussed here and the subject of Chapter 2: the secularization of the First World prevents secularization elsewhere following the same course because imposition, emulation, and resistance are now possible. Or, to put it another way, while the first societies to secularize could experience only emergent secularization, the rest can experience all four types.

## Modernization

Before discussing a selection of the changes in the religious cultures of various developing countries, I want to dampen enthusiasm for using the vitality of religion outside the West as rebuttal of the secularization paradigm. First, 'modern' means more than just 'extant'. All the world has changed, but not all change is modernization. Some

---

[7] G. Tazmini, *Khatami's Iran: The Islamic Republic and the Turbulent Path to Reform* (London: Tauris, 2009).

fragments of affluent culture—football, Coca-Cola, mobile phones—are ubiquitous, but much of sub-Saharan Africa and Asia remains agrarian, and, as Collier shows, many nations are as poor as they were when they gained their independence in the early 1960s.[8] In the 1930s, when the attentions of pioneering anthropologist Edward Evans-Pritchard made them famous, the Nuer of southern Sudan were a pastoralist people whose way of life had changed little for centuries.[9] That they now have jeeps and Kalashnikov rifles tells us that their world has changed, but it has not been as a result of the sort of modernization we expect to produce secularization. Over half the population of Morocco—just 9 miles from Europe—now lives in cities, but an almost equal proportion is uneducated and illiterate.[10] In some countries the Wahbenzi (so-called because of their fondness for Mercedes-Benz limos, preferably in a cavalcade) have prospered but left the majority little better off in absolute terms and relatively deprived. And, for some unfortunates, the combination of great potential wealth and a weak state has produced the opposite of development. However one describes and explains the current condition of the mineral-rich Democratic Republic of Congo, plundered by a succession of corrupt rulers and invaded by all its neighbours, it would be difficult to say that it has modernized in any sense that might test the secularization paradigm.[11]

A further reason for caution is that such modernization as we do find is often very recent. If we suppose that structural differentiation weakens ambient religion, that the combination of individualism, egalitarianism, and diversity undermines religious certainty, and that the spread of effective technology increases what Martin calls a sense of 'mastery over fate', we must expect the secularizing impact of modernization to be slow. In Britain, for example, these changes

[8] Collier, *Bottom Billion*.

[9] E. E. Evans-Pritchard, *The Nuer* (Oxford: Clarendon Press, 1940); *Nuer Religion* (Oxford: Clarendon Press, 1956).

[10] S. Hegasy, '"Fourteen Kilometres from Europe": Islam and Globalization in Morocco', in in M. Rieger (ed.), *What the World Believes: Analyses and Commentary on the Religion Monitor 2008* (Gutersloh: Verag Bertelsmann Stiftung, 2009), 257–70.

[11] K. Hock, 'The Omnipresence of the Religious: Religiosity in Nigeria', in Rieger (ed.), *What the World Believes*, 271–300, regards Nigeria's religious vitality and prosperity compared to its neighbours as proof that the secularization paradigm is wrong. The comparison seems hollow when one realizes that Nigeria's GDP is less now than it was in 1950.

were evident in the eighteenth century—more than a full century before we saw church adherence start to decline. Add to that two important features of the European situation. First, the reduction of religious commitment tends to be generational. Secondly, as Voas argues, changes in individual belief and behaviour tend to be gradual, with a considerable period of 'fuzzy fidelity' between the religious and the secular. Brazil may be close in many aspects of modernization to the European timeline, but many developing and non-developing countries are only three generations away from the first serious encounter with the modern.

I do not want to suggest that we can learn nothing about the secularization paradigm from the non-Western world. The point is that, even if only Demerath's emergent secularization was in play, we would as yet expect to see little sign of it. But, of course, the reality is far more complex, because in a wide variety of ways the political powers of the West (and their culture) intrude on the rest of the world in ways that hasten some elements of secularization but retard others.

## Major Trends

With these reservations, we can turn to a sample of religious trends, which I have chosen because they show the wide variety of religious responses to tentative modernization. Two observations have widespread application, and these will be made first.

In the most minimal sense, there has been widespread secularization at the level of government and constitution. Iran and Pakistan declare themselves to be Islamic Republics, but all the other countries discussed below are formally secular. There is, of course, still much government interference in religion, especially where religioethnic minorities are seen as potential threats to the stability of the state: China is an example. But generally governments do not claim divine mandates.[12]

---

[12] Jonathan Fox has constructed a detailed and sophisticated model of various forms of government interference in religion (J. Fox, *A World Survey of Religion and the States* (Cambridge: Cambridge University Press, 2008).

Although most societies show a degree of social-structural differentiation—in the relative autonomy of the economy, legal system, and polity, for example—theoretical separation is not the key element in the link between modernization and secularization. The presumed effective cause is religion's loss of salience and contact. The less religious institutions do, and, the more that the secular state does, the less acquaintance people will have with religious culture and the less their faith will be implicitly reinforced. As we will see in the discussion of Africa, for example, many governments in the developing world have been unable to provide effective state education, health, and welfare systems. If the only form of education available to many people is the madrassa or Quran school, we cannot expect notional structural differentiation to have significantly changed the level of ambient religion.

## Asia

China and Japan raise an interesting question about the limits of the secularization paradigm. In the standard account, diversity weakens religion by making everyone a heretic (that is, aware that they are choosing God, rather than the other way round) and by encouraging relativism. Those two things are a problem, because Christianity is monotheistic and exclusivist and lays great store on doctrine. That other people think differently is a threat, because the religion is predicated on the idea that there is one truth that we must believe in. Richard Madsen notes that millions of temples have been built or rebuilt in the Chinese countryside by people who would 'be hard-pressed to give a consistent and coherent account of the Daoist or Buddhist philosophies that one might think were behind this revival'.[13] Apparently what they want is a place for shared ritual. Ditto for Chinese Catholics, many of whom are sceptical about doctrines, do not regularly pray, and do not follow the socio-moral teachings of their church, but nonetheless want to be buried with Catholic funeral rituals. 'Collective ritual, in this and many Asian contexts, comes before personal faith, as do collective myths—stories about gods or

[13] R. Madsen, 'Embedded Religion in Asia', *The Immanent Frame* (2009), http://blogs.ssrc.org/tif/2009/02/09/embedded-religion-in-asia (accessed 14 Mar. 2010).

spirits or blessed events such as apparitions, healings, or miraculous occurrences.'[14]

Winston Davis makes a related point with the term 'theological nonchalance'.[15] In Japan, elements of Buddhism, Confucianism, and Shinto form a web of culture in which it is difficult to separate the sacred and profane and in which many people live without feeling the need to commit themselves exclusively to one particular theology: hence, 'in Japan, where praxis, aesthetics, and feelings are the core of religion, the problem of secularization can be more fruitfully studied by examining changing religious customs rather than by dilating on the decline of religious beliefs'.[16] If theological nonchalance is at all common, a key element of the secularization paradigm is rendered somewhat irrelevant.

However, Davis does accept that 'educated, middle-class Japanese seem to entertain fewer specific religious ideas, and commit themselves to religious institutions with less enthusiasm than do their counterparts in the country',[17] and we can speculate as to how long a culture can display indifference to core ideas before that lack of enthusiasm undermines what Davis summarized as 'the praxis, the aesthetics and the feelings'. It is difficult to see how rituals can survive for many generations without people nurturing the beliefs that make those rituals any more important than a well-choreographed dance routine or an infantry platoon's drill routine. After all, Tai Chi is now enjoyed as an exercise programme by many in the West who have no interest in its supernatural justifications or purposes. That is, while the distinction between orthodox and orthoprax religions is useful, a religious culture that stresses praxis still requires some sort of supernatural 'doxy' to prevent it from becoming secularized.

Although the conflict between the Chinese government and the Uighur population in the West and the Tibetans shows that religion remains alive and well when it is embedded in competing ethnic interests, both China and Japan show signs of religious cultures 'secularizing' in the sense of becoming more individualistic in

---

[14] Madsen, 'Embedded Religion in Asia'.
[15] I am grateful to Robert Hefner for drawing this to my attention.
[16] W. Davis, *Japanese Religion and Society: Paradigms of Structure and Change* (Albany, NY: State University of New York Press, 1992), 250.
[17] Davis, *Japanese Religion*, 251.

epistemology and more therapeutic in orientation. It is not easy to characterize Falun Gong. Leaving aside the Chinese government's interest in depicting it as politically radical, we still have a choice between stressing its traditional mix of psycho-medicine and beliefs about the spirit worlds and an alternative interpretation of it as a modern rewriting of tradition that empowers the individual for entirely this-worldly purposes. Much the same could be said for a large variety of new religious movements that have been created in Japan since 1945. The best known of these, Soka Gakkai, has reduced the teaching of Buddhism to an undemanding formula that promises that chanting a short phrase will deliver inner peace and desired material goods. Soka Gakkai's website describes it as a 'practical philosophy of individual empowerment and inner transformation that enables people to develop themselves and take responsibility for their lives'.[18]

Although Arabs created Islam, they now form only some 15 per cent of the world's Muslims. Indonesia has the largest Muslim population. The state that General Sukarno's 1945 rebellion against colonial rule created is a vast amalgam of some 150 linguistic groups: 3,000 miles east to west. Although majority Muslim, Indonesia's military rulers aimed to create a new 'sacred canopy' for their new country. *Pancasila* or the Five Principles claimed to unite all the monotheisms and the indigenous Javanese religious traditions. Although Indonesians might express their belief in God in the manner of their particular religion, atheism and agnosticism were outlawed. Despite considerable state resources being put into its promotion, *Pancasila* never diverted Indonesians from their primary religious commitments, and since the 1990s Muslims have become increasingly assertive in demanding that Islam be given pride of place in the operations of the state, and religio-ethnic violence has become increasingly common and severe.

Indonesia is important because, as Robert Hefner suggests, it offers a better site for considering Islam's response to modernization than the Middle East or Afghanistan.[19] Fundamentalism attracts most attention but it is not the main current in the Islamic world. What is much more prevalent is what he calls 'religionification'—a process

---

[18] www.sgi-uk.org (accessed 12 Dec. 2009).
[19] The following remarks are from my notes of three delightful lectures Robert Hefner gave at the UCSIA summer school in 2009.

that has some parallels with the Protestant Reformation in sixteenth-century Europe. There are two elements. The institutions of Islam are becoming more formal, and teaching and rituals are being standardized. There is also a discernible change in the individual's relationship to the religious culture. Casual and occasional participation in an easy-going all-pervasive religious culture, often demonstrated through adherence to local saint cults, is being replaced by the model of the believing well-informed active Muslim.

Whether the process of Muslims becoming individually more literately and thoughtfully 'religious' will be followed, as it was in Protestant Europe in the nineteenth and twentieth centuries, by people becoming more assertive and selective remains to be seen. Although Indonesia is more prosperous and stable than many post-1945 states, it has not yet established a culture of political democracy that ensures the peaceful resolution of internal conflicts. Primarily ethnic disputes over, for example, government-sponsored population movements easily acquire a religious dimension and thus encourage people to continue to see their faith as an important part of their ethnic identity. That is, the exterminate-the-aliens option that many European states tried before settling to tolerate diversity has not yet been completely eliminated.

## Latin America

As the name suggests, Latin America was until the 1960s overwhelmingly Catholic Christian. Since then a Protestant Reformation has been sweeping the continent, as large numbers have converted to evangelical or Pentecostal Protestantism. The picture is varied. Between 20 and 30 per cent of the people of Guatemala are now Protestant, the vast majority Pentecostal. About 20 per cent of Brazilians are Protestant, about two-thirds Pentecostal. At the low end, only 5 per cent of Uruguayans are Protestant.[20]

The rapid growth of Pentecostalism is often presented as a rebuttal of the secularization paradigm, but there is another plausible

[20] These data come from P. Freston, 'Religious Change and Economic Development in Latin America', www.bezinningscentrum.nl/Religion_Development/PaulFreston1.pdf (accessed 24 Nov. 2009).

interpretation. David Martin[21] and others see the shift from a shared communal organic Catholicism, in which the laity play little part, to a lay-led individualistic personal faith, as demonstrating many parallels with the growth of Methodism in Britain in the late eighteenth and early nineteenth centuries. The explanation is largely functional. The shift from a rural agrarian economy based on the organic community of the village and the hacienda to an urban industrial economy undermined the old social ties and created a demand for a new kind of persona: the self-reliant self-directed individual. Pentecostalism also fits well with the growing assertiveness of women and the demands for gender equality. Although it is patriarchal in its rhetoric, Pentecostalism's critique of the sexual irresponsibility and wastefulness of machismo culture makes it popular with women.[22] In the sense of encouraging personal autonomy and self-direction, 'Pentecostalism is not generally a reaction against modernization but rather a manifestation of it'.[23] In Britain, Methodism and related sectarian alternatives to the national churches grew for a century before starting to decline. It may be that the same cycle in Latin America will be shorter.

Finally, there is evidence of single-step disaffiliation from Christianity. Freston notes: 'Despite the increasing social flexibility of Pentecostalism, there are good reasons for thinking that its current headlong growth will reach a ceiling within the next two or three decades. In both Brazil and Chile, only half of those ceasing to call themselves Catholic convert to Protestantism.'[24]

## Sub-Saharan Africa

About a third of the people of sub-Saharan Africa are Muslim. Most of the rest are Christian—generally Catholic, Anglican, Presbyterian, or Methodist, depending on which missionary society provided the initial stimulus to conversion. From the 1920s there was a variety of

[21] D. Martin, *Tongues of Fire: Explosion of Protestantism in Latin America* (Oxford: Blackwell, 1993).
[22] E. Brusco, *The Reformation of Machismo: Evangelical Conversion and Gender in Columbia* (Austin: University of Texas Press, 1993).
[23] Freston, 'Religious Change', 6.     [24] Freston, 'Religious Change', 7.

'Spirit-filled' churches—the Aladura churches in western Nigeria, for example—that filtered pre-Christian African belief in healing and witchcraft through the filter of American Pentecostalism.[25] But such alternatives to the European traditions were rare until the late 1960s, when American television evangelists such as Kenneth Copeland inspired a new generation of entrepreneurial pastors with his 'prosperity gospel'.[26]

Although physical and psychological healing remained part of the repertoire of the new Pentecostal churches, they also promised relief from poverty. According to the Gospel of Matthew (19: 29), Christ promised: 'And every one that hath forsaken houses, or brethren, or sisters, or father, or mother, or wife, or children, or lands, for my name's sake, shall receive an hundredfold, and shall inherit everlasting life.' The prosperity gospel takes this literally: God wants us to be rich, only a lack of faith holds us back, and gifts given to God (well, to his earthly representative) will be returned multiplied by 100. One might imagine the dire economies of Africa and the spread of HIV/AIDS would be powerful refutation of what its critics deride as the 'health and wealth' gospel, but Pentecostalism does, in a roundabout way, work. Churches sometimes attract funding from American sponsors. More importantly, pastors visibly prosper, as their large congregations donate a tenth of their incomes. And, although the opportunities for Weberian entrepreneurs are fewer in Ghana or Zambia than they were in colonial America, the puritanism of some Pentecostal churches helps adherents harbour their scant resources and offers some protection against AIDS.

As in the Latin American case, we can see some elements of Pentecostalism in Africa—the more middle-class churches—as a modernizing adaptation of the religious culture: the self-directed and goal-setting member of a voluntary association replacing the passive individual in a communal organic community. But, as Paul Gifford argues, much of the appeal is very different. Pentecostal churches are exploding because the mainline churches are now so secularized that they do not attempt to cater for the religious problems of Africans.

---

[25] A. Hastings, *The Church in Africa: 1450–1950* (Oxford: Clarendon Press, 1994), 513–18.

[26] S. Brouwer, P. Gifford, and S. D. Rose, *Exporting the American Gospel: Global Christian Fundamentalism* (London: Routledge, 1996), 151–78.

The Catholic Church is so busy clearing slums and laying drains and educating people that, for people who see their main problems as the spiritual forces acting on them, the Catholic Church offers no solutions at all. Pentecostal churches reverse the curses, neutralize the witchcraft, break the spells, and exorcize the evil spirits that are blocking people's destiny.[27] And the organic community is not far away. As the ease with which some African countries have fallen into brutal tribal conflict shows, there is a great deal of diversity but there is little of the individualism and egalitarianism that, in the West, combined with diversity to undermine dogmatism and cause people gradually to evolve a more liberal, tolerant, and ecumenical version of their faith. Periodically African peoples have displayed the pre-modern response to 'the other': expulsion, murder, and mass rape.[28] The bitter conflict between Hutis and Tutsis in Rwanda and Burundi suggests an attitude very far from that which, in Chapter 2, was offered as a driver for first tolerance and then relativism and finally indifference to one's faith.

We can also note that an important part of the appeal of religious organizations is their ability to fill the gap left by the failure of successive governments to create stable institutions for delivering health care, social support, and education. Many African governments are now less effective than they were at the point of independence. Although there is formal socio-structural differentiation, in practice the churches (and, for Muslims, mosques and Sufi orders) remain central to most people's well-being because there is little else that works.

Finally we can note that most sub-Saharan African states also lack the components of the rationalization part of the secularization explanation. Education is rare, science hardly a feature of the culture, and there is little or no technological production.

---

[27] P. Gifford, *Christianity, Politics and Public Life in Kenya* (London: Hurst, 2009), 46–54.

[28] It is common for scholars of a left-leaning persuasion to claim that Western rationalism or capitalism is responsible for 'othering'. Edward Said makes that case in his *Orientalism* (Harmondsworth: Penguin, 1995). The obvious riposte is that, the Nazi treatment of the Jews aside, the xenophobia of modern rationalistic capitalist Western Europe rarely matches the brutality common in the Middle Ages. The 'discipline' that Foucault despises is generally nicer than pre-modern indiscipline.

## The Middle East

As the rise of Islamic fundamentalism is routinely presented as refutation of the secularization paradigm, it is worth stressing that no Middle Eastern country was secular before the 1979 Iranian Revolution, the 1981 assassination of President Sadat of Egypt, or the 1990s career of Osama Bin Laden brought radical Islam to our attention. There was a superficial secularity at an elite level in those states taken over by army officers. Egypt, Syria, and Iraq briefly espoused the ideology of secular Arab nationalism, but Ba'athism was short lived. It was (and still is) common for wealthy Arabs to wear their faith very lightly: conforming in public but deviating abroad and in the privacy of their own homes. But the majority of people in the Arab and North African countries of the former Ottoman empire remained relatively pious Muslims.

Islamic fundamentalism is a response to unpopular change by religious people rather than the conversion of secular people to religion. The explanation of fundamentalism is complex, with important local variations, but the basic themes are simple enough. In the West industrialization took centuries and the accompanying social changes were slow, but even they generated enough periods of political conflict. In many of the newly independent states carved out of the Ottoman Empire development was rapid and chaotic and its benefits unevenly distributed. It disrupted traditional social orders and raised expectations of economic prosperity that could not be met. It is not an accident that militant movements recruit from the ranks of the educated and the urban.[29] The massive expansion of further and higher education in many developing countries produces more professional workers than the economy can employ. The frustrated then seek scapegoats for their condition and secularization is a convenient target. Unstable governments were frequently replaced and progressive regimes that first alienated the conservative economic, political, and religious elites then alienated the progressive elements of the population by becoming authoritarian.

---

[29] Roy has noted parallels between the support for transnational Islamism and the support for the radicalism of Paris 1968 (O. Roy, *Globalized Islam: The Search for a New Ummah* (London: Hurst, 2004) ).

Often people were confronted in one generation with changes that took centuries to occur in the West: the creation of polities based on a universal franchise, for example, or the granting of equal rights to women. Such rapid change inevitably provoked opposition when the rewards were meagre or unevenly distributed. It is not hard to imagine that opposition to the Shah of Iran's White Revolution in the 1960s and 1970s would have been much weaker if those who lost power and status under the old order had been rewarded with larger economic and political gains under the new. What destroyed the Shah (in addition to his dependence on outside force) was the failure of change to deliver benefits large enough to make it worthwhile.

Among the many differences between the modernization of the West and the twentieth-century changes in the Muslim Middle East is the relative absence of any great need for religious toleration: most states are homogenously Muslim.[30] Also absent is one key condition for the emergence of a notion of the individual separate from his or her religious identity. As I argued in Chapter 2, in the West the acceptance that people had a right to be wrong about God came in the context of states and governments strong enough to survive without requiring that all subjects or citizens share a common faith. In the absence of any perceived internal need for religious tolerance (or an inegalitarian unwillingness to see the need), fragile states tended to look for more, not less, religious legitimation. When the military dictators of Pakistan found themselves threatened by revolt, they played the Green card, which, given the enduring conflict with India, was always popular. In the latter days of his regime, Saddam Hussein cynically burnished his Islamic credentials to ward off dissent. The military rulers of Egypt alternated between encouraging and repressing the Muslim Brotherhood, depending on their perceived need for new bases of popular support.

One further element of the 'emergent secularization' explained in Chapter 2 was also rare in the Muslim countries that have produced the strongest fundamentalist movements: effective structural differentiation. In the West, the emergence of such distinct relatively autonomous spheres as the economy, the law, the polity, education,

---

[30] The sort of toleration being discussed here should not be confused with the Ottoman model of permitting a degree of social and cultural independence to 'blocs'.

and social welfare was gradual. In the successors to the Ottoman Empire, a degree of structural differentiation was imposed by the British and the French or was adopted by local rulers, but religious institutions remained much more central to large parts of life. One particular example, which had considerable consequences, was the inability of the nascent states to replace the religious obligations to give alms (usually to or via religious bodies) by a secular obligation to pay taxes to the state. This meant that, unless there was oil or a populace wealthy enough for sales tax to be effective (and the two combine in the Arab Emirates), governments could provide only the most rudimentary education, health, and social welfare, and religious associations were able to perform important social functions that in the West are generally secular. One of the reasons for the success of the Muslim Brotherhood in Egypt, Hamas in the Gaza Strip, and Hezbollah in southern Lebanon is the ability of such movements to provide (not always on a voluntary basis) the services that the Christian churches provided in agrarian societies in Western Europe.

One feature of the Middle East that keeps religion at the heart of politics and that has no parallel in modernizing Europe is the presence of, and reaction to, the state of Israel. Over its course, the Arab–Israeli conflict has gradually become more religious. In 1914, about 40 per cent of the area now covered by Israel, Palestine, Egypt, Jordan, Lebanon, Syria, Iraq, and Turkey was Christian. Mass emigration has reduced that, so that probably less than 2 per cent of those who live in the Palestinian territories are Christians. The 1979 Islamic revolution in Iran both inspired and funded radical Islamic movements elsewhere in the region. Hamas, which developed from the local Muslim Brotherhood, displaced the secular Palestinian Liberation Organziation in the Gaza Strip. Hezbollah displaced the secular Amal as the main Shi'ite militia in Lebanon and gained considerable local credibility from its war against Israeli in southern Lebanon. The success of Israel in defeating Arab forces in 1948 and 1967 was once seen as a blow to Arab prestige. Now it is widely seen as an insult against Islam. Muslim fundamentalists see the destruction of Israel, which not only represents a wrong religion but is also a surrogate for the crusader USA, as a primary policy goal. That at least a third of the originally displaced Palestinians were Christians has not stopped the plight of the Palestinians becoming an internationally popular cause with jihadi Muslims.

International politics brings me to my final point about Islam in the Middle East and modernization. The contrast between Muslim countries and Latin America and sub-Saharan Africa highlights an important consideration. A religious response to social dislocation was possible because the imams and ayatollahs had been the losers in, not the promoters of, social change. This left them free to sound an authentic note of dissent. Their hand was strengthened because they could offer a consistent explanation of problems. The West was Christian. The problems of Lebanon or Egypt or Iran—and we can add Pakistan here—were caused by Christian interference or by local leaders emulating Christianity. Identifying the Crusaders as the source of all problems also provided the solution: the imposition of a radical puritanical Islam. In Latin America and sub-Saharan Africa, Christianity formed a bond with the West, and the large number of local indigenous religions could not provide the base for anti-Western sentiment, because they were each tiny and offered no grand vision of an alternative society. So, although there was some promotion of indigenous religions, the main religious response to modernization was to embrace a more 'modern' version of Christianity that was partly funded and heavily promoted by American churches.

In brief, the rapid social change that the Middle East has experienced weakened the traditional religious culture and institutions. One possible reaction (and it competes with three others: Hefner's 'religionization', membership of revived Sufi cults, and increasing indifference to religion) is radical Islamism. Which brings me to one final thought. Though fundamentalism clearly has considerable appeal as a movement of opposition, it is not at all clear that it has a viable long-term future. Since 1979, when the Iranian Revolution took over the Shah's repressive state institutions, the ayatollahs have had vastly more power over their people than Cromwell's Puritans had in England during the Civil War. They also had the loyalty-inducing war with Iraq to cement their position. Yet, thirty years after Khomeini came to power, Iran is now deeply divided, with many young people seeking greater freedom from religious control.

## The Bigger Picture

The world outside Western Europe is vastly complex. Societies differ enormously in religious tradition, political history, and level and type of economic development. It is tempting to conclude that, even if it offers a convincing account of Europe's past, the secularization paradigm offers little clue as to what is now occurring in the rest of the world. However, there is an alternative to the country-by-country and religion-by-religion case study. We can perhaps regain some enthusiasm for grand narratives by considering the results of the largest exercise in comparative empirical social science: the World Values Survey (WVS). Led by Ronald Inglehart, the WVS has carried out representative national surveys of beliefs and values in four sweeps between 1981 and 2001. The first surveyed twenty-two European countries and later sweeps broadened the base to fifty-six nations. Pooling the data allows the analysis of over a quarter of a million respondents.

To explore the relationship between modernization and religion, Norris and Inglehart construct a variety of measures of religiosity: frequency of religious participation, frequency of prayer, stated importance of religion, and claimed belief in heaven, hell, life after death, and souls. They then classify the religious culture of each society in the WVS as Eastern, Muslim, Orthodox, Protestant, or Roman Catholic. They also construct a variety of measures of modernization and human development. In the simplest presentation of the data, societies are divided by the nature of their characteristic economic activity: agrarian, industrial, and post-industrial (by which they mean the provision of services being more important than the manufacture of material objects). There is a clear and straightforward connection between the type of society and all the measures of religiosity. For example, the proportion of the population that attends church (or the equivalent) at least weekly is 44 per cent for agrarian, 25 for industrial, and 20 for post-industrial societies. Those who 'pray each day' declines from 52 per cent in agrarian to 34 in industrial to 26 in post-industrial societies. A similar gradient is found for all measures, with a considerable drop from agrarian to industrial and then a smaller drop from industrial to post-industrial. 'By any of these measures, therefore, religious participation, values and beliefs remain widespread in poorer developing nations, but today they engage less than the majority of the publics in the most affluent post-industrial societies.'[31] So far, this is what the secularization paradigm has argued.

---

[31] P. Norris and R. Inglehart, *Sacred and Secular: Religion and Politics Worldwide* (Cambridge: Cambridge University Press, 2004), 59.

Norris and Inglehart then correlate measures of religiosity with two measures of modernization: the UNDP Human Development Index (which combines income, literacy, education, and longevity) and a narrower measure of economic development (based on the proportion of people living in urban areas and the GINI coefficient of income inequality). The correlations are strong: 'The extent to which sacred or secular orientations are present in a society can be predicted by any of those basic indicators of human development with a remarkable degree of accuracy, even if we know nothing further about the country.'[32]

The analysis is pursued with increasingly sophisticated statistical modelling. Taking the aggregate level of religious participation in each of fifty-six societies as the thing to be explained, the Human Development Index and the GINI coefficient scores explain 46 per cent of the variation: a strong result considering the measurement error built into a project as complex as the WVS. Other analyses produce further support for the idea that modernization reduces religiosity. However, there is a demographic sting in the tail.

Despite modernization being associated with a decline in religiosity, the world has recently become more, not less religious, because the most modern and hence least religious people have fewer children. Between 1975 and 1997, the twenty-five most secular societies in Norris and Inglehart's survey had an annual population growth rate less than half that of the twenty-four most religious: 0.7 to 2.2 per cent.[33] Norris and Inglehart are clearly right about the immediate future, but it is difficult to draw firm conclusions about the longer term because it is difficult to predict the economic changes that bear on fertility rates or the cultural changes that, even in a conservatively religious society, will encourage women to restrict fertility.

[32] Norris and Inglehart, *Sacred and Secular*, 61. These results are supported by other survey work. The 2002 Pew Global Attitudes survey of 44 nations and the Gallup International Millennium study of 60 countries found a similar strong inverse relationship between religiosity and development (Pew Research Center for the People and the Press, 'Among Wealthy Nations, US Stands Alone in its Embrace of Religion', 19 Dec. 2002, http://people-press.org/reorts/display.php3? ReportID=167 (accessed 7 Mar. 2003); Gallup International, 'Religion in the World at the End of the Millennium' (2000), www.gallup-international.com/survey15. htm (accessed 12 Mar. 2003)).

[33] Norris and Inglehart, *Sacred and Secular*, 234.

### The Explanation: Purpose versus Plausibility

We can have many technical reservations about Norris and Ingle-hart's analysis of the WVS data, but I am more interested in their explanation for secularization, because it allows me to clarify what, if anything, is distinctive about my own approach.[34]

Norris and Inglehart explain the deleterious impact of moderniza-tion on religious belief and practice via the notion of existential security: 'societies become less responsive to the appeals of the meta-physical world when people's lives are lifted out of dire poverty and its life-threatening risks, and life in this world becomes more secure.'[35] That is entirely plausible, but it is a guess, because none of their survey data bears directly on the issue: the WVS does not ask people why they are religious, nor does it directly ask how secure or insecure people feel. It is also a guess that is barely elaborated. It is not clear whether the imagined causal link is protection or compensation. Do those whose lives are poor, nasty, brutish, and short seek to enlist the practical assistance of the deities now or do they seek their rewards in heaven or in a better rebirth?

Monocausal theories of the origins or purposes of religion are notoriously difficult. When they are specific, as in Karl Marx's drug-dealer view of the divine, they are patently false. When they are broad, as in Rodney Stark and William S. Bainbridge's compensators theory, they are vacuous. I prefer to avoid the issues of origins, take the fact of religion as given, and try to explain why its popularity varies in a way that can encompass a wide variety of propositions about the functions or purposes of religion. I assume that popularity is largely, though not necessarily entirely, a reflection of belief and hence, if we turn from the attitudes of adherents to characteristics of the system, a matter of the plausibility of key ideas. Even if we explain the popularity of religious rituals by their social benefits, it seems reasonable to assume that most of those involved to some consider-able extent believe in the ideas that inform the rituals. We can

---

[34] For those who like to locate their theorists, what follows is pretty much a rewriting in a Bergerian/Schutzian mode of the functionalist tendencies in Wilson's approach.

[35] Norris and Inglehart, *Sacred and Secular*, 71.

imagine that some people are just going through the motions or merely conforming, but widespread fictions cannot be maintained. In Belfast I had a Jewish friend who attended prayers though he was an agnostic. He attended to make up the quorum, so that the believers could have their prayer meeting. Had only a minority actually believed, the meetings would not have gone ahead, and my friend would not have felt obliged to pretend to something he did not actually believe. Furthermore, while some secondary benefits of religious involvement might be enjoyed by people who did not actually believe, most religions confine the key benefits to believers. The prayers of the faithful will be answered; the prayers of the person going through the motions will not.

We can arrive at the same point by considering the importance of social interpretation. Whether or not something has worked often involves a considerable degree of interpretation. An adherent of Soka Gakkai chants for a car. She does not get it and continues to cycle to work. She is disappointed but is then diagnosed with a mild heart condition and is assured by her doctor that her regular exercise was vital in preventing the problem becoming dangerous. So the chanting really worked! Strong faith can often allow the true believers to find victory where observers see only failure.

If that reasoning allows us to construe the maintenance of a faith as resting on plausibility rather than functionality, then we can consider what makes a faith more or less plausible. This is no simple matter and there is no single answer, but weight of numbers clearly has much to do with it. People born into a society that is pervaded by a belief system to which all members subscribe are as likely to acquire the shared faith as they are to acquire the common tongue. Constant interaction with others who share one's faith is strong reinforcement. Hence circumstances (such as ethnic conflict) that strengthen group ties will reinforce the plausibility of the group's religion for its members, while circumstances (such as political stability and affluence) that allow people to pursue their own preference at the expense of group loyalty will weaken attachments to the common faith. This theory, if that is not too grand a term, fits what we know about the way that cultural defence retards secularization. It fits our observations about the relativizing impact of diversity: where people are strongly bound to a group with a particular belief system, outsiders are likely to be dismissed or demonized by being seen through shared invidious stereotypes. Whether or not some alternative culture weakens our faith depends on whether the members of our group are sufficiently well socialized into our faith to be unimpressed as an alternative. This formulation in terms of group loyalty versus individual preference has the advantage over the Norris and Inglehart version of encompassing their explanation while retaining a necessary focus on the power of the social.

We can postulate two sources of fragmentation: one constant, the other more variable. The constant is the fact that any body of ideas or practices will randomly generate variation and hence requires social control and discipline to retain cohesion. The variable source is individualism. Societies clearly differ in the extent to which they see individual autonomy as valuable: it is rare in traditional agrarian societies and it is common (indeed, it is almost a defining characteristic) of modern consumerist societies. Norris and Inglehart see the need for existential security as explaining why people want to be religious; once such security is provided by this-worldly means, the demand for religion declines. I can encompass the same sort of argument in a broader and less contentious manner, which does not lose sight of plausibility or imply cynical opportunism, by suggesting that what prosperity and peace bring is a general weakening of social bonds and with it a general decline in the plausibility of all shared beliefs and values. In any culture, individual autonomy (or, if you like, personal freedom) is in tension with group loyalty. The greater the power of the group, the greater the plausibility of its shared beliefs and values. Although some of the separate elements of the secularization paradigm as outlined in Chapter 2 can be read as propositions about individual needs for, and benefits from, religion, even these are better understood as propositions about the circumstances in which people feel able to loosen their ties to their community and thus become less subject to its ideological control and its socialization processes. For example, the rationalization line that I trace through science and technology to a general sense of 'mastery over fate' can be taken both as a statement about the culture as a whole—humanity has increased its collective mastery over fate—and also as an individual statement: the general cultural confidence makes more people willing to reject (though more usually it feels more like just ignoring) social pressure.

The weakening of the social consensus need not produce the secular. It also produces religious rebellions and revivals. In that sense we could imagine the tension between social conformity and individual autonomy as simply regular oscillation that in any one society will produce periods of religious stagnation and religious enthusiasm. What makes the secularization story directional (and that will be progressive or regressive according to one's tastes) is the fact that some system-level changes (structural differentiation, for example) weaken religious institutions and some cultural changes (for example, the widening range of what is permitted to be a matter of personal preference) narrow the range of what the social can demand of the individual. The gradual decline in ideological coercion allows alternatives to proliferate, either through invention or through 'tariff-free' imports. When other conditions are right, increased diversity allows toleration, which in turn becomes relativism, which in turn becomes indifference.

In summary, while Norris and Inglehart's explanation of secularization as the rise of this-worldly forms of existential security seems generally sensible, I think we can usefully recast it so that we think not of the purposes that religion serves but of the circumstances in which supernatural belief systems gain, retain, or lose plausibility. At its most general, modernization increases the autonomy of the individual, increases the degree of variation in the religious culture, and weakens the plausibility of religious belief systems.

## Conclusion

This chapter's brief review of some salient changes in the religious cultures of societies outside Europe and its settler offshoots is not, in any immediate sense, a test of the secularization paradigm. Those who believe that the paradigm postulates the universal and inevitable decline of religion simply misunderstand the nature of the paradigm and, worse, the nature of social science. At best, social science can hope only to produce some general observations from the explanation of specific events. For very many reasons (including the human capacity for reflection and learning and the shortage of comparable cases), it cannot produce general laws of the sort found in physics.

Nonetheless considering patterns of connection between modernization and changes in religion in the developing world can deepen our understanding of the secularization paradigm by identifying similarities and differences.

Nowhere in the world is unchanged. The second half of the twentieth century saw every part of the globe brought into economic, political, social, and cultural contact. There has been much convergence; there has also been divergence, as groups within societies rebel, revolt, and react against particular aspects of the rapid change in which they are engulfed. Many parts of Latin America seem to be going through much the same changes as Europe post-Reformation and are showing similar reactions: the replacement of an organic communal taken-for-granted Catholic Christianity by an individualistic voluntary Protestantism with a therapeutic this-worldly orientation that we can well imagine will, in a few generations, produce a religious climate very similar to that of most European countries. Many other societies, in particular the fifty or so failed states inhabited by Collier's 'bottom billion', are patently lacking crucial elements of the European experience of modernization and hence show little signs of secularization.

And, of course, there is the major difference that stems from the uniqueness of history. The modernization of Europe and its subsequent secularization were what Demerath calls 'emergent'. The modernization of everywhere else cannot avoid owing much—as imposition, emulation, or rejection—to the Western experience.

It would be quite sensible to stop the analysis at that point and to say that we live in a world of multiple modernities: societies with very different cultures will modernize in different ways, and some of those ways will allow religion to retain pride of place in the public culture and keep levels of personal religiosity high.[36] Given the relative recent onset of modernization, that would be the safest answer, but I think there is already in sources such as the World Values Survey evidence to warrant a slightly bolder prognosis.

First, however, we need to recognize that modernization is not inevitable.[37] It is no insult to Congo or Afghanistan (or even to Europe of the 'Dark Ages') to say that Congo and Afghanistan are hardly more economically or socially developed than was Europe between

---

[36] S. N. Eisenstadt, *Multiple Modernities* (New Brunswick, NJ: Transaction, 2002).

[37] I am grateful to Paul Gifford for persuading me of this point.

the fall of Rome and the Renaissance. That a jihadi Muslim group was willing to murder the first cohort of medical students to graduate in Somalia for twenty-two years is a stark reminder that there are people who reject modernization, and there are settings in which such groups are likely to prevail.[38] If we want to extend the secularization paradigm outside its European base, the key prediction is not that all societies will modernize with the results for religion seen in Europe. It is that, *if other places modernize* in ways similar to the European experience, then we can expect the nature and status of religion also to change in similar ways.

In those societies that enjoy peace, political stability, and prosperity, it is likely both that elements of the European experience will be repeated and that the finished products of that experience will be emulated. The changes will take generations, but increased social-structural differentiation will see the emergence of spheres that are relatively free of religious influence. Organic communal faiths will become more individualistic. This-worldly and therapeutic concerns will gradually displace the worship of an authoritarian creator God. Social fragmentation will produce increased religious diversity. Combined with positive contact with other cultures, that will gradually shift people from dogmatic to tolerant versions of their faith, which in turn will gradually create indifference. In particular, women will become more socially and politically active, and gender roles will gradually become more egalitarian. Given the almost universal preference for greater personal autonomy and the strong international pressures that promote it, it is difficult to see how any religious tradition, no matter how popular, can remain immune.

[38] BBC News, 3 Dec. 2009.

# 10

# Will Conflict Reverse Secularization?

## Introduction

Early discussions of secularization rarely mention non-Christian religions. Bryan Wilson's *Religion in Secular Society*, for example, contains only one reference to Islam and that was in a discussion of the historical sociology of Max Weber.[1] There is nothing reprehensible in that narrow focus. The secularization paradigm was developed to explain the changing nature and status of religion in modernizing liberal democracies and that religion was Christian.

Since the 1960s migration has brought sizeable non-Christian populations to the West. Those populations are still small enough that representative national sample surveys generally include too few members for meaningful analysis. Nonetheless, as we will see shortly, because their views of the proper place and reach of religion often differ from those of the natives, the novel presence of Muslims, Hindus, Sikhs, and Buddhists does introduce new issues into debates about the secularization paradigm.

This chapter is concerned narrowly with those debates. I first present some basic demographic data on the settlement and growth of non-Christian populations in the West and review some of the issues that arise from the changes in the cultural composition of European societies. As the major clashes concern Islam, the section

[1] B. R. Wilson, *Religion in Secular Society* (London: C. A. Watts, 1966), p. xiv.

on beliefs and attitudes will focus on Muslims. I then consider the responses of Christian groups to arguments about religious rights before turning to my main concern. Since Jürgen Habermas popularized talk of a 'post-secular Europe', there has been much confusion between religion becoming more troublesome and people becoming more religious.[2] In the final part of the chapter I will consider the possibility that religion becoming more controversial will inspire a Christian revival.

## Changing Religious Composition of the West

Most countries of the European Union now have significant numbers of Hindus, Buddhists, Sikhs, and—the most numerous group—Muslims. Muslims make up 3 per cent of the population of Britain, between 4 and 5 per cent of the people of Belgium, Denmark, Germany, Austria, and Sweden, and about 9 per cent of the population of France.[3] Britain has attracted migrants from its former colonies in the Caribbean, Africa, and from India, Pakistan, Bangladesh, and Sri Lanka. France has large numbers of migrants from North Africa.[4] Germany has a large Turkish population.[5] Sweden's immigrants have mostly been refugees: in the 1980s from Iraq, Iran, and Lebanon and in the 1990s from Somalia, Bosnia, and Kosovo.[6] During the 1960s and 1970s the Netherlands recruited workers from Turkey and Morocco. Official work immigration ended in 1973, but the number of Moroccans and Turks continued to rise, as workers moved their families. A number of Surinamese Muslims came to the Netherlands before and after the independence of Suriname in 1975. More

[2] J. Habermas, 'Notes on a Post-Secular Society', Sign and Sight, 18 June 2008; http://print.signandsight.com/features/1714.html (accessed 12 Dec. 2009).

[3] H. Knippenberg (ed.), The Changing Religious Landscape of Europe (Amsterdam: Het Spinhuis, 2005).

[4] J. Cesari, 'Islam in France: The Shaping of a Religious Minority', in Y. Y. Haddad (ed.), Muslims in the West: From Sojourners to Citizens (Oxford: Oxford University Press, 2002), 36–51.

[5] B. F. Stowasser, 'The Turks in Germany: From Sojourners to Citizens', in Haddad (ed.), Muslims in the West, 52–71.

[6] A. S. Roald, 'From "People's Home" to "Multiculturalism": Muslims in Sweden', in Haddad (ed.), Muslims in the West, 101–20.

recently, the Netherlands has accepted people from Bosnia, Somalia, Iran, Pakistan, and Afghanistan as refugees and asylum-seekers.

Non-Christians form only small proportions of national populations, often smaller than the totals of Christian migrants, but they are disproportionately notable because they are concentrated in metropolitan areas, score high on indices of deprivation, and raise important policy issues about the public place of religion.

The rhetorical impact of current figures can be enhanced by extreme projection. The *Sunday Telegraph*, Britain's leading right-wing paper, gave a neat example of paranoid demography in August 2009 when it ran a two-page spread under the headlines 'Muslim Europe: The Demographic Timebomb Transforming our Continent'. As 55 people had been killed and some 700 injured in the July 2005 suicide bombing of the London Underground, one might think the use of the time-bomb metaphor a little tasteless, but what is the basis for the estimate that 'A fifth of Europe will be Muslim by 2050'?[7]

The first trick is to take the most extreme estimates of fertility. Assume that the Christians and ex-Christians of Europe will continue to have very few children and that Muslim immigrants and their children will have more and more children. It is more likely that, as non-Christians prosper, all their characteristics—including family size—will move from the Turkish or Pakistani or African norm towards the European norm. But, even if Muslims continue to have larger families, it does not follow that Europe will become significantly more religious. The second trick in the paranoid demography is to assume that all those who describe themselves as Muslims in surveys and censuses are so in any religiously meaningful sense. As we will see shortly, they are not. The third trick is to take a well-supported observation and reverse it. Almost all regular churchgoers were raised by churchgoing parents; if you did not learn a faith from your parents, you are unlikely to acquire one later in life. It does not follow that all the children of churchgoing parents will be churchgoing. All panda cubs become pandas, but not all children of Catholic parents become Catholics. A major 2004 British survey showed that 4 per cent had been raised with a non-Christian religion, but only

    [7] www.telegraph.co.uk/news/worldnews/europe/5994047/Muslim-Europe-the-demographic-time-bomb-transforming-our-continent.html (accessed 3 Mar. 2010).

3 per cent claimed the same identity. This is a slippage of 25 per cent, which is better than the 36 per cent slippage for the Church of England and the 35 per cent for Catholics, but the same as the loss rate for the 'other Christian' category.[8]

As the majority of migrants come from countries that are more traditionally religious than their new homes, the immediate impact of these population movements has been to make Europe slightly more religious than it would otherwise be (though not more religious than it was in 1900). This, of course, has no bearing on the secularization paradigm as an explanation of Europe's past; it just tells us that other places are different.

The plausibility of the paradigm would be threatened by evidence that non-Christian populations were growing by converting the natives. Certainly the claim that we are all 'essentially' religious would be strengthened by evidence that significant numbers of ex-Christians convert to Islam, Hinduism, Buddhism, or Sikhism. Estimating the size of the convert population is not easy, but the 2001 census in Scotland asked for current religion and religion of upbringing. The proportions of Muslims, Hindus, and Sikhs who had been raised as such were 94, 90, and 85 per cent respectively. Only for Buddhists, much fewer in number, was conversion significant: just over half of those who identified as Buddhists were converts.[9] Around the period of the 2001 census, Britain, for example, was estimated to have about 10,000 converts to Islam, most of them women who married Muslim men. A 2007 German government report estimated that less than 1 per cent of German Muslims were converts.[10] French sources produce a similar figure, though they also note what probably applies in other countries: the traffic is not all one way. There may be as many Muslims who convert to Christianity.[11]

When my great-aunts left Aberdeenshire for Canada in the 1920, they left for good. Cost of travel and slowness of communication

[8] Data from British Social Attitudes Survey, 2004, reported in P. Brierley, 'Changing your Religion', www.religiousintelligence.co.uk/news/?NewsID=4759 (accessed 10 May 2009).

[9] www.scotland.gov.uk/Publications/2005/02/20757/53570 (accessed 12 Oct. 2009). Unfortunately the England and Wales census did not ask for religion of upbringing.

[10] C. Whitlock, 'Converts to Islam Move up in Cells', Washington Post, 15 Sept. 2007.

[11] 'France: Muslims Convert to Christianity', Islam in Europe, 11 Mar. 2007.

meant that they settled to become Canadians with no expectation that they would return or maintain ties beyond the occasional letter and postcard. Some of their grandchildren have visited Scotland, but they come as Canadians exploring their roots. Now cheap air fares, phone calls, and Internet communication and easy access to home-land television channels via satellite allow non-Christians resident in Europe to retain strong ties to their ancestral homeland. They can return frequently. When they seek suitable marriage partners, they find them in the old country.[12] They can retain dual citizenship. Until recently migrants had little choice but to settle, and, even if migrants were sufficiently distinctive to form a community, it was very obvi-ously socially as well as geographically in a new land. For most migrants to the United States, the retention of a dual identity was confined to thin cultural associations, such as the Irish colouring their beer green on St Patrick's Day.

A further difference between the situation of my Scottish relatives in Canada in 1920 and that of non-Christians in contemporary Europe is that many of the latter have an interest in and take an interest in foreign-policy conflicts. Another personal anecdote: in the 1930s my soldier father served on what the British called the North-West Fron-tier in what is now Pakistan. He was stationed in Kohat, which in September 2009 was the site of a suicide bombing by supporters of the Afghani Taliban. By the 1930s British interest in the Empire was waning. Few Britons enthusiastically supported our presence in India and Afghanistan. Some on the Left (George Orwell, for example) opposed it. But almost no Briton supported those against whom my father was fighting, and none did so because they shared a common religious bond with the other side. European countries, either directly or indirectly, are involved in conflicts that involve Muslim states or Muslim minority populations, and many have suffered terrorist attack by radical Muslims keen to punish the West. This adds an extra dimension to the already complex questions of how Muslims adapt to living in Europe and how Europeans adapt to Islam.

[12] Even relatively cosmopolitan and 'secular' migrants may find themselves pressed through family ties and traditions to accept, if not exactly 'arranged', then 'heavily promoted' marriages with a member of the extended family from the old country. For a very well-described autobiographical example, see Z. Sardar, *Balti Britain: A Provocative Journey through Asian Britain* (London: Granta Books, 2008).

# Points of Conflict

The details vary from society to society, but most liberal democracies have evolved a settlement between the religious and the secular that has two distinct elements. First, there is a public–private divide.[13] Modern societies have responded to religious diversity (and to the increasingly large numbers who have no faith) by tolerating a great deal of religious variety in private and by excluding religion from the public sphere. Secondly, where once-dominant churches retain some vestige of their privileges, it is generally on the understanding that they do not take advantage of them. In England, for example, the state church manages schools that are funded by the tax-payer, but those schools do not aggressively proselytize or promote a distinctive socio-moral agenda. Indeed, they are often preferred over state schools by Muslim parents, who like the generally conservative ethos.

That settlement works well when the diverse religions to be accommodated are liberal, tolerant, and ecumenical, and either have no particular social mores or can translate these into some secular surrogate such as conservatism. It runs into trouble in three analytically separable circumstances: when a minority rejects the principle of a public–private divide, when it does not like where the line is drawn, and when what it wishes to do in private offends against some important shared principle. The first two are clear. The third can be illustrated with the example of the Mormon Church, which was forced by US federal action to end polygamy and to accept the ordination of blacks. Gender equality is another principle that generates demands for intervention in what minorities might reasonably describe as a private matter. In Britain in 2004, Muslim women were unusually likely to be what government statisticians record as 'economically inactive': 69 per cent of them as compared to less than 40 per cent for other non-Christian women and 25 per cent for Christian women. As the comparable figure for Muslim men was around 30 per cent, we know this is not a function of discrimination. It is largely a result of

---

[13] K. Dobbelaere, 'Secularization Theories and Sociological Paradigms: A Reformulation of the Private–Public Dichotomy and the Problem of Societal Integration', *Sociological Analysis*, 46 (1985), 377–87.

Muslim women forgoing opportunities for education and employment outside the home.[14] Many critics of Muslim attitudes towards women (seen also, for example, in arranged marriages, polygamy, divorce without protection for ex-wives, and restrictive clothing codes) argue that these are forms of patriarchal oppression that Christian or secular people would not tolerate and hence that they should not be accepted when given a religious justification. At its most general, this can become an argument about individuals versus groups. This simplifies, but, although modern societies recognize groups when they legislate to protect individuals who suffer because of some identity attributed to them, they do not generally accord rights to groups. They do not generally accept the idea that religious groups should enjoy positive rights that trump the protections given to every individual. The case made by deviant Mormon groups, for example, that preventing their polygamy infringes their religious freedom is defeated by the argument that the protection of adolescent girls from sexual exploitation trumps any religious interest.

The issue of public secularity is complicated by the fact that in many societies the current church–state settlement involves a degree of disguised collusion. France and the USA are unusual in their open and forthright commitment to public secularity. Elsewhere nonconformists battled to remove the real privileges of the state churches but then stopped short once they had achieved a working accommodation. The Church of England, for example, still has bishops sitting in the upper house of the Westminster legislature and the monarch is the head of the Church. This can easily be misunderstood, as it was by the scholar who wrote of 'the case in the United Kingdom where the Crown is the head of the Anglican Church, giving it power and legitimacy'. When neither Queen nor Church has any power or much legitimacy, it is hard to decide which is more flattered by the claim.[15] What the parties to the current settlement understand is that the 'Lords ecclesiastical' have not had any power since universal suffrage stuffed the lower, and vastly more powerful, House of Commons

---

[14] Office of National Statistics, National Statistics Online, www.statistics.gov. uk/cci/nugget.asp?id=979 (accessed 3 Mar. 2010).

[15] D. T. Kücükcan, 'Looking at Religions and Religious Education in Secular National Contexts in Western Europe', *Centrum Voor Islam in Europe*, www. flwi.ugent.be/cie/kucukcan2.htm (accessed 3 Mar. 2010).

with dissenters and atheists. However, that the Church of England superficially enjoys certain legal privileges encourages non-Christian groups to demand equal protection and advantage.

One area in which Muslims may challenge the evolved relations of church and state is in the teaching of religion in state schools. In France and a number of post-communist countries, the state plays no part in religious education. A second model, found in England, Wales, Scotland, Denmark, Sweden, and Norway, does not offer religious instruction but as part of the normal curriculum has classes about religion in general and about a variety of religions, taught by the school's staff. A third model, found in most parts of Germany and in Italy, Finland, Austria, Belgium, and Poland, involves the state legitimating confessional religious education by providing the time and space (though usually not the funding) for the dominant religion (or religions) to promote its beliefs, while also allowing parents to withdraw their children. The larger the number of alternatives that are so legitimated by the state, the less valuable that legitimation. In Berlin, for example, children may choose between Catholic, Lutheran, Jewish, and Science of Life (given by the Humanist Union) lessons, but two-thirds of children choose to attend none of these and just go home early.

While Muslims are not disadvantaged in the first two models, they are in the third. The proposal that Islam be added to the list of confessional alternatives has sometimes met organized resistance, but more often the obstacle is low numbers and the lack of a central organization that can play the part of the Catholic or Lutheran Church in managing the religious education opportunity. A third obstacle—and this is relevant to an important point I will make shortly—is that any proposal for change may provoke resistance from liberals, atheists, and agnostics who wish to abandon rather than update an anachronism.[16] The representatives of Christian churches are more likely to favour expansion because they appreciate that their historic privilege is precarious, they know they must now base their claim for state support on the democratic rights of believers

[16] A 2009 referendum in Berlin to consider making religion classes compulsory and adding Islam to the religions with a right to mount such classes failed because too few people bothered to vote, and polls suggest the plan would have been rejected, though we cannot separate liberal from Islamophobic reasons for opposition ('Berlin Rejects Religious Lessons', *BBC News*, 26 Apr. 2009).

rather than on divine obligation, and hence they have an interest in championing this new entry to the field.

It is not just Islamophobia (though there is plenty of that) that makes the presence of Muslim minorities potentially awkward. There are two significant differences between the strands of Christianity that colluded in the evolution of a largely secular society and Islam. Non-Christian migrants and their offspring potentially challenge the secular accommodation because they are often unusually religious. A major British survey in 2005 asked 'What is your religion even if you are not practising?' and 'Do you consider you are actively practising your religion?' Of the Muslims, Hindus, and Sikhs, just over 70 per cent were actively practising; for Christians the figure was only 31 per cent.[17] As we will see shortly, more detailed analyses suggest lower levels of observance, but all studies suggest that nominalism is lower among non-Christians than among Christians.

The second source of potential conflict stems from the difference between orthoprax and orthodox styles of religion. It is often hard to separate these two things, but it is analytically useful to distinguish between social mores that are Islamic and those that are Afghani, Pakistani, or the like. Liberal Muslims, for example, argue that much of what is presented as Sharia is simply secular local culture and thus can be dispensed with. But, even if we imagine away the cultural accretions, it remains the case that Islam requires more by way of distinctive behaviour (and more public behaviour at that) than Christianity. For Christians the ritual requirements of faith are few and are readily confined to leisure time; especially for Protestants, what matters is correct belief. Ritual plays a large part in Hinduism, but most rituals make no demands on the public sphere. One of the key elements of Islam is the law and that law covers every aspect of private behaviour and public policy. In the interpretations that have been current in the Middle East and South East Asia for centuries, much of that law is at odds with the culture of Western Europe. Another way of making the same point is to note that the European notion of religious liberty tends to concentrate on words rather than deeds.

[17] Home Office Citizenship Survey 2005, cited in R. Gale and P. Hopkins, 'Introduction', in P. Hopkins and R. Gale (eds), *Muslims in Britain: Race, Place and Identities* (Edinburgh: Edinburgh University Press, 2009), 10.

The right to say you are a witch is protected: the right to ritual slaughter of animals in a pagan rite is not.

Another common area for conflict is censorship. All Muslim majority states protect the prestige of Islam by prohibiting a great deal of what European countries would regard as free speech, and some Muslims in Europe expect their faith to be protected from insult and blasphemy. Here again the fact that the secularization of the public sphere has been incomplete in most European societies—stopping at the point where the hegemonic faith loses most of its power—encourages non-Christians to see themselves as the victims, denied the protection still notionally accorded Christians. Actually there has been no prosecution for blasphemy in Scotland since 1843, and the last state prosecution in Britain was in 1921. The last use of any sort was a 1977 private prosecution brought by conservative Christians against *Gay News* for publishing a poem that depicted Christ as homosexual. It had to be a private prosecution, because the state refused to act. But many European states still have blasphemy laws, so Muslims can claim state protection from the publication of Salman Rushdie's *The Satanic Verses* or the 2006 Danish cartoons of the Prophet and feel victimized when they do not get it.

Over the last few paragraphs the focus has narrowed from non-Christian religions to Islam, and that is a reasonable reflection of the degrees of tension. Buddhists have little difficulty with the secularity of European states and are not seen as a threat. Hindus and Sikhs have more tension points—dietary requirements, competing religious holidays, and dress-code issues—but neither faith offers a general challenge to European secularity nor do their adherents have foreign-policy disagreements. Although diasporic groups continue to take sides in Indian politics, European countries are not currently involved in Indian affairs and are therefore not seen as an enemy of Hindu or Sikh interests. Indeed, a number of Hindu and Sikh organizations now reject any imputation of a shared Asian identity in order to distance themselves from Muslims.[18]

---

[18] P. Gopal, 'Prey for the BNP', *Guardian*, 23 Nov. 2009; R. Berkeley, *Connecting British Hindus: An Enquiry into the Identity and Public Policy Engagement of British Hindus by the Runnymede Trust* (London: Runnymede Trust, 2007).

# Islamic Communities

It is difficult to generalize about millions of people from diverse backgrounds, in a variety of countries, united only by the religion of their ancestors. But we can make some observations, though their implications are often paradoxical.

First there has been a shift from sojourner to citizen. Turks who went to work in Germany, North Africans in France, and refugees from Yugoslavia in Scandinavia often saw themselves as temporary residents. Now with children and grandchildren they have settled— hence the process of institution-building since the 1980s. Cesari says of mosque building: 'the Muslims in question were not becoming more observant. Having resolved upon permanent residence in France, they were simply changing their attitude in favor of greater participation in French society.'[19] Even those who retain strong ties to the old world see themselves as dual citizens rather than as temporary visitors.

Secondly, there has been a great deal of assimilation. Many non-Christians are successful entrepreneurs and professional people distinguished, if at all, only by ethnicity.[20] Even those Muslims who do live in relatively distinct communities have lost many of the characteristics of their parents and acquired those of their host country. Distance between the generations is hardly surprising, when many of the settler generation (especially of women) had little or no formal schooling, while their children and grandchildren have been schooled in state schools. A German Interior Ministry survey found, somewhat to its authors' surprise, that more than half of Germany's Muslims belonged to some sort of German club or association. Muslims girls were much more involved in school and social activities than had been expected: 90 per cent of Muslims girls went on school trips and 93 per cent took part in swimming lessons. They were also less religiously observant than had been imagined. Although over 80 per cent described themselves as religious, only a third chose

[19] Cesari, 'Islam in France', 37.
[20] J. Klausen, *The Islamic Challenge: Politics and Religion in Western Europe* (Oxford: Oxford University Press, 2005).

the 'very religious' designation, while half said they were 'somewhat religious'. And only a third claimed to attend the mosque regularly.[21] A number of studies suggest that French Muslims can be roughly divided into three equally large groups: the 'personally pious' (who, for example, regularly attend the mosque); the 'communally observant', who will keep Ramadan and join the family for 'Islamic holidays, feasts, commemorations and life-cycle events';[22] and those whose faith is largely nominal. A 2009 poll of Muslims in Birmingham found that only 10 per cent consistently prayed five times a day, 67 per cent did not, and 23 per cent said they did so 'sometimes'.[23]

Cesari makes an important point about Muslims in France that is generally applicable: they now choose their faith. Although living in a relatively introverted minority community makes the fact of choice less of the 'heresy' that Peter Berger had in mind when he spoke of the relativism-inducing consequences of modern religious diversity, it is far more of a conscious choice than their ancestors enjoyed in their homelands.[24] Most choose to be less observant than their parents and grandparents. A few choose to be more observant, and some of those also choose to become politically radical, culturally confrontational, or both. For example, they may respond to the demands that they integrate and adopt European privatized models of religiosity by wearing a veil, headscarf, or other forms of symbolically significant clothing. The rise of Islamic fundamentalism, terrorist attacks on Western targets, and the Western wars in Iraq and Afghanistan offers all Muslims in Europe a cause that they can support and an identity—as a member of a global radical Islam—that they can adopt. Studies suggest no common pattern to identify those to whom radicalization appeals. Neither class, gender, deprivation, or level of education has any consistent relationship with radicalization, which seems an idiosyncratic choice.[25]

[21] 'Challenging Stereotypes: Germany has 1 Million More Muslims than Previously Thought', *Speigel Online*, 24 June 2009.

[22] Cesari, 'Islam in France', 41, and various surveys mentioned in the Wikipedia entry 'Islam in France', http://en.wikipedia.org/wiki/Islam_in_France (accessed 1 Dec. 2009).

[23] http://britishbornmuslims.wordpress.com/british-muslim-poll.

[24] P. L. Berger, *The Heretical Imperative: Contemporary Possibilities of Religious Affirmation* (London: Collins, 1980).

[25] For a good account of the variety of backgrounds from which British radicals may come, see K. Malik, *From Fatwa to Jihad* (London: Atlantic, 2009).

What we do know is that the political radicalization that so scared governments in the aftermath of the World Trade Center attacks is rare. It is no surprise that newspapers exaggerate; 'news' encourages selective reading of evidence and even more selective reporting. The few who demonstrate in favour of some extreme position are always more newsworthy than the many who do not. But we do now have a body of survey data. The London bombings of 2005 stimulated a series of polls of British Muslims, and the responses hardly suggest widespread radicalization. Typical is the poll in which 96 per cent—that is, nearly everyone—said that Muslims were wrong to bomb London. The proposition 'Western society may not be perfect but Muslims should live within it and not seek to bring it to an end' was accepted by 80 per cent; only 7 per cent thought that 'Western society is decadent and immoral and Muslims should seek to bring it to an end, if necessary by violent means'.[26] In a poll that used the same pair of statements but divided the second by adding a version in which the last phrase read 'by peaceful means only', the percentage who approved of the violent option dropped to just 1.[27]

Even this rather moderate result may be a distortion because the poll did not include a non-Muslim control group. One poll asked for views on the statement 'It is never justified for anyone to attack British civilians because of Britain's activities in Iraq and Afghanistan'. Seventy-three per cent of Muslims agreed and 10 per cent disagreed, which might seem like a lot of Muslim support for terrorism until one knows that 7 per cent of non-Muslims also disagreed.[28]

Polls also show little evidence of general alienation. In responses to the question 'How loyal do you feel to Britain?', 91 per cent chose 'very loyal' and 'quite loyal'.[29] Almost two-thirds of Muslims said they thought of Britain as 'my country'.[30] When asked if they would

---

[26] Sunday Telegraph/ICM Research, 'Muslims Poll—February 2006', www. icmresearch.co.uk/pdfs/2006_february_sunday_telegraph_muslims_poll.pdf (accessed 1 Dec. 2009).

[27] A. King, 'One in Four Muslims Sympathises with Motives of Terrorists', Independent, www.telegraph.co.uk/news/uknews/1494648/One-in-four-Muslims-sympathises-with-motives-of-terrorists.html (accessed 3 Mar. 2010).

[28] Anthony Wells, 'One Year on', http://ukpollingreport.co.uk/blog/archives/265 (accessed 1 Sept. 2009).

[29] Sunday Telegraph/ICM Research, 'Muslims Poll—February 2006'.

[30] GfK/NOP, 'Attitudes to Living in Britain' (Apr. 2006), www.imaginate. uk.com/MCC01_SURVEY/Site%20Download.pdf (accessed 1 Apr. 2008).

like to live in areas governed by Sharia or by British laws, the sample split evenly—40/41 per cent, with 19 per cent undecided. But, when another poll added the clarificatory 'Sharia law, as practised in such countries as Saudi Arabia and Iran', the percentage in favour dropped to 31. In summary, while some Muslims in Europe have values and preferences that set them at odds with the Christian-tinged but largely secular cultures of most European societies, the reality is a long way from the xenophobe's fear of a jihadi enemy within the gates. Indeed, though I will not pursue the point, it may well be that the willingness of some governments (the British, for example) to think of, and wish to deal with, non-Christian minorities as blocs rather than as collections of somewhat disparate individuals exaggerates the apparent distinctiveness of Muslims, Hindus, and Sikhs. By treating what is only one part of people's identity as a master status, the logic of multiculturalism is to amplify that characteristic.[31]

## Christians are a Minority Too

In 1900 Christianity enjoyed considerable cultural power and prestige in Europe. Now it is a minority religion, and, encouraged by the example of Muslims, Hindus, and Sikhs pressing for their cultural distinctions to be recognized, some Christians feel driven to try to regain what they once took for granted. An official Church of England report asserted that the government was giving preferential treatment to the Muslim community: 'There can be little doubt that the terrorism agenda has seriously unbalanced government relations with the faith communities.'[32] Such suspicions, of course, find their own confirmation. Contrary to the views of some Muslims, the terrorist bombing of the London tube network in 2005 did actually happen, but the 'Muslim-conquest' trope is sufficiently attractive to

---

[31] The case is well made in M. Mirza, 'Multiculturalism and the War on Terror: Religiosity and the Politics of Identity', *Rising East Online*, 4 (May 2006), www.uel.ac.uk/risingeast/archive04/academic/mirza.htm (accessed 5 July 2009).

[32] Church of England, *What Makes a Good City*, quoted in *Observer*, 12 July 2009.

the conservative wing of the British press that the very rare acts of terrorism are routinely plumped up by the exaggeration of trivia. For example, the *Daily Telegraph* ran the headline: 'Bacon "Ban" for Residents of Care Home Run by a Muslim'. An aggrieved relative was reported as saying: 'This is a disgrace. The old people who are in this home and in their final years deserve better. They are paying customers who are making profits for this man. The least he can do is give them their favourite food.' Actually all that had happened was that the owner had switched contracts for meat supplies and the new supplier—a British firm that could supply all sorts of meat—had once delivered halal meat.[33]

The following are just a selection of some of 2009's religion news stories in Britain. A bus driver refused to drive his bus because it had an advert for atheism on its side. A Christian doctor was removed from a local council's adoption panel because she refused to recommend that gay couples be allowed to adopt.[34] A registrar was demoted for refusing to administer a civil partnership ceremony to a gay couple.[35] A member of the staff of British Airways insisted on wearing a large crucifix in defiance of a rule that said staff should not wear conspicuous jewellery.

A further stimulus to Christian umbrage is the increasing willingness of governments and supra-national bodies such as the European Union to intrude in what had previously been regarded as the private. For example, in 2009 the Commission of the European Union told the British government that it had misinterpreted an EU equality directive. The British version allowed religious organizations to refuse a position to a homosexual 'so as to avoid conflicting with the strongly held religious convictions of a significant number of the religion's followers'.[36] The EU has now directed that such discrimination can be permitted only if the job involves promoting or practising the religion in question. So the Church of England can refuse to ordain homosexuals, but it can no longer refuse to hire homosexuals to teach in church schools or to work in church offices. Increasingly, public bodies have been actively promoting equality in a way that infringes on the rights of minorities to voice discriminatory views. For example, a Christian couple who wrote to their council to complain about its

[33] *Daily Telegraph*, 18 July 2009.   [34] *Sunday Telegraph*, 19 July 2009.
[35] *Daily Telegraph*, 22 June 2009.   [36] *Observer*, 23 Nov. 2009.

support for gay rights were visited by the police and warned that their actions might constitute a public-order offence. I can now summarize the argument thus far. Exactly how long varies from country to country, but the public privileges of religion have not been newsworthy for a long time. The arguments between nonconformists and state churches were generally settled in the late nineteenth or early twentieth centuries. The tensions caused by anti-Semitism were largely resolved by the Second World War, which also marked the Catholic Church's acceptance of liberal democracy. From the 1950s to the 1980s religion was of little interest to European social scientists, because it was not interesting to anyone else. That some scholars now talk of a post-secular Europe is largely a result of the migration of non-Christians making religion newsworthy again. Some adherents of religions that were not party to the gradual evolution of church–state relations challenge those arrangements, and in so doing they stimulate conservative Christians to see themselves as disadvantaged. Through the game of competitive victimhood, religion has once again become troublesome.

## Nativist Reaction

The possibility that the growth of non-Christians religions in the West refutes the secularization paradigm because it involves large-scale conversion of the previously secular has been addressed. There is another way in which the novel presence of non-Christian religions in Europe might undermine the paradigm and that is through large numbers of currently ex-Christians returning to their heritage faith in reaction against what they see as alien religion. As a political scientist put it: 'Muslim growth...may lead to a renewed emphasis on Christian identity.'[37] There are certainly conservative Christian

[37] E. Kaufmann, 'Breeding for God', *Prospect*, 128, 19 Nov. 2006, www.pros pectmagazine.co.uk/2006/11/breedingforgod (accessed 4 Jan. 2008). Kaufmann misrepresents my comments on the 2001 census results when he says that the proportion of white British people describing themselves as Christian was higher in districts with large Muslim populations. My contrast was actually between Scotland and England and was far less specifically concerned with Muslims.

groups that hope that dislike of Islam will cause nominal Christians to rediscover their faith.

Unlikely as it seems, there is a precedent for such a reaction in what political scientists call 'nativism'. In the first half of the nineteenth century, western New York State experienced a series of popular religious revivals in which large numbers of young men were recruited to evangelical Protestantism.[38] The causes of that revival were complex, but historians believe it was in part inspired by anti-immigrant sentiment. Waves of poor and ill-educated Catholics were moving into an area that still had some of the chaos of a frontier and they were blamed for an increase in such forms of anti-social behaviour as gambling, prostitution, and alcoholism. Preachers used the new immigrants as a rhetorical device to press the case for the true faith of evangelical Protestantism. The good life is threatened by people who are socially defective because they have the wrong religion. How can we preserve the good life? By recommitting ourselves to the true faith. It is that drama—with Muslims taking the part of Catholics—that some European Christians hope will be repeated when they remind us of the Christian roots of Western liberal society.

Is there any sign of contemporary European nativism taking a religious form? There is certainly plenty of anti-immigrant sentiment in Europe (much of it misdirected, because probably half the targets were born in Europe). The French National Front; the Italian Northern League; Lisjt Fortuyn in Holland; Vlaams Bloc in Belgium; the British National Party; the Austrian Freedom party; there is no shortage of opposition to non-Christians. However, it is significant that none of these movements seeks to mobilize on the basis of a shared Christianity. When the British National Party criticizes Muslims, it does not do so on the grounds that they worship the wrong God. Instead it claims that Islam seeks social domination and that Muslims have a variety of secular vices. Jorg Haider[39] in Austria argued that:

---

[38] P. E. Johnson, *A Shopkeeper's Millennium: Society and Revivals in Rochester, New York, 1815–1837* (New York: Hill and Wang, 2004); W. Cross, *The Burnt-Over District: The Social and Intellectual History of Enthusiastic Religion in Western New York State 1800–1850* (Ithaca, NY: Cornell University Press, 2006 (1950)).

[39] P. Ignazi, *Extreme Right-Wing Parties in Western Europe* (Oxford: Oxford University Press, 2003), 107–23.

'The social order of Islam is opposed to our Western values. Human rights and democracy are as incompatible with the Muslim religious doctrine as is the equality of women. In Islam, the individual and his free will count for nothing; faith and religious struggle—jihad, the holy war—for everything.'[40] Pym Fortuyn in Holland avoided basing his criticism of Islam on the superiority of Christianity and openly attacked Protestantism. When asked by the Dutch newspaper *Volkskrant* whether he hated Islam, he replied:

I don't hate Islam. I consider it a backward culture. I have travelled much in the world. And wherever Islam rules, it's just terrible. All the hypocrisy. It's a bit like those old Reformed protestants. The Reformed [Protestants] lie all the time. And why is that? Because they have standards and values that are so high that you can't humanly maintain them. You also see that in that Muslim culture.[41]

There are two reasons why European xenophobes cannot use Christianity as a recruiting device: they are not Christians and most Christians are not xenophobes. A theological critique of Islam, Hinduism, or Sikhism would do nothing for the British National Party because its members and likely supporters are very rarely churchgoing Christians. Looked at from the other end, the Christian churches in Western Europe have generally been supportive of non-Christian minorities and of immigrants. In Britain, the Archbishop of Canterbury argued that certain activities of informal sharia courts should be supported. And, in settings where churches negotiate with government agencies (for example, over chaplaincy rights in prisons), Church of England officials have taken a lead in pressing for non-Christian clergy to be included. When the Swiss in a 2009 referendum voted 58 to 42 per cent for a ban on minarets, the Vatican described the decision as 'a blow to religious freedom'.[42]

In brief, although there is considerable suspicion of, and some hostility towards, non-Christian minorities in West European societies, there is no evidence of that nativist response taking a religious form. Nor, as the evidence presented in Chapter 1 shows, is there any sign of

[40] P. H. Merkl and L. Weinberg (eds), *Right-Wing Extremism in the Twenty-First Century* (London: Routledge, 2003), 84.

[41] Quoted in http://en.wikipedia.org/wiki/Pim_Fortuyn (accessed 12 Oct. 2009).

[42] *Daily Telegraph*, 1 Dec. 2009.

the decline in indices of religious interest or involvement being reversed. The new competition is not stimulating a Christian revival in Europe.

## Strengthening the Secular State

Even if there is no reversal of the decline in the popularity of religion, the novel presence of non-Christian religions in Europe might still challenge one element of the secularization paradigm: the privatization of religion. When Eric Kaufmann speculated that the growth of Islam in Europe might trigger a Christian revival, he also hedged his bets by offering as an alternative the strengthening of liberal commitment to a secular state.[43] It is certainly possible that renegotiating the public presence of religion will confirm rather then reverse the privatization of religion.

As I argued in Chapter 2, the marginalization of religion was more often a reluctant adjustment to circumstances than the product of an enthusiastic campaign for secularism, and many of those circumstances were unintended consequences of changes promoted for quite different purposes. Or, to put it more generally, things are rarely as they are just because that is what most people wanted, though we do have a happy knack of making virtue out of necessity. As the privatization of religion was not simply the consequence of popular wishes, so any reverse will not simply reflect changing attitudes. Nonetheless, it is hard to imagine religion regaining public presence or political influence unless there is a considerable shift of opinion in that direction. So there is some value in looking at survey data on attitudes to the public place of religion.

Throughout the twentieth century in Britain, declining personal involvement in the Christian churches had been accompanied by continued sympathy for religion as an idea. In 1947 a detailed Mass Observation survey of residents in a London suburb found that

broad and uninterested tolerance of religion is common—much more so than hostile feelings. . . . Many people look upon religion as something quite

---

[43] Kaufmann, 'Breeding for God'.

harmless and purely personal—an innocuous hobby, like collecting stamps. One of the results of this attitude is that these same people often feel that religion is exceeding its legitimate grounds if it 'interferes' with more practical matters. Religion to them is all right in its place, but shouldn't get involved in everyday affairs outside the private life of believers.[44]

That religion has become increasingly controversial has stimulated a large number of opinion polls. Taken as a whole, they suggest an increasingly negative attitude. For example, a 2007 poll offered respondents a choice between describing religion as beneficial and describing it as harmful: only 17 per cent thought it beneficial and 42 per cent regarded it as harmful.[45] Unfortunately, such polls generally report just the spread of answers to specific questions and do not permit detailed analysis, so, to test whether recent religious conflict has produced any change in British attitudes, Tony Glendinning and I examined a variety of items in the 1998 and 2008 British Social Attitudes survey. We found six propositions that seemed relevant: 'Religious leaders should not try to influence how people vote in elections'; 'Religious leaders should not try to influence government decisions'; 'Looking around the world, religions bring more conflict than peace'; 'People with very strong religious beliefs are often too intolerant of others'; 'How much confidence do you have in Churches and religious organisations?'; and 'Do you think that churches and religious organisations in this country have too much power or too little power?' Statistical testing showed that, taken together, the six items identified a reasonably coherent attitude and allowed us to construct a simple five-point scale where 5 was sympathetic to religion having a strong public presence, 1 was unsympathetic, and 3 was the neutral mid-point. As well as being able to see how such attitudes were related to demographic variables such as age, class, and gender (and the answer is 'not much'), we were able to divide respondents according to their degree of religious practice.

The first observation is that the mean score for the entire sample, from both the 1998 and 2008 survey, is less than the neutral or indifferent mid-point score. That is, general support for public

---

[44] Mass Observation, *Puzzled People: A Study in Popular Attitudes to Religion, Ethic, Progress and Politics in a London Borough* (London: Gollancz, 1947), 84.

[45] YouGov poll, reported in J. Humphries, *In Gods We Doubt* (London: Hodder and Stoughton, 2007).

religion was low in 1998 and it was low in 2008. Crucially, although the mean scores are significantly higher for those people who say they attend church weekly or more often, they are still less than 3: even the religious people in Britain accept the privatization of religion. Our second observation, and this is vital for testing the claim that there may now be pressure for the deprivatization of religion, is that scores on our attitude scale remained static or declined slightly between 1998 and 2008. The scores for the non-religious people and for the most religious remained the same (at 2.1 and 2.9 respectively), while for the occasional attenders they declined from 2.6 to 2.5.

In summary, while British church leaders now frequently complain about the marginalization of their faith, there is no sign that their feelings are shared by any significant part of the British people. Were it the case that increasing concern about jihadi Muslims or about equality legislation constraining religious organizations was stimulating a desire for religion to be given greater public influence, we should see some evidence of that in a change in attitudes between the 1998 and 2008 surveys. We see no such evidence, not even from the regular churchgoers.

## Conclusion

That nominally Christian Europeans have not been stimulated by the growth of non-Christian religions into returning to the faith of their fathers is hardly a surprise. It was never likely, and, were the possibility not raised in attempts to refute the secularization paradigm, I would not have devoted a chapter to it. Xenophobia has not triggered a Christian revival because secular people do not interpret the problem within the right framework to produce a religious response. As I argued in explaining the notion of cultural defence in Chapter 2, people who already share a common religious world view may well interpret some new threat (especially from a competing religion) in theological terms and may feel confirmed and strengthened in their faith. It is perfectly understandable that some Dutch Catholic schools responded to the 2004 murder of a Dutch filmmaker by an Islamic fundamentalist by increasing the number and visibility of signs of the Catholic identity: after all, they are staffed by committed Catholics, competitors in a contest for attention and approval.[46] People who do not share a common religion lack the necessary prerequisite to think in those terms or to see 'becoming Christian' as an appropriate response to any problem, even one with putatively religious roots. Even if they lacked no more attractive response, they would not get converted. But they do not lack a more attractive response. There is an obvious explanation and solution to hand. Most Europeans do not, as the conservative Christian might wish they did, interpret terrorist attacks or public arguments about veils as proof that only Islam is dangerous. They interpret them as proof that any religion taken too seriously is dangerous. Britons or Swedes in 1850 may have made a clear distinction between correct and false religion. Their contemporaries are much more likely to distinguish between privatized tolerant and liberal religion, which is fine, and any religion that makes demands on them and that insists on a public presence. To the extent that some Christians now behave like a disadvantaged minority and make a fuss about their rights, they simply confirm the view of the secular or only nominally Christian majority that religion is more trouble than it is worth.

[46] H. Knippenberg, 'The Netherlands: Selling Churches and Building Mosques', in H. Knippenberg (ed.), *The Changing Religious Landscape of Europe* (Amsterdam: Het Spinhuis, 2005), 104.

# Select Bibliography

Aarts, O., Need, N., Te Grotenhuis, M., and de Graaf, N. D., 'Does Belonging Accompany Believing? Correlations and Trends in Western Europe and North America between 1981 and 2000', *Review of Religious Research*, 50 (2008), 16–34.

Abercrombie, N., Baker, J., Brett, S., and Foster, J., 'Superstition and Religion: The God of the Gaps', *A Sociological Yearbook of Religion*, 3 (1970), 93–129.

Asad, T., *Genealogies of Religion: Discipline and Reasons of Power in Christianity and Islam* (Baltimore: Johns Hopkins University Press, 1993).

Aupers, S., *In de ban van moderniteit: De sacralisering van het zelf en computertechnologie* (Amsterdam: Aksant, 2004).

Barna, G., 'The Year's Most Intriguing Findings', *Barna Research Online* (2000).

Beck, G., and Lynch, G., ' "We are all one, we are all gods": Negotiating Spirituality in the Conscious Partying Movement', *Journal of Contemporary Religion*, 24 (2009), 339–55.

Becker, G., 'The Economic Approach to Human Behaviour', in J. Elster (ed.), *Rational Choice* (Oxford: Basil Blackwell, 1986), 108–22.

Bellah, R., *Tokugawa Religion: The Values of Pre-Industrial Japan* (Glencoe, Ill.: Free Press. 1957).

Berger, P. L., *The Social Reality of Religion* (London: Faber and Faber, 1969).

——, *The Heretical Imperative: Contemporary Possibilities of Religious Affirmation* (London: Collins, 1980).

——, and Luckmann, T., 'Secularization and Pluralism', *International Yearbook for the Sociology of Religion*, 2 (1966), 73–84.

——, and Luckmann, T., *The Social Construction of Reality* (Harmondsworth: Penguin, 1973).

——, Berger, B., and Kellner, H., *The Homeless Mind: Modernization and Consciousness* (Harmondsworth: Penguin, 1974).

——, Davie, G. R. C., and Fokas, E., *Religious America, Secular Europe: A Theme and Variations* (Aldershot: Ashgate, 2008).

Berkeley, R., *Connecting British Hindus: An Enquiry into the Identity and Public Policy Engagement of British Hindus by the Runnymede Trust* (London: Runnymede Trust, 2007).

Bezilla, R., *Religion in America 1992–93* (Princeton: Princeton Religion Research Centre, 1993).

Bibby, R., *Fragmented Gods* (Toronto: Stoddart, 1987).

——, *Unknown Gods* (Toronto: Stoddart, 1991).

——, *Restless Gods* (Ottawa: Wood Lake Books, 1995).

Blau, J. R., Land, K. C., and Rudding, K., 'The Expansion of Religious Affiliation: An Explanation of the Growth in Church Participation in the United States, 1850–1930', *Social Science Research*, 21 (1991), 329.

Brierley, P., *Religious Trends* (London: Christian Research, 1999).

——, *Pulling out of the Nosedive: A Contemporary Picture of Churchgoing: What the 2005 English Church Census Reveals* (London: Christian Research, 2006).

Brisett, W. N., 'Secularization in the Global South: The Case of Ethiopia', *Hedgehog Review* (Spring/Summer 2006), 147–51.

Brouwer, S., Gifford, P., and Rose, S. D., *Exporting the American Gospel: Global Christian Fundamentalism* (London: Routledge, 1996).

Brown, C. G., 'Did Urbanization Secularize Britain?', *Urban History Yearbook* (1988), 1–14.

——, *The Death of Christian Britain: Understanding Secularization 1800–2000* (London: Routledge, 2001).

Brown, F. K., *Fathers of the Victorians* (Cambridge: Cambridge University Press, 1961).

Boice, J. L., *At One with All Life: A Personal Journey in Gaian Communities* (Findhorn: Findhorn Foundation Press, 1989).

Bruce, S., *Religion in the Modern World: From Cathedrals to Cults* (Oxford: Oxford University Press, 1996).

——, 'The Pervasive World-View: Religion in Pre-Modern Britain', *British Journal of Sociology*, 48 (1997), 667–80.

—— *Fundamentalism* (Cambridge: Polity Press, 2008).

——, *A House Divided: Protestantism, Schism and Secularization* (London: Routledge, 1990).

——, *Pray TV: Televangelism in America* (London: Routledge, 1990).

——, *Choice and Religion: A Critique of Rational Choice* (Oxford: Oxford University Press, 1999).

——, 'Praying Alone? Church-Going in Britain and the Putnam Thesis', *Journal of Contemporary Religion*, 17 (2002), 317–28.

——, *God is Dead* (Oxford: Blackwell, 2001).

——, 'Defining Religion', *Revue internationale de sociologie* (2010).

——, and Glendinning, T., 'Religious Beliefs and Differences', in C. Bromley, J. Curtice, K. Hinds, and A. Park (eds), *Devolution: Scottish Answers to Scottish Questions* (Edinburgh: Edinburgh University Press, 2003).

Brusco, E., *The Reformation of Machismo: Evangelical Conversion and Gender in Columbia* (Austin: University of Texas Press, 1993).

Bryant, J. M., 'Cost-Benefit Accounting and the Piety Business: Is Homo Religiosus, at Bottom, a Homo Economicus?', *Method and Theory in the Study of Religion*, 12 (2001), 520–48.

Campbell, C., 'The Easternization of the West', in B. R. Wilson and J. Cresswell (eds), *New Religious Movements: Challenge and Response* (London: Routledge, 1999), 35–48.

Caplow, T., Bahr, H. M., and Chadwick, B. A., *All Faithful People: Change and Continuity in Middletown's Religion* (Minneapolis: University of Minnesota Press, 1983).

Casanova, J., *Public Religions in the Modern World* (Chicago: University of Chicago Press, 1994).

Cesari, J., 'Islam in France: The Shaping of a Religious Minority', in Y. Y. Haddad (ed.), *Muslims in the West: From Sojourners to Citizens* (Oxford: Oxford University Press, 2002), 36–51.

Chaundler, C., *Everyman's Book of Superstitions* (London: A. R. Mowbray, 1970).

Chaves, M., and Gorski, P., 'Religious Pluralism and Religious Participation', *Annual Review of Sociology*, 27 (2001), 261–81.

Chirot, D., 'The Rise of the West', *American Sociological Review*, 50 (1985), 181–95.

Clark, D., *Between Pulpit and Pew: Folk Religion in a North Yorkshire Fishing Village* (Cambridge: Cambridge University Press, 1982).

Collier, P., *The Bottom Billion: Why the Poorest Countries are Failing and What Can Be Done about It* (Oxford: Oxford University Press, 2007).

Condran, J. G., and Tamney, J. B., 'Religious "Nones" 1957–1982', *Sociological Analysis*, 46 (1985), 415–23.

*The Congregational Yearbook* (London: Congregational Union of England and Wales, 1966).

Cox, Jeffrey, *The English Churches in a Secular Society: Lambeth, 1870–1930* (Oxford: Oxford University Press, 1982).

Cressy, D., *Birth, Death and Marriage: Ritual, Religion, and the Life-Cycle in Tudor and Stuart England* (Oxford: Oxford University Press, 1997).

Cross, W., *The Burnt-Over District: The Social and Intellectual History of Enthusiastic Religion in Western New York State 1800–1850* (Ithaca, NY: Cornell University Press, 2006 (1950)).

Currie, R., Gilbert, A. D., and Horsley, L., *Churches and Churchgoers: Patterns of Church Growth in the British Isles since 1700* (Oxford: Oxford University Press, 1977).

Davie, G. R. C., *Religion in Britain since 1945: Believing without Belonging* (Oxford: Blackwell, 1994).

——, *Religion in Modern Europe: A Memory Mutates* (Oxford: Oxford University Press, 2000).

——, 'Vicarious Religion: A Methodological Challenge', in N. T. Ammerman (ed.), *Everyday Religion: Observing Modern Religious Lives* (New York: Oxford University Press, 2006), 21–35.

Davis, W., *Japanese Religion and Society: Paradigms of Structure and Change* (Albany, NY: State University of New York Press, 1992).

De Graaf, N. D., Need, A., and Ultee, W., 'Losing my Religion? A New and Comprehensive Examination of Three Empirical Regularities Tested on Data for the Netherlands in 1998', in A. Crockett and R. O'Leary (eds), *Patterns and Processes of Religious Change in Modern Industrial Societies: Europe and the United States* (Lampeter: Edwin Mellen Press, 1998).

Demerath, N. J., III, 'Secularization and Sacralization Deconstructed and Reconstructed', in J. A. Beckford and N. J. Demerath III (eds), *The Sage Handbook of the Sociology of Religion* (London: Sage, 2007).

Dobbelaere, K., 'Secularization Theories and Sociological Paradigms: A Reformulation of the Private–Public Dichotomy and the Problem of Societal Integration', *Sociological Analysis*, 46 (1985), 377–87.

Durkheim, E., *The Division of Labor in Society* (Glencoe, Ill.: Free Press, 1964).

——, 'Concerning the Definition of Religious Phenomena', in W. S. F. Pickering (ed.), *Durkheim on Religion* (London: Routledge and Kegan Paul, 1975), 74–99.

Eccleston, Jean, and Eccleston, Peter, *A History and Geology of Staithes* (Staithes: Jean and Peter Eccleston, 1998), 118.

Eisenstadt, S. N., *Multiple Modernities* (New Brunswick, NJ: Transaction, 2002).

Elster, J., *Sour Grapes: Studies in the Subversion of Rationality* (Cambridge: Cambridge University Press, 1983).

——, 'Introduction', in J. Elster (ed.), *Rational Choice* (Oxford: Basil Blackwell, 1986), 1–33.

Evans-Pritchard, E. E., *The Nuer* (Oxford: Clarendon Press, 1940).

——, *Nuer Religion* (Oxford: Clarendon Press, 1956).

Field, C. D., 'Joining and Leaving British Methodism since the 1960s', in L. J. Francis and Y. J. Katz (eds), *Joining and Leaving Religion: Research Perspectives* (Leominster: Gracewing, 2000).

Finer, S. E., *Comparative Government* (Harmondsworth: Penguin, 1982).

Finke, R., 'An Unsecular America', in S. Bruce (ed.), *Religion and Modernization: Sociologists and Historians Debate the Secularization Thesis* (Oxford: Oxford University Press, 1992), 145–69.

——, and Iannaccone, L. A., 'Supply-Side Explanations for Religious Change', *Annals of the American Academy of Political and Social Science*, 527 (1993), 27–39.

Finke, R., and Stark, R., 'Religious Economies and Sacred Canopies', *American Sociological Review*, 53 (1988), 41–9.

Finke, R., and Stark, R., *The Churching of America, 1776–1990: Winners and Losers in Our Religious Economy* (New Brunswick, NJ: Rutgers University Press, 1992).

Foucault, M., *Discipline and Punish* (Harmondsworth: Penguin, 1991).

——, *The Birth of the Clinic* (London: Routledge, 1994).

Fox, J., *A World Survey of Religion and the States* (Cambridge: Cambridge University Press, 2008).

Gale, R., and Hopkins, P., 'Introduction', in P. Hopkins and R. Gale (eds), *Muslims in Britain: Race, Place and Identities* (Edinburgh: Edinburgh University Press, 2009).

Gallie, D., 'The Labour Force', in A. H. Halsey and J. Webb (eds), *Twentieth-Century British Social Trends* (London: Macmillan, 2000), 281–323.

Garnett, J., Grimley, M., Harris, A., Whyte, W., and Williams, S., *Redefining Christian Britain* (London: SCM Press, 2006).

Geertz, C., 'Thick Description: Towards an Interpretative Theory', in his *The Interpretation of Cultures: Selected Essays* (New York: Basic Books, 1973), 3–32.

Gellner, E., *Nations and Nationalism* (Oxford: Basil Blackwell, 1983).

——, *Relativism and the Social Sciences* (Cambridge: Cambridge University Press, 1985).

——, *Plough, Sword and Book: The Structure of Human History* (London: Collins Harvill, 1988).

——, *Postmodernism, Reason and Religion* (London: Routledge, 1992).

General Registrar for Scotland, *Statistics on Marriage* (Edinburgh: GRS, 2007).

George, C. V. R., *God's Salesman: Norman Vincent Peale and the Power of Positive Thinking* (New York: Oxford University Press, 1994).

Gifford, P., *Christianity, Politics and Public Life in Kenya* (London: Hurst, 2009).

Gill, R., *The 'Empty Church' Revisited* (Aldershot: Ashgate, 2003).

——, Hadaway, C. Kirk, and Long Marler, P., 'Is Religious Belief Declining in Britain?', *Journal for the Scientific Study of Religion*, 37 (1998), 507–16.

Glendinning, T., and Bruce, S., 'New Ways of Believing or Belonging: Is Religion Giving Way to Spirituality?', *British Journal of Sociology*, 57 (2006), 399–413.

Goodridge, M. R., 'The Ages of Faith: Romance or Reality', *Sociological Review*, 23 (1975), 381–96.

Gorer, G., *Exploring English Character: A Study of the Morals and Behavior of the English People* (New York: Criterion Books, 1955).

Grant, D., O'Neil, K., and Stephens, L., 'Spirituality in the Workplace: New Empirical Directions in the Study of the Sacred', *Sociology of Religion*, 65 (2004), 265–83.

Graves, C., *Women in Green: The Story of the WVS in Wartime* (London: Heinemann, 1948).

Greeley, A., *Religious Change in America* (Cambridge, Mass.: Harvard University Press, 1989).

Hadaway, C. K., Marler, P. L., and Chaves, M., 'What the Polls don't Show: A Closer Look at US Church Attendance', *American Sociological Review*, 58 (1993), 741–52.

Halsey, A. H., and Webb, J., *Twentieth-Century British Social Trends* (London: Macmillan, 2000).

Hamberg, E., 'Christendom in Decline: The Swedish Case', in H. McLeod and W. Ustorf (eds), *The Decline of Christendom in Western Europe 1750–2000* (Cambridge: Cambridge University Press).

Hanley, P., *Finding Faith Today: The Technical Report* (London: Bible Society/Churches Together in England, 1992).

Harrell, D. E., *Oral Roberts: An American Life* (Bloomington, Ind.: Indiana University Press, 1985).

Harris, C., *Women at War 1939–1945: The Home Front* (Stroud: Sutton Publishing, 2000).

Hastings, A., *The Church in Africa: 1450–1950* (Oxford: Clarendon Press, 1994).

Heelas, P., *The New Age Movement* (Oxford: Blackwell, 1996).

——, *Spiritualities of Life: New Age Romanticism and Consumptive Capitalism* (Oxford: Blackwell Publishing, 2008).

——, and Woodhead, L., *The Spiritual Revolution: Why Religion is Giving Way to Spirituality* (Oxford: Blackwell, 2004).

——, and Seel, B., 'An Ageing New Age?', in G. Davie, P. Heelas, and L. Woodhead (eds.), *Predicting Religion* (Aldershot: Ashgate, 2003), 234.

Hegasy, S., '"Fourteen Kilometres from Europe": Islam and Globalization in Morocco', in M. Rieger (ed.), *What the World Believes: Analyses and Commentary on the Religion Monitor 2008* (Gutersloh: Verag Bertelsmann Stiftung, 2009), 257–70.

Heine, P., and Spielhaus, R., 'What do Muslims Believe?', in M. Rieger (ed.), *What the World Believes: Analyses and Commentary on the Religion Monitor 2008* (Gutersloh: Verag Bertelsmann Stiftung, 2009), 585–605.

Hepburn, A. C., *The Conflict of Nationality in Modern Ireland* (London: Edward Arnold, 1980).

Hervieu-Leger, D., *Religion as a Chain of Memory*, trans. Simon Lee (New Brunswick, NJ: Rutgers University Press, 2000).

Hill, M., and Bowman, R., 'Religious Adherence and Religious Practice in Contemporary New Zealand', *Archives de science sociales des religions*, 58 (1985), 91–112.

Hock, K., 'The Omnipresence of the Religious: Religiosity in Nigeria', in M. Rieger (ed.), *What the World Believes: Analyses and Commentary on the Religion Monitor 2008* (Gutersloh: Verag Bertelsmann Stiftung, 2009), 271–300.

Hoggart, R., *The Uses of Literacy* (London: Chatto and Windus, 1957).

Hornsby-Smith, M. P., *Roman Catholics in England: Studies in Social Structure since the Second World War* (Cambridge: Cambridge University Press, 1987).

Horwood, T., *The Future of the Catholic Church in Britain* (London: Laicos, 2006).

Hout, M. A., Greeley, A., and Wilde, M. J., 'The Demographic Imperative in Religious Change in the US', *American Journal of Sociology*, 107 (2001), 468–500.

Howard, John, *Staithes: Chapters from the History of a Seafaring Town* (Scalby: John Howard, 2000).

Humphries, J., *In Gods We Doubt* (London: Hodder and Stoughton, 2007).

Hunt, D., *Journeys to Faith: A Survey of People Baptised in Scottish Baptist Churches June 1996–May 1997* (self-published, 1997).

——, *Reflecting on our Past: A Statistical Look at Baptists in Scotland 1892–1997* (self-published, 1997).

Hunter, J. D., *Evangelicalism: The Coming Generation* (Chicago: University of Chicago Press, 1987).

——, *Culture Wars: The Struggle to Define America* (New York: Basic Books, 1992).

Hutton, R., *The Triumph of the Moon: A History of Modern Pagan Witchcraft* (Oxford: Oxford University Press, 1999).

Hylton, S., *Their Darkest Hour: The Hidden History of the Home Front 1939–45* (Stroud: Sutton Publishing, 2001).

Iannaccone, L. A., 'Religious Practice: A Human Capital Approach', *Journal for the Scientific Study of Religion*, 29 (1990), 297–314.

——, 'The Consequences of Religious Market Structure', *Rationality and Society*, 3 (1991), 156–77.

Ignazi, P., *Extreme Right-Wing Parties in Western Europe* (Oxford: Oxford University Press, 2003).

Jelen, T. (ed.), *Sacred Markets, Sacred Canopies: Essays on Religious Markets and Religious Pluralism* (Lanham, MD: Rowan and Littlefield, 2002).

Jenkins, T., *Religion in English Everyday Life: An Ethnographic Approach* (Oxford: Berghahn Books, 1999).

Johnson, P. E., *A Shopkeeper's Millennium: Society and Revivals in Rochester, New York, 1815–1837* (New York: Hill and Wang, 2004).

Kelley, J., and de Graaf, N. D., 'National Context Parental Socialization, and Religious Belief: Results from 15 Nations', *American Sociological Review*, 62 (1997), 639–59.

Klausen, J., *The Islamic Challenge: Politics and Religion in Western Europe* (Oxford: Oxford University Press, 2005).

Knippenberg, H. (ed.), *The Changing Religious Landscape of Europe* (Amsterdam: Het Spinhuis, 2005).

——, 'The Netherlands: Selling Churches and Building Mosques', in H. Knippenberg (ed.), *The Changing Religious Landscape of Europe* (Amsterdam: Het Spinhuis, 2005).

Kramer, A., *Land Girls and their Impact* (Barnsley: Pen and Sword Books, 2008).

Land, K. C., Deane, G., and Blau, J. R., 'Religious Pluralism and Church Membership', *American Sociological Review*, 56 (1991), 237–49.

Larkin, P., 'Annus Mirabilis', *High Windows* (London: Faber and Faber, 1979).

Le Roy Ladurie, E., *Montaillou: Cathars and Catholics in a French Village, 1294–1324* (Harmondsworth: Penguin, 2002).

Levey, G. B., and Modood, T. (eds), *Secularism, Religion and Multicultural Citizenship* (Cambridge: Cambridge University Press, 2009).

Levy, M., *Modernization: Latecomers and Survivors* (New York: Basic Books, 1972).

Lipset, S. M., and Raab, E., *The Politics of Unreason: Right-Wing Extremism in America 1790–1977* (Chicago: University of Chicago Press, 1978).

Luckmann, T., *The Invisible Religion: The Problem of Religion in Modern Society* (New York: Macmillan, 1967).

Luhmann, N., *Funktion der Religion* (Frankfurt: Suhrkamp, 1977).

Lynd, R. S., and Lynd, H. J., *Middletown: A Study of Contemporary American Culture* (New York: Harcourt, Brace and Co., 1929).

McCloud, S., 'Popular Culture Fandoms, the Boundaries of Religious Studies, and the Project of the Self', *Culture and Religion*, 4 (2003), 187–206.

McLeod, H., *The Religious Crisis of the 1960s* (Oxford: Oxford University Press, 2000).

Madeley, J. T. S., and Enyedi, Z. (eds), *Church and State in Contemporary Europe: The Chimera of Neutrality* (London: Cass, 2003).

Malik, K., *From Fatwa to Jihad* (London: Atlantic, 2009).

Malinowski, B., *The Argonauts of the Western Pacific* (New York: E. P. Dutton, 1961).

Mann, M., *The Sources of Social Power*: i. *A History of Power from the Beginning to AD 1760* (Cambridge: Cambridge University Press, 1986), and ii. *Rise of Classes and Nation States, 1760–1914* (Cambridge: Cambridge University Press, 1993).

Maple, E., *Superstition and the Superstitious* (London: W. H. Allen, 1971).

Marler, P. L., and Hadaway, C. K., 'Testing the Attendance Gap in A Conservative Church', *Sociology of Religion*, 60 (1997), 175–86.

Marshall, G., *In Search of the Spirit of Capitalism* (London: Hutchinson, 1982).

Martin, D., *The Religious and the Secular* (London: Routledge and Kegan Paul, 1969).

Martin, D., *The Dilemmas of Contemporary Religion* (Oxford: Blackwell, 1978).

Martin, D., *Tongues of Fire: Explosion of Protestantism in Latin America* (Oxford: Blackwell, 1993).

——, *On Secularization: Toward a Revised General Theory* (Aldershot: Ashgate, 2005), 3–7.

Mass Observation, *Puzzled People: A Study in Popular Attitudes to Religion, Ethic, Progress and Politics in a London Borough* (London: Gollancz, 1947).

Melton, J. Gordon, *Encyclopaedic Handbook of Cults in America* (New York: Garland, 1992).

Merkl, P. H., and Weinberg, L. (eds), *Right-Wing Extremism in the Twenty-First Century* (London: Routledge, 2003).

Messner, T. F., *Tammy: Telling it my Way* (New York: Villard, 1996).

Michels, R., *Political Parties: A Sociological Study of Oligarchic Tendencies* (New York: Free Press, 1962).

Millbank, J., *Theology and Social Theory: Beyond Secular Reason* (Oxford: Blackwell, 1990).

Niebuhr, R. H., *The Social Sources of Denominationalism* (New York: Meridian, 1962).

Norris, P., and Inglehart, R., *Sacred and Secular: Religion and Politics Worldwide* (Cambridge: Cambridge University Press, 2004).

Obelkevich, J., *Religion and Rural Society in South Lindsey, 1825–1875* (Oxford: Oxford University Press, 1976).

Olson, D. V. A., 'Religious Pluralism in Contemporary US Counties', *American Sociological Review*, 63 (1998), 757–61.

——, 'Religious Pluralism and US Church Membership: A Reassessment', *Sociology of Religion*, 60/2 (1999), 149–73.

Opie, I., and Tatem, M., *A Dictionary of Superstition* (Oxford: Oxford University Press, 1989).

Parsons, T., *Structure and Process in Modern Societies* (Glencoe, Ill.: Free Press, 1960).

——, and Bales, R. F., *Family, Socialization and Interaction Process* (Glencoe, Ill.: Free Press, 1955).

Partridge, C., *The Re-Enchantment of the West Vol. 1.* (Edinburgh: T and T Clark, 2004).

—— (ed.), *New Religions: A Guide: New Religious Movements, Sects and Alternative Spiritualities* (Oxford: Oxford University Press, 2004).

Pollack, D., and Pickel, G., 'Religious Individualization or Secularization', in D. Pollack and D. V. A. Olson (eds), *The Role of Religion in Modern Societies* (New York: Routledge, 2007), 191–200.

Prince, R., and Daiches, D., *The New Age in Glastonbury* (Oxford: Berghahn Books, 2000).

Quebedeaux, R., *The Worldly Evangelicals* (New York: HarperCollins, 1980).

Ramet, S. P., 'Politics and Religion in Eastern Europe and the Soviet Union', in G. Moyser (ed.), *Politics and Religion in the Modern World* (London: Routledge, 1991).

Richter, P., and Francis, L. J., *Gone but not Forgotten: Church Leaving and Returning* (London: Darton, Longman and Todd, 2005).

Riesebrodt, M., *Pious Passion: The Emergence of Modern Fundamentalism in the United States and Iran* (Chicago: University of Chicago Press, 1993).

Roald, A. S., 'From "People's Home" to "Multiculturalism": Muslims in Sweden', in Y. Y. Haddad (ed.), *Muslims in the West: From Sojourners to Citizens* (Oxford: Oxford University Press, 2002), 101–20.

Robbins, T., and Lucas, P. C., 'From "Cults" to New Religious Movements', in J. A. Beckford and N. J. Demerath III (eds), *Sage Handbook of the Sociology of Religion* (London: Sage, 2007), 227–47.

Roof, W. C., 'God is in the Details: Reflections on Religion's Public Presence in the United States in the Mid-1990s', *Sociology of Religion*, 57 (1996), 149–62.

Roth, G., 'Rationalization in Max Weber's Developmental History', in S. Lash and S. Whimster (eds), *Max Weber, Rationality and Modernity* (London: Allen and Unwin, 1987), 75–91.

Roud, S., *A Pocket Guide to the Superstitions of the British Isles* (London: Penguin Books, 2004).

Roy, O., *Globalized Islam: The Search for a New Ummah* (London: Hurst, 2004).

Said, E., *Orientalism* (Harmondsworth: Penguin, 1995).

Sardar, Z., *Balti Britain: A Provocative Journey through Asian Britain* (London: Granta Books, 2008).

Sawkins, J., 'Church Affiliation Statistics: Counting Methodist Sheep', *Soundings* (Mar. 1998), 17.

Scott, D., and Hirschkind, C. (eds), *Powers of the Secular Modern: Talal Asad and his Interlocutors* (Stanford: Stanford University Press, 2006).

Shibley, M. A., *Resurgent Evangelicalism in the United States* (Columbia, SC: University of South Carolina Press, 1996).

——, 'Contemporary Evangelicals: Born-Again and World-Affirming', *Annals of the American Academy of Politics and Social Science*, 558 (1998), 67–93.

Sica, A., 'Rationalization and Culture', in B. S. Turner (ed.), *The Cambridge Companion to Weber* (Cambridge: Cambridge University Press, 2000), 42–58.

Smith, C. (ed.), *The Secular Revolution: Power, Interests, and Conflict in the Secularization of American Public Life* (Berkeley and Los Angeles: University of California Press, 2003).

Smith, D., *Transforming the World? The Social Impact of British Evangelicalism* (Carlisle: Paternoster Press, 1998).

Stark, R., 'German and German–American Religiousness', *Journal for the Scientific Study of Religion*, 36 (1997), 182–93.

——, and Bainbridge, W. S., *A Theory of Religion* (New York: Peter Lang, 1987).

——, and Finke, R., *Acts of Faith: Explaining the Human Side of Religion* (Berkeley and Los Angeles: University of California Press, 2000).

Stowasser, B. F., 'The Turks in Germany: From Sojourners to Citizens', in Y. Y. Haddad (ed.), *Muslims in the West: From Sojourners to Citizens* (Oxford: Oxford University Press, 2002), 52–71.

Sutcliffe, S., 'Unfinished Business: Devolving Scotland/Devolving Religion', in S. Coleman and P. Collins (eds.), *Religion, Identity and Change: Perspectives on Global Transformations* (Aldershot: Ashgate, 2004), 84–106.

Sykes, Richard, 'Popular Religion in Decline: A Study from the Black Country', *Journal of Ecclesiastical History*, 56 (2005), 288.

Szajkowski, B., *Next to God ... Poland: Politics and Religion in Contemporary Poland* (New York: St Martins Press, 1983).

Tamney, J. B., and Johnson, S. D., 'The Popularity of Strict Churches', *Review of Religious Research*, 39 (1998), 2109–23.

Tazmini, G., *Khatami's Iran: The Islamic Republic and the Turbulent Path to Reform* (London: Tauris, 2009).

Thiessen, J., and Dawson, L. L., 'Is there a "Renaissance" of Religion in Canada? A Critical Look at Bibby and beyond', *Studies in Religion*, 37 (2008), 389–415.

Thomas, K., *Religion and the Decline of Magic* (Harmondsworth: Penguin, 1978).

Tönnies, F., *Community and Association* (London: Routledge and Kegan Paul, 1955).

Tschannen, O., 'The Secularization Paradigm: A Systematization', *Journal for the Scientific Study of Religion*, 30 (1991), 395–415.

Voas, D., 'Intermarriage and the Demography of Secularisation', *British Journal of Sociology*, 54 (2003), 83–108.

——, 'The Continuing Secular Transition', in D. Pollack and D. V. A. Olson (eds), *The Role of Religion in Modern Societies* (New York: Routledge, 2007).

——, 'The Rise and Fall of Fuzzy Fidelity in Europe', *European Sociological Review*, 25 (2009), 155–68.

——, and Bruce, S., 'The Spiritual Revolution: Another False Dawn for the Sacred', in K. Flanagan and P. C. Jupp (eds), *A Sociology of Spirituality* (Aldershot: Ashgate, 2007), 43–62.

——, and Crockett, A. D., 'Religion in Britain: Neither Believing nor Belonging', *Sociology*, 39 (2005), 11–28.

Wallis, R. *The Elementary Forms of the New Religious Life* (London: Routledge and Kegan Paul, 1984).

Walliss, J., ' "Loved the wedding, invite me to the marriage": The Secularisation of Weddings in Contemporary Britain', *Sociological Research Online*, 7 (2002).

Weber, M., *The Protestant Ethic and the Spirit of Capitalism* (London: George Allen and Unwin, 1976).

Wickham, E. R., *Church and People in an Industrial City* (London: Lutterworth Press, 1957).

Williams, S., *Religious Belief and Popular Culture* (Oxford: Oxford University Press, 1999).

Williams, W. M., *The Sociology of an English Village: Gosforth* (London: Routledge and Kegan Paul, 1956).

Wilson, B. R., *Religion in Secular Society* (London: C. A. Watts, 1966).

——, *Sects and Society* (London: Heinemann, 1978).

——, *Religion in Sociological Perspective* (Oxford: Oxford University Press, 1982).

——, 'Secularization: The Inherited Model', in P. E. Hammond (ed.), *The Sacred in a Secular Age* (Berkeley and Los Angeles: University of California Press, 1985).

——, 'Morality in the Evolution of the Modern Social System', *British Journal of Sociology*, 36 (1985), 315–32.

Wolffe, J. (ed.), *Evangelical Faith and Public Zeal: Evangelicals and Society in Britain 1780–1980* (London: SPCK Press, 1955).

Wood, M., *Power, Possession and the New Age* (Aldershot: Ashgate, 2007).

Woodhead, L., 'Why So Many Women in Holistic Spirituality?', in K. Flanagan and P. Jupp (eds), *A Sociology of Spirituality* (Aldershot: Ashgate, 2008), 115–25.

Wuthnow, R., *The Restructuring of American Religion* (Princeton: Princeton University Press, 1988).

Yamane, D., 'Secularization on Trial: In Defense of a Neosecularization Paradigm', *Journal for the Social Scientific Study of Religion*, 36 (1997), 109–22.

*The Yorkshire Congregational Yearbook* (York: Yorkshire Congregational Union, 1952).

Young, L. A. (ed.), *Rational Choice Theory and Religion* (London: Routledge, 1997).

# Index

Lightning Source UK Ltd.
Milton Keynes UK
UKOW041456011012

199912UK00001B/4/P